"*Digital Transforr* .... *tructing bridges*
to disseminating .... *ainable change.*
*Herbert recognizes that the challenge is not the tools but the culture – the vital
ingredient for the digital shift from customer experience to back office systems.*"
– Perry Hewitt, Vice President of Marketing, ITHAKA

"*This book contains rarely found and rarely used common sense for the over
hyped and jargon fuelled trend of digital transformation. Lindsay uses her
experience and communications skills to provide clear guidance for this important
element of business evolution in a well-structured logical format.*"
– Paul Hoskins, Chairman, Precedent

"*This book is the 'Quora' of Digital Transformation. Lindsay Herbert has done a
superb job of outlining and answering so many questions that arise from Digital
Transformation, both for business leaders and for consultants. In digital we need
to question everything and look for the answer…luckily much of it is here.*"
– Peter Abraham, Co-founder, Crank

"*For once here is a practical and unbiased guide to corporate digital
transformation. Lindsay has managed to pull together a great mix of evidence-
based analysis and a clear roadmap to follow that in my experience actually
works. I recommend any modern, serious business leader reads it.*"
– Adam Freeman, Co-founder, Freeformers

"*I was privileged to work with Lindsay and see her undoubted skills in action
in live digital transformation projects, she was simply brilliant. And under the
sub-headings of Bridge, Uncover, Iterate, Leverage and Disseminate she does
a wonderful job on explaining how it should be done in today's digital world. A
great read.*"
– Phil Jones, Founder and Organiser, Podge Events

"*Lindsay's clear-headed approach to digital transformation sweeps away the
misconceptions and demystifies the jargon surrounding it. She provides hugely
useful suggestions with the BUILD model and has delightfully counterintuitive
advice, such as reigning in the urge for PR campaigns until you have actually
delivered tangible change. Her insights will prove valuable to anyone on this
challenging (and rewarding) journey.*"
**– Eva Appelbaum, Founder and Consulting Partner, The Arc Group;
Ex-Head of Digital Transformation at the BBC**

"Lindsay breaks down what can be intimidating concepts of digital transformation, but without understating its complexity and difficulty. She emphasizes the importance of fundamental mind shift – one that embraces change as a constant."
– Mike Giresi, Chief Information Officer, Royal Caribbean Cruises

"Transforming your organisation can be a terrifying prospect, full of fear and stress. This book makes it into a thrilling one, full of hope and purpose."
– Ben Hammersley, futurist

"In today's business world, there is nothing more essential and at the same time more confusing and intricate than the concept of Digital Transformation. With an astute and engaging style, Lindsay Herbert unravels one of the most important challenges for the futureproofing of organisations. An obliged reading for all executives."
– William Confalonieri, Australia's first Chief Digital Officer

DIGITAL
TRANSFORMATION

DIGITAL TRANSFORMATION

Build Your Organization's Future
for the Innovation Age

LINDSAY HERBERT

Bloomsbury Business
An imprint of Bloomsbury Publishing Plc

B L O O M S B U R Y
LONDON · OXFORD · NEW YORK · NEW DELHI · SYDNEY

Bloomsbury Business
An imprint of Bloomsbury Publishing Plc

50 Bedford Square	1385 Broadway
London	New York
WC1B 3DP	NY 10018
UK	USA

www.bloomsbury.com

BLOOMSBURY and the Diana logo are trademarks of Bloomsbury Publishing Plc

First published 2017

British Library Cataloguing-in-Publication Data
A catalogue record for this book is available from the British Library.

ISBN: PB: 978-1-4729-4037-7
ePDF: 978-1-4729-4039-1
ePub: 978-1-4729-4038-4

Library of Congress Cataloging-in-Publication Data
Names: Herbert, Lindsay, author.
Title: Digital transformation : B.U.I.L.D your organization's future / by Lindsay Herbert.
Description: London ; New York, NY : Bloomsbury Business, 2017. |
Includes bibliographical references and index.
Identifiers: LCCN 2017020394 | ISBN 9781472940377 (pbk.) |
ISBN 9781472940384 (epub) | ISBN 9781472940407 (exml)
Subjects: LCSH: Information technology–Management. |
Technological innovations–Management. | Customer relations–Technological innovations. |
Internet marketing. | Internet in public relations.
Classification: LCC HD30.2 .H465 2017 | DDC 658/.05–dc23
LC record available at https://lccn.loc.gov/2017020394

Cover design by Eleanor Rose
Cover image © Getty Images

Typeset by Integra Software Services Pvt. Ltd.
Printed and bound in Great Britain

To find out more about our authors and books visit www.bloomsbury.com.
Here you will find extracts, author interviews, details of forthcoming
events and the option to sign up for our newsletters.

CONTENTS

ACKNOWLEDGEMENTS

The effort of writing a book is surprisingly similar to that needed to lead a major digital transformation programme. Both are fraught with false starts, wrong turns, and are equally likely to cause deep resentment towards anyone with free-time or regular access to sunlight and fresh air.

But the other common factor is that neither can be accomplished without help. Whether it's specialist knowledge from experts, or just well placed empathy from loved ones, success comes from building on the support you find around you, in every form it might take.

In my case, my biggest source of support came from Joseph Da Silva, my husband, who moonlighted as both proofreader and research assistance, and whose unflappable optimism and unwavering belief in me was the only light I needed to guide me through the bleakest and weariest of times.

My mother, Cathy Davis-Herbert, was also an incredible source of support, even with thousands of miles between us. In the spirit of Design Thinking, she was also my representative audience member, shouting 'jargon' or just nodding off when things got too dry or technical.

Jen Janzen, dear friend and – to my great fortune – professional editor and writer, is to thank for translating many of my words into those of a coherent person. No small feat under normal circumstances, but Jen managed it under a deadline shorter and less forgiving than an Agile sprint.

My publisher, Ian Hallsworth, was also an incredible source of support because without his advice and fortifying professional belief, my ideas and research would still be sitting undeveloped on a laptop, and not in the hands of people leading change for their own organizations around the world.

Finding time to write while working a more than full-time new role was thanks to Debbie Vavangas, Global Partner at IBM and all-round superhuman. Debbie helped me safeguard just enough of my personal time that I avoided needing hospitalization, or moving the publishing date to 2027.

I also must profoundly thank the many professionals who shared their lessons of innovation over the past three years. Each person's contributions made the book what it is, and repeatedly reignited my own passion for the topic – a necessity among the hundreds of lonely hours spent writing in a windowless, soundproofed room (the by-product of having a professional musician for a spouse).

Lastly, I want to thank my biggest inspiration when it comes to embracing change itself. My grandmother, Pamela Herbert, raised six children across almost as many countries, treating each move with the same adventurous spirit that she continues to treat new challenges today. I grew up on stories of how she adapted and thrived – whether fending off real danger, including an attempted kidnapping, or managing everyday trials, like trying to find OXO cubes in 1960's Benghazi. My grandmother continues to inspire me to embrace change today, and I tried to write this book in her spirit in the hopes it will help others do the same.

INTRODUCTION:
How to Digitally Transform

Turn your company into one that thrives in a changing environment by using the five stages followed by all successful digital transformations.

The essentials of digital transformation

Digital transformation. It's a buzzword that appears on boardroom agendas everywhere, but anxieties about what it is, how it works, and what it means for business processes are still crippling many organizations into inaction, with many struggling to even articulate 'what' is it they're failing to do.

For this reason, I want to dive straight in to getting you the most critical information about successful digital transformation – starting with the three biggest misconceptions about it.

Misconception 1: 'Digital transformation needs a big budget before it can even start.'
It doesn't matter its sector or size; your organization can absolutely afford to 'do' digital transformation. In fact, there are more examples of failed digital transformations that start with big budgets than those who started with small investments in critical areas.

As you'll see in the examples throughout this book, the vast majority of success cases never attribute money specifically to 'transforming'. Digitally savvy organizations simply tackle the job on a more manageable project-by-project basis.

This leads to a second point, which is actually more of a request: Please put down the 'We're transforming' posters for the company breakrooms, and don't hit send on that all-staff email.

You'll see later in this book that the time to start the PR campaign isn't until you're well into the programme, when you have tangible examples showing

I disagree with the thinking that you need a huge transformation budget to start anything. What you have to do is say 'we're not going to try to create the Holy Grail here. This is our business model, so what do we think is most important? How do we drive value and what does the organization design need to look like to enable that?' Start with that.

The intent of our digital transformation is for someone to be able to maximize their discretionary time that they have granted to us. No one needs to go on a cruise. The cruise business is less than 3 per cent of the entire hospitality spend in North America, so it's still a really small segment of the broader business.

I am absolutely positive that by making it easier for people to digest the product and maximize their time within the product, this concept of 'frictionless vacation' will allow us to grow the segment.

That transformation is all about understanding how to talk to people in a much more curated and personalized fashion so they get that we're relevant. They don't feel intimidated or overwhelmed, and they can act on the information we're providing them.

Interview with Mike Giresi, Chief Information Officer,
Royal Caribbean Cruises
Former Chief Information Officer, Tory Burch, 2011–2015

digital transformation is already happening, working, and benefiting both staff and customers. Before that, unveiling your grand innovation plan will only trigger a flurry of worried staff emails to HR, or in a best-case scenario, a bunch of eager-to-please employees volunteering to get involved before there's anything to get involved in.

Misconception 2: 'Everyone knows what I'm talking about when I say "Digital Transformation".'

I speak a lot about digital transformation, from keynotes at conferences with thousands of attendees to leadership retreats with an organization's executive suite. I've never once witnessed instant consensus on what digital transformation means.

I'll go into more detail in the next section 'What is real digital transformation', but here's the condensed version: everyone you've spoken to about digital transformation has a slightly different definition of the focus, extent, and purpose of doing it – and this is one of the biggest reasons for programmes to fail.

Misconception 3: 'When the digital transformation is over, we can go back to business as usual.'

This misconception is the most baffling to me because the word 'transform' means something is no longer the thing it was before. Somehow so many

'Digital transformation' is to understand the rules of the game have essentially changed. You're not just trying to transform your business by putting your existing practices on the internet. And it's not just for one big initiative either. It's not for a 'big bang' launch. It's not for the quarterly report to shareholders. It's something that you have to be able to sustain through culture and practice throughout the years.

Interview with Perry Hewitt, Vice-President of Marketing, ITHAKA
Former Chief Digital Officer, Harvard University, 2011–2016

companies think 'digital transformation' will allow them to continue doing what they've always done, just with new technology thrown into the mix.

The truth is that digital transformation is actually not about adapting to new technology at all – it's about directing an organization to be more adaptive to change itself.

You'll see throughout the cases used in this book that the companies that succeed are the ones that adopt a new mindset and new ways of working, not just to meet the changed needs of their customers today, but to become more flexible and able to accommodate changes in the future as well.

And that's just the beginning.

Throughout my years working with organizations and speaking to others leading their own company's transformation across all sectors and geographies, I've seen so many different versions of the same rough beginnings, bumpy middles, and epiphany-laden ends to notice patterns emerge.

It's from these patterns that I've distilled the framework of successful transformation, complete with tasks, objectives, outcomes, and tips to enhance the journey. By the end of this book, you'll have the tools to adapt the framework to guide your own transformation.

Before we get ahead of ourselves though, there is still one important concept to tackle. It's time to delve into what *real* digital transformation actually looks like, so you can know it when you see it, and so you can start to picture your own company's 'before and after'.

What is real digital transformation?

What it is and how to spot it

Real digital transformation isn't about getting your company to use a specific set of new technology; it's about your company's ability to react and successfully utilize new technologies and procedures – now and in the future.

For most, this includes adopting processes that allow your company's leadership and staff to investigate, experiment, and strategically employ new technology on an ongoing basis.

In other words: Real digital transformation is something you only have to do once.

New gadgets, new networks, new capabilities – everything new in our digital age poses equal threat and opportunity, and like a boxer in the ring, the company that can react quickly with concentrated force wins the title. The company that ducks and dodges the punches without a proactive strategy is only delaying its inevitable defeat.

The average company today though is nothing like a boxer. The average organization is stuck in its ways, isolated, slow to react, and bogged down by old processes. It's locked in a state of slow decision making, thanks to hierarchies that have enlarged over time, creating internal silos of people and processes, with complex approval processes that make it difficult to reach consensus, let alone pursue a collective goal.

Real digital transformation is about breaking down these barriers, removing the constraints imposed by outdated logic, and leveraging technology to create new revenue streams, drive down costs, and enhance the user experience.

Like a boxer going through rigorous training, successful digital transformation begins with a series of small changes that accumulate until the organization can cope with bigger demands. When training – or transformation – is finished, neither the boxer nor the company will behave, look, or move the way it did at the start.

Essentially, this is your *Rocky* moment. Training starts today and depending on your current fitness, in a few weeks or months, you'll be ready for your first match.

Tell-tale signs of real digital transformation

Boxing metaphors are good at setting the scene, but there are many tangible signs of real digital transformation. Regardless of the size of your company or the sector it's involved in, real digital transformation includes using new devices, platforms, systems, and networks to create:

- More profitable business models
- More efficient operating processes
- Greater access to markets
- Enhanced offerings to users
- New sources of revenue

Because these elements are intrinsically linked to your business as a whole, to achieve success in these goals, your transformation programme is going to have to tackle three critical areas of your organization:

1 **Business model**: How revenue is generated, and how customers are acquired and retained
2 **Customer experience**: Core product and services, and the processes by which customers transact and engage with you
3 **Internal processes**: Ways of working, operations, analysis, and decision making

After you've completed a true digital transformation, here's what it will look like at a top level:

1 **Increased revenue:** Bigger share of market, new markets acquired, and/or lower costs to acquire and maintain customers
2 **Increased competitive advantage:** Better products or services than the competition and/or filling a new need/want category no one else caters to
3 **Getting more done faster and with less:** Increased efficiency, coordination, and a new ability to quickly tap into strengths

How you achieve it will depend on the specifics of your organization, its unique barriers and assets, and the landscape you operate in. A small charity's digital transformation looks radically different (and a lot cheaper) than the transformation of a major bank – but the difference each can make on the future sustainability of their own organization is equally game-changing.

Separating jargon from reality

So why shouldn't you call your programme 'digital transformation', talk about it at meetings, or announce it to staff, customers, and shareholders? Because like most business terms, 'digital transformation' has moved into the dangerous territory of *jargon*.

Digital transformation is ongoing. It's a commitment that a company makes, not a single fiery hoop that it jumps through once. At its most basic level, I see digital transformation as being an acknowledgement within a company that the previous way of doing business will no longer suffice for their continued ability to succeed within their sector.

The common thread is always that there's a new disruptive capability has come along, whether it is in communication, in data, in acknowledging development, which forces an organization to make a significant change which they otherwise would not have done.

Interview with Bryan VanDyke, Managing Director & Head of Digital,
Morgan Stanley

Back in the days when 'synergy' and 'thinking outside the box' were the hot topics in business management, jargon was an annoying but mostly harmless part of day-to-day professional life. Consultants used it to make standard recommendations sound like radical new concepts; managers used it to make old decisions sound like a bold new direction; and employees used it to sound like mangers and consultants.

Most jargon starts innocently: a group of professionals in the same field start using a term as shorthand to refer to complex concept they're all familiar with, but the term starts to catch on. People start using it because they think they understand it, or because they think it helps them sound like an expert. Either way, the effect is the same. The number of 'definitions' increase as do the number of misunderstandings, because no one likes to admit when they don't know something – especially when it's in the middle of a management meeting and everyone else is nodding along knowingly.

The danger comes when digital-related jargon slips into the decision-making process for how to run a company.
This is because 'digital' (a word which in itself is jargon) is actually a catch-all term for the new technologies and capabilities embedded across every aspect of modern life.

Defining 'digital'
From a consumer's perspective, digital includes everything on the Internet (websites, social media, advertising, etc.) and literally anything you can do, see, or engage with through connected devices, such as smart TVs, mobile phones, laptops, wearables (like smartwatches that track your heart when you run), and

I think one of the responsibilities of a CIO is to bring people together and at least come up with rules of engagement as to what digital transformation is and what it isn't. That we're actually looking for things beyond 'hey, we want to go paperless'.

To me digital transformation, and the way I've run my career, is having a constantly improving mindset. I set the bar very high for my teams so that we are constantly evolving. That doesn't mean change for change sake, but we are always pointing the finger at ourselves to see how we can get better. How can we leverage new technologies? How can we leverage existing technologies better in a strategic way?

Interview with Jay Ferro, Executive Vice President, EarthLink
Former Chief Information Officer, American Cancer Society, 2012–2016

Wi-Fi-enabled appliances (like fridges that re-order your milk for you when the sensors detect spoilage).

Digital is everywhere, but it becomes truly powerful when you extend its definition to the enterprise level. In this sense, 'digital' also includes every element of your company's entire IT infrastructure – from product and inventory management and running the supply chain to every aspect of marketing, communications, and HR. In fact, you'd be hard-pressed to find an element of your business that doesn't have a digital component integral to its operations; how sophisticated or well implemented it is – that's another matter.

Because the realm of digital is so vast, it's useful to think of it as an enabler of capabilities rather than a set of things. For example, digital can enable any company to:

- Automate insight gathering and decision making
- Rapidly handle complex transactions and processes
- Facilitate large-scale engagement and communication

But perhaps the most important thing to note in all this is that digital is also a democratizer of power. It's the sole cause for what's shifted from the time when big companies held the currency – the supply chains, the means of mass production, the giant inventories – to today, when anyone can command a market from their garage-based start-up.

Because of digital, normal people – not just giant brands – can attract and retain customers, simply by figuring out clever ways to create and deliver value through digital. We've all heard the stats: Uber is the biggest global taxi service, yet owns no cars. Airbnb is the biggest hotel chain, yet doesn't own a single piece of rentable real estate (McRae 2015). And this is where transformation and challenge factor in for the big companies. They don't want to democratize because that's not how you traditionally control a vast supply chain. They don't want to network because that's not how value has historically been created or held.

Where the danger of jargon comes into play

Technology can raise a start-up from humble garage beginnings to Fortune 100 status in less time than it takes to run a typical IT upgrade project and without the usual overspend (45 per cent, in case you were wondering) (Bloch et al. 2012). But because of the murky nature of jargon and the many interpretations of digital, companies are making these decisions based on poorly understood principles, which leads to embarrassing, expensive, and often, irreversible mistakes.

On the extreme end, you have the dot-com bubble of the 1990s, when nearly every company with '.com' in the name instantly shot up in investment value without any evidence of a real product, service, or marketable asset. People didn't really understand what 'dot-com' meant and instead of properly investigating, they invested out of fear they were going to miss out on the next big thing. When the bubble burst in 2001, people were shocked to find out that just because a company is 'online' doesn't mean it can survive without a solid business plan and revenue model (Leckart 2010). That's the power of jargon.

Following the dot-com crash, you'd think people would be less swept up by the magic of a catchy term. Not so.

For example, working at an agency in 2008, I'd regularly receive request for proposals asking for 'Web 2.0' with a single cost line item to fill in. Now, the term 'Web 2.0' actually referred to the social capabilities enabled by the web and the value it can help generate. But like all jargon, what started as shorthand for a complex concept soon got co-opted and people decided to implement it without realizing they've each ascribed it a different meaning. Fast-forward to pitch day. My team would be faced with a panel of perplexed clients asking why we were trying to sell them a new website with social media feeds, a forum, and blogging capabilities when they just wanted a website that's 'Web 2.0'. I shudder to think of the money lost on websites built during those years by opportunistic agencies who were more than happy to add 'Powered by 2.0' in the footer of every webpage for a small fee. But what's far more disturbing is what's happening now with the briefs asking for 'digital transformation'.

> All lot of buzzwords are driven by commercial gain. With digital
> transformation, a lot of the language ends of being driven by third parties
> trying to capitalize for different products and services. Self-interest tends to
> drive terminology.
>
> My experience is that digital transformation is that lots of little bits can
> add up to big bits. Because of digital transformation, we're faster, cheaper,
> have a much better customer experience, and perform better commercially.
> Culturally, we're operating in a way that the entire company wants to mimic.
> What more do you want?
>
> Interview with Ash Roots, Director of Digital, Direct Line Group

What people really mean when they say 'digital transformation'

The first time I remember seeing the term 'digital transformation' written on a brief was for a major global financial firm in 2010. Despite the rest of the brief asking only for a new website, the pitch panel included the entire senior executive board as well as the CEO. This was a strangely senior panel for a large, but fairly standard, website. Just a few years before, the same pitch would have been attended by IT Director and Marketing Director at best.

So what changed so quickly for this UK-based financial firm? 2008's housing market crash in America triggered a global recession and the firm's bottom line was now hurting. So, like many other companies, the senior executives had decided to turn to 'digital transformation' to stretch budgets, find new customers, and generally solve decades' worth of indifference to technology and outdated ways of working, but sadly, their definition of 'transformation' only extended as far as redesigning the firm's website.

What quickly became clear to me was how many other organizations were trying to implement major innovation programmes without fully understanding the costs, complexities, or company-wide implications. Basic answers to core questions were being skipped over as huge investments were made, and in some cases lost as projects failed and staff bailed out.

As such, 'digital transformation' has turned into business jargon that's best avoided. Some think of it as shorthand for 'don't be like Blockbuster', whose bankruptcy followed years of ignoring companies like LoveFilm and Netflix, which gained market share using the web to outperform the Blockbuster video rental empire at its core business (Satell 2014).

In case you can't help but use the term (perhaps it's already become ubiquitous at board meetings), Table 1.0 is a cheat sheet of what people tend to think it means, depending on the role they're in.

Table 1.0

People who talk about digital transformation	What they really mean
CEO: 'This year is about digital transformation'	We're doing a series of IT and website upgrades to try to boost revenue and keep our investors happy.
CMO: 'We're digitally transforming our marketing'	We're going to spend more on digital marketing this year – and we're redesigning the website.
CIO: 'We're running a digital transformation programme'	We're finally buying an enterprise Customer Relationship Management system and re-platforming our website.
CFO: 'We're investing in digital transformation'	We need to automate and shift low-skilled work offshore to reduce our costs.
Top-tier consultant: 'We're crafting a digital transformation strategy'	You need to pay us a lot of money for a set of recommendations that tell you to spend even more.
Digital agency: 'This project is your first stage of digital transformation'	We'll develop your new website using a method called 'Agile' but without properly preparing you or your teams for the new ways of working it requires.

The challenge of real transformation

The struggle of digital transformation is rooted in our DNA.
As humans, we all love convenience. Every piece of technology that has existed, or will ever exist, is created to reduce or eliminate the labour required to achieve a desired outcome – all for the purpose of reducing effort and freeing time for more worthy pursuits.

But there's a catch. We seek convenience, but we also naturally avoid new processes. Change brings risk, uncertainty, and effort (convenience's natural enemy). Tell your staff they have to learn a new skill that will make their work easier in the future, and their blood pressures will rise. Even the people who like learning and actually volunteer for training opportunities will feel the flutter of adrenalin and anxiety at the mention of an altered routine.

Five stages of personal digital transformation

Stage 1: Denial

I don't really need a new phone. So what if the new ones now have more features. They're really expensive, harder to use, and I only really use my phone for a few things anyway.

Stage 2: Fear

There are too many choices and they're all so expensive! I'll get a cheaper price if I sign a contract for two years but what if I hate it after a month??

Stage 3: Anger

What does this button do?! And where have all my contacts and calendar appointments gone?! I knew this was a mistake!

Stage 4: Delight

These photos are incredible! I'm going to post this one online ... using the voice commands! This feature is going to be really handy when I'm on the road.

Stage 5: Attachment

I turned on my old phone the other day and it feels so heavy and runs so slowly compared to my new one. I can't believe I waited so long to get it.

These hard-wired genetic attributes make new technology slow to take off initially when the change is the part that stands out most. Once the new system has been adopted, this same evolutionary trait makes the system hard to leave because it's a comfortable, known, and therefore convenient process.

This is why changing to keep up with technology isn't the real problem. The real challenge is changing attitudes towards change itself.

To help understand how your staff, managers, and customers are going to feel and react to the changes you'll be proposing, think about the digital transformations you've already undergone in your own life. Every time we get a new phone, laptop, or car, we all go through the same natural, human reactions to digital transformation.

Given the ubiquity of this experience, you might think digital transformation is about getting your company and its people through a big period of upgrades, and then it's back to business as usual. But all this does is set yourself up for another round of 'transforming' in two years' time when what you upgraded to is now woefully out of date.

This is why the real challenge of digital transformation is about putting new ways of working in place that ensure a process of continuous change and improvement is at your company's core.

As a movement, digital transformation will influence all stages of humankind. For instance, I'm fifty-five and I can still remember going to the postal office with a sheet of paper. I had a number and the number was to a theatre in London. I remember the guy gave me back the sheet of paper and said 'now it's in London', and I was amazed. That was a fax and it was 1984. My kids who are seventeen and early twenties, grew up with digital. They can't imagine what it is to live without a mobile phone or the internet. My generation has only just made the change from the analogue world to the digital world, and then digital became mobile. Mobile makes it 24/7 and personal – in dating, in paying your bills, or in monitoring your health. If you're open to digital, there's a whole new world waiting.

Interview with Wim Pijbes, Director, Stichting Droom en Daad
Former General Director, Rijksmuseum, 2008–2016

Common digital challenges and their typical root causes

There are five common challenges this book is designed to circumnavigate.

1   **Fears from staff**

    Resistance from staff can take many forms, but the reason most often is a fear the business is moving away from the existing employees' core skills. Worries about being replaced by young 'digital natives' or even replaced by machines and automation are reasons enough for staff to resist, and, in extreme cases, sabotage digital transformation efforts.

2   **Resistance from management**

    Mid-level managers pose a greater risk to digital transformation efforts than senior leaders or new staff because of their ability to discourage staff, deny resources, and generally obstruct progress at every level of the organization. The standard cause is a perceived threat to their autonomy and area of responsibility. It's understandable that a programme aimed at fundamentally changing ways of working and increasing accountability among staff is going to threaten the power and responsibility a manager has worked hard to acquire.

3 **Loss of revenue from non-digital customer segments**

This refers to the potential loss of revenue or value from customers who currently rely on traditional channels to transact, access services, and engage with your organization. This is when the digital transformation programme has to weigh the risk of taking resource away from these traditional channels in favour of experimenting with new ones.

4 **Decreases in business-as-usual productivity**

One of the biggest overlooked areas is the loss of time and resource a business will incur, while those assets are diverted to the digital transformation programme. This is especially true for companies that aren't able to hire more staff or generate additional investment for the transformation efforts.

5 **Inconsistencies in the quality of customer and staff experiences**

It's impossible to transform everything at once, but it can become glaringly obvious that some areas of the business are lagging behind once digital transformation has already taken place in some parts of the organization. This usually happens at the senior leadership level where a fracturing has occurred in the executive team. Those in favour of transformation have given the go-ahead for the areas they can control, while the others hold back to see the results before committing for their own teams.

In pretty much every organization I've seen, the block to transformation is not at the board level or the CEO level. It's certainly not at the bottom either because that's made up of people in their 20s and 30s who grew up using digital technologies.

The block is almost always middle managers who are one or two rungs down from the top job. These people have twenty-five years of their career invested in doing it one way, and they'll be buggered if they're going to change anything now because they're about to get the corner office. So, the very senior leadership have to say to the people just below them: suck it up.

Interview with Ben Hammersley, Futurist, BBC World Presenter
'Cybercrime, with Ben Hammersley' & WIRED Contributing Editor

The best ways to doom any digital transformation

The purpose of this book is to show you how to implement a successful digital transformation programme, but it's impossible to explain the good practice without also talking about what you shouldn't do. For this reason, you'll see many examples of digital transformation done badly, along with rationale explaining why certain approaches just don't work.

There is one sure-fire way to doom your digital transformation programme that's worth addressing right from the start, especially as it's the most common: targeting the wrong thing for transformation.

Don't transform to preserve the 'how', transform it to match the 'why'
The most famous example of failed digital transformation is Blockbuster, and for good reason, because it happens to feature the best way to doom your transformation from the start. The now-bankrupt video rental company went from controlling the market in home-based media entertainment to being the referenced cautionary tale (and often, punchline) in business strategy, all because it prioritized its business model (the 'how' you do business) over delivering its mission statement (the 'why' you do business'). In doing so, Blockbuster failed to use newly available technology to fulfil its own corporate mission statement, which was 'to provide customers with the most convenient access to media entertainment' (Alfredo 2012).

I always explain that digital transformation is not about all the cool sexy things that we are doing to change the way we engage with customers, our students. Digital transformation is about acquiring digital maturity. Digital maturity comes from following two parallel processes. The first is the one people focus on, which is to use technology and innovation to take engagement with stakeholders and customers to a new and different frontier. But the other process and the most important one, is the change that is invisible from outside the organization, and is really the most difficult and most painful change.

You are not going to be able to sustain that ecosystem of cool things if the organization isn't set-up to manage it.

Interview with William Confalonieri, Chief Digital Officer, Deakin University

Don't forget what the cause and the commercial side of it is, but do so in a way that's brave. Too frequently, and Blackberry and Blockbuster might be examples, it's easy to be complacent when you own a market. That's when you really have to be brave and you may have to give up revenue, especially if you see the market is going to start giving something away that you charge for, or that you make most of your money on now. Are you better to wait till they eat all your market share because they're giving it away free, or are you better off starting to give yours away free while you still have the brand and find other ways to monetize?

One must wonder where the market would be today if Barnes & Noble and other competitors responded differently when Amazon first started out as an online bookseller. What if the then market leaders had aggressively discounted to that level and created a dominate online defence, who would have even heard of Amazon now?

Those who are brave enough to take what may appear to be a financial hit to the benefit of their future are probably more on a path to the right way to transform, than those who steadfastly hold to their path because it's where their margins have been. You've got to be tough enough to stomach when 'The Street' tells you your margins are going down relative to your peers. You've got to be able to articulate why that's ok, and how in say two years' time you're going to be twice as profitable as those peers because you're going to make them irrelevant.

Interview with Jan Babiak
Board of Directors, Walgreens Boots Alliance & Bank of Montreal

To avoid Blockbuster's fate befalling your own transformation programme, you have to strip your organization's mission back to its basics and identify its true mission – the real answer to 'why do you exist?'

It might sound obvious in hindsight, but when you're in the midst of the day-to-day within a company, it's easy to fixate on how you do things, and forget completely why you started doing them in the first place. You need to take a step back and look at the bigger picture because how can you transform when you don't know what you're trying to become?

Answering the question: Why do you exist?

Many companies get the focus of transformation wrong for two reasons.

First, it's common for a company to underestimate the need for a driving mission and/or confuse the need for a mission with a need for a catchy marketing campaign. For example, utilities companies often claim their purpose is to help people save money and conserve energy, yet very few have the outputs to match – their prices keep going up and usage among their customers stay the same. For these companies, either the purpose is false (e.g. they don't really care about conservation but think it makes for good PR) or the system they're using is flawed (e.g. they do want to help people conserve but they aren't good at doing it). Either way, digital transformation can help both types of companies, but only after the companies agree on the actual purpose they're striving to fulfil for their users, so that leaders and staff can align themselves to deliver outputs that actually match.

Second, it's common in companies that have been in business for a long time for outputs to stop matching the founding mission, but because the company is still reasonably profitable, no one thinks to question the misalignment. Even the customers are used to old way of consuming the products and services, and won't think there's anything that needs improvement – until another company comes along with a better way of doing it.

This brings us back to Blockbuster, whose mission was to provide customers with the most convenient means of accessing media entertainment. Before it became common to shop online, going to your neighbourhood video store was the most convenient way, but as soon as people started to shift towards buying certain products online (e.g. books, DVDs and other standardized products that don't need to be felt or tried on), Blockbuster's leadership should have used digital transformation to answer the question 'how can we increase the convenience of accessing films?'

Instead, they poured money into trying to grow their current output by asking 'how can we get more people renting from our stores?' (Salem Baskin 2013) As such, the digital transformation that ensued focused entirely on driving more people to keep visiting the physical stores. Eventually, the money started to run out, branches were forced to close, and more and more Blockbuster customers switched to online services like Netflix.

As a final caution, sometimes people get confused about digital transformation and think its purpose is to put everything online. This isn't true at all, as you'll see from many examples throughout this book. But even in Blockbuster's case, if its mission had been 'to provide the most enjoyable access to media entertainment', then transforming its shops to include virtual reality, gaming stations with enhanced screens and sound, and interactive video feeds with celebrities from the latest films, would have been a great way to better align its outputs with its purpose – and without having anything to do with enabling people to buy its content online.

Maybe that will be the next digital transformation opportunity in home entertainment. Everyone's come to expect the endless scrolling of film titles on Netflix, so the competitor that offers an immersive film selection experience that takes place in a physical store could be the welcome break from today's experience of never leaving the sofa on Friday and Saturday nights.

I'm very fortunate to have be in digital since 1994, which means I've had the benefit of making many of the big mistakes myself. I've worked in large publishing organizations where we took a big bang approach to brand and internet strategy in which we spent a great deal of money with a very large agency. We thought the one-time boost would get us over the edge and after that we would magically be digital. Having been there on the frontlines and having seen every organization I've worked with from a start-up of twelve people to multi-thousand for-profit corporations to educational cultural sector, that the lessons remain true. If you optimize for a moment, you're not optimizing for your future.

Interview with Perry Hewitt, Vice-President of Marketing, ITHAKA
Former Chief Digital Officer, Harvard University, 2011–2016

Distilling success into five stages: BUILD

Why is it called BUILD?

The five stages form the acronym 'BUILD' for two reasons. First, BUILD symbolizes the scale, permanence, and impact of digital transformation itself.

You should think of digital transformation in the same way you would a physical one, because the goal for both is the same: securing your company's future success. If your company was constructing new buildings – ones that had to be sturdy, secure, and stand the test of time – your engineers and architects would follow a standardized, collaborative, and systematic approach. This is similar to what it takes to plan, execute, and scale a digital transformation. You need your future digital platforms and the innovation processes your staff follow to be as secure and robust as the floors and walls around you.

The second reason is because five steps that spell something meaningful is easy for others to remember, and that significantly helps when you're winning support for the method from colleagues, executives, and stakeholders. In developing BUILD, I've reviewed many different frameworks, and most either list too many steps (more than ten in some cases) or don't even attempt to put it into a framework – opting to cluster best practices and case studies in a laundry list sort of approach. Anyone who's ever had to get buy-in at boardroom level knows the effectiveness of presenting a concise plan versus a list of to-dos – the BUILD model is that concise plan but with all best practice and case studies to support it contained within each stage.

Where did the stages come from?

The five stages of BUILD come from the distinctive phases that are present in most large-scale digital transformations. Interestingly, these phases are also present in small-scale transformation, just with fewer steps occurring within each stage.

BUILD: The five stages of all successful transformations

Before diving in, here's a synopsis of the five stages, so you know in advance what's coming and what you'll get out of each part.

1 Bridge

Bridge the gaps between your company, the people it's meant to serve, and the changes happening around it.

The first step of any digital transformation is figuring out how much you need to change and how quickly. The only way to accomplish this is to go outside your company.

After BUILD Stage 1: 'Bridge', your company will have:

1   Tangible evidence of how digital technology and new ways of working are being used by peers and competitors to win market share, increase revenue, and decrease costs.

2   Consumer and customer insights into the new offerings and experiences that are already winning a greater share of their time, spend, and loyalty.

3   Knowledge of technologies that could improve and add value to your existing business as well as insights into those that pose an immediate threat to your core business.

4   A vision that succinctly describes the kind of transformation needed to address these opportunities and threats, and that helps you win support from needed stakeholders, partners, and investors.

5   A leadership group willing to sponsor and guide transformation by providing oversight, evaluating progress, and mitigating barriers throughout the programme.

2. Uncover

Uncover your company's hidden barriers, useful assets, and needed resources to plan and prioritize its routes to transformation.

The second stage of digital transformation is figuring out the best routes for making the changes needed to achieve your vision. This involves investigating your company, challenging any outdated logic, and prioritizing needed fixes.

After BUILD Stage 2: 'Uncover', your company will have:

1 Revealed the internal barriers that could prevent your company from achieving its transformation vision.

2 Found assets you can leverage to get started sooner or with less funding.

3 Identified the business outcomes individual projects will need to achieve in order to achieve the overall vision.

4 Identified missing skills and resources, and begun the process of filling them.

5 Created the first cross-functional teams to begin iteratively working to achieve the project outcomes defined by the routes to transformation.

3. Iterate

Build in short cycles, test with real users, and improve as you go to know which innovations can scale.

The third stage of digital transformation is switching from insight gathering and consensus building to producing actual results. This involves cross-functional teams working collaboratively in cycles of ideate, build, test, learn, and improve to achieve meaningful and measurable business goals.

After BUILD Stage 3: 'Iterate', your company will have:

1 Cross-functional project teams that work collaboratively to iteratively create solutions that achieve goals aligned to the objectives.

2 Solutions that start as simple prototypes and get bigger and more complex incrementally as they're tested and improved with real users.

3 Results and evaluation processes that reveal which solutions carry the biggest business value and, therefore, should be scaled.

4 Benchmarks from testing that will inform each solutions' key performance indicators to make the case for why it should be scaled and what value it should bring.

5 New ways of working that have been trialled by the iterative teams, proving which are successful in the context of your organization.

4. Leverage

Leverage successes to access greater resources, influence, and space to scale new solutions, ways of working, and the innovation mind set.

The fourth stage of digital transformation is entirely focused on preparing to take each of the successful solutions from the previous stage to scale by leveraging successes internally and externally. Then, by evaluating where these new assets, resources, and skills have most successfully been leveraged, you can decide more easily where to scale and by how much.

After BUILD Stage 4: 'Leverage', your company will have:

1   Shared successes internally to win influence from previously resistant parties, and access greater resources and freedoms to expand.

2   Marketed successes externally to attract new partners, new hires, and new customers in preparation to scale.

3   Identified the best areas to scale based on the amount of influence, resources, assets, and support gained.

4   Won buy-in from staff and management to increase the instances of organic adoption as the programme grows into new areas of the business.

5   Anticipated and mitigated threats, such as retaliation from the competition, that often accompany an organization announcing transformation successes.

5. Disseminate

Disseminate new innovations and ways of working systematically to make thriving in changing environments the new business as usual.

The final stage is about incrementally scaling digital transformation across every area of the business to achieve sustainable adaptability in changing and complex environment. This includes the formalization of new ways of working and rewards, and establishing the BUILD model as the new business as usual.

After BUILD Stage 5: 'Disseminate', your company will have:

1   New innovations launched and localized in new markets by incrementally scaling the cross-functional team model and iterative project approach.

2   Established flexible systems for supporting scaling across the key digital disciplines: Customer Experience, Design, DevOps, and Insights.

3   Created universal goals for achieving your company's mission with a focus on customer experience and continuous improvement.

4   Established clear rewards and incentives for cooperating with others to produce original work as well as processes for recognizing individual contributions.

5   Formalized supports for innovation, and made strategic investments in platforms, people, processes, and partnerships to enable future adaptability.

You come into an organization and you're the CEO, CTO or Head of Digital, or whatever the role, and yes there are nuances that are sector-specific, but so many of the same tenants of digital transformation are absolutely identical. We all have to deal technical debt and legacy debt. You walk in and there are alignment issues, there are communication issues, there are transparency issues, there are cultural challenges, authority is set-up incorrectly, or the wrong people are in the wrong seats.

Every CIO and CTO wants to talk about digital transformation. But the reality is once the doors close, we're all going to lament the amount of technical debt that we still have to deal with. The business runs day to day and there is no company ever on the planet that allows you to just completely stop business and say 'ok CIO, go digitally transform for a couple of years and then come back to us. We're just going to put the business and the customers on hold while you fix everything'.

Interview with Jay Ferro, Executive Vice President, EarthLink
Former Chief Information Officer, American Cancer Society, 2012–2016

Before you dive in

BUILD is cyclical and repeatable

Whether you have already started your transformation programme or not, every organization has its own quirks, and some areas will need more transformation than others. The good news is that the stages of BUILD are intended to repeat, allowing you to achieve your vision incrementally at a pace your organization can sustain.

If your company hasn't started its digital transformation whatsoever – and your first step is just trying to convince others of the benefits – then read through each stage before you do anything else. That will help you decide upfront what overall effort will be needed and where you're likely to encounter the greatest opposition, so you can use the methods featured to establish yourself as the voice of transformation and help win support from the people whose skills and influence you'll depend on.

BUILD is adaptable to every type of organization

Whether you're in a business-to-consumer (B2C) company with 500,000 staff globally or a business-to-business (B2B) firm with fifty staff in one building, the core lessons of digital transformation are the same. This is also true for public sector organizations like government bodies, and non-profit organizations like universities and charities.

For this reason, you'll see the terms 'company', 'business', and 'organization' used interchangeably throughout. Where there are differences, or techniques that work particularly well for certain sectors or sizes of operation, they're called out specifically – usually alongside relevant examples, and the differences between implementations of approaches for different types of organizations are addressed specifically where needed. As such, don't worry about whether a chapter or section is referencing 'companies' or 'organizations' because the tasks, objectives, and outcomes it describes will apply to both.

A note on company size and geography

If your company is particularly large and global, there will be a tendency to think of just your part of the business or just the territory you're in as an 'organization' in itself. This is a mistake.

For digital transformation to actually result in long-term sustainable change, you must address the goals and weaknesses of the entire company. Failing to do so will mean the vision you create will be too small in scope to accomplish any goals bigger than those in your division, or win support for implementing changes that require support or cooperation from other areas. That said, it's very likely the first instances of change will appear only in your area or territory – just don't confuse this with a transformation programme in itself.

If your company is already on this fragmented path – for example, multiple 'transformation projects' are already running on a department-by-department basis with no overarching vision or leadership, you'll benefit hugely from the tasks, objectives, and outcomes detailed in 'Part 1: Bridge' to bring these programmes together.

Everyone is a 'consumer' and the people you serve are all 'customers'

The sooner you can get your company thinking about the people you serve as 'consumers' and 'customers', the faster you'll be able to start seeing past the outdated logic and sector-specific biases that often cause the need for digital transformation programmes in the first place.

This is because the specialized terms – 'clients', 'supporters', 'patients', 'students' – all imply those people are defined by their interactions with you, and that their expectations and behaviours are shaped by what experiences you offer them. This couldn't be further from the truth.

The drastically increased speed with which new technology and digitally enabled services are introduced to us as general consumers – along with the proliferation of high-speed Internet – means our expectations and behaviours are being shaped faster by what new experiences enter our personal lives than what happens to us at work, school, or in the context of any one organization's experience.

Further to that, thanks to social media, review sites, and communication technology like instant messaging and email, every organization is required to keep people it serves using those services efficiently and happily to avoid them complaining, causing problems, or just going somewhere else. This is because of transparency enabled by these channels. They all act as means for people to share bad experiences, see better experiences elsewhere, and be empowered to challenge even the biggest of brands one-on-one in a public setting.

A note on B2B companies

In my years as a consultant, the worst sector for failing to appreciate these principles, opting to cling to sector-specific terms, are businesses in the B2B sector because, using their logic, these firms sell to companies and not individuals. Not true: You are selling to individuals; they just all work for the same company.

In billion-dollar deals, for example, your customers might include the people who make up your client's procurement department, the heads of its distribution centres, its supply-chain management team, its legal team, its operations management team, its IT and infrastructure management team, and its entire senior leadership team – and that's not including the 'customers' of the client company itself.

That's a lot of people to think about in terms of meeting needs and adapting your organization to suit the behaviours and technology preferences they adopt. It's critical, though, because until artificial intelligence replaces all the people I've just listed, there's no such thing as selling to a company – only to the humans inside it.

You don't have to be the CEO to spark change

Whether you're a CEO trying to lead change, a director wanting to try new ideas, or a member of staff wanting to influence the boss, the principles of BUILD apply. In fact, it's rare to encounter a digital transformation that starts entirely at CEO or board level. Most often, transformation starts with pockets of innovation getting results that win support and willingness to make bigger changes. Once it's embraced by senior leadership, however, the true start date of the digital transformation gets forgotten. This is why there is a misconception that you have to be the leader of a company to be successful in starting the programme.

If you aren't the leader of your company, your first task is to evaluate where your organization currently sits in its transformation journey and decide how receptive senior leadership already is towards taking the transformation further. Critically though, you can't approach transformation selfishly from the perspective of just your department or area of remit. This is where most non-executive directors fail to win senior leadership support. Unless your goal is to advance the company's success as a whole, you'll just come across as another department head asking for more budget without understanding the bigger demands on the company, or being aware of the dozens of similar pitches made by your counterparts across the company.

Real transformation has to be driven from the top

If your senior leadership team is completely unaware of – or even against – the need for major change, you can and should use the stages of BUILD to run your own small-scale digital transformation to make the case. Some of the methods described in 'Part 4: Leverage' will help you achieve this outcome of winning support and influence from senior leadership. Just be sure to engineer your area's digital transformation in a way that helps you make the case for greater change to senior leadership, and don't stray from this goal. This is because, while digital transformation doesn't have to start from the top, any progress made will not be sustainable if it's not adopted across the company – something that takes the power, resources, and influence held only by the person or people ultimately in charge.

At Tory Burch, we grew up as a digital business. There wasn't so much 'legacy to new' transformation, it was much more about how do we stay relevant and agile, and as we got bigger, how do you maintain that edge. In fact the challenge was kind of the reverse, we had to establish enterprise capabilities because we didn't have any!

At Royal Caribbean Cruises, it's completely the opposite. Monolithic, legacy based, large applications, very complicated, organization model doesn't fit anything we're trying to do – and you have this cultural chasm you need to overcome.

To me the hardest part of this work is the culture. The technology if it's done right, normally does what it's supposed to, it's really the culture of the organization that's the biggest challenge. If it's not supported at the very top of the business, it's not going to get done. I don't care who you are or what you say, the CEO has to be completely behind it. If they're not, it's going to fail.

Interview with Mike Giresi, Chief Information Officer, Royal Caribbean Cruises
Former Chief Information Officer, Tory Burch, 2011–2015

BUILD Stage 1: Bridge

Bridge the gaps between your company, the people it's meant to serve, and the changes happening around it

Why Bridge?

No company is an island, but many act like one

Many failed innovation programmes stem from managers, directors, and CEOs thinking the first step of digital transformation is to look within the company for solutions. They audit their operational efficiencies, analyse past performance, brainstorm new customer ideas, identify IT upgrades, and gather budget requests from each department until they've amassed a giant report with detailed requirements for suppliers to bid on and implement.

This is equivalent of a captain trying to predict the next storm by gathering detailed weather readings from inside the ship.
As someone regularly brought in to lead transformation programmes, a company that has already assembled a 'Transformation Plan' document (or worse, a 400+ slide PowerPoint deck with accompanying Excel spreadsheets) is holding up a major red flag for three reasons.

First, it's guaranteed the company has spent a lot of time and money creating the plan, which means there will be major sensitivities and objections to deviating from it – even if its validity or usefulness is already under suspicion by the same people raising those objections.

Second, by the time a plan like this has been prepared, edited, vetted, and approved, most of it has already fallen out of date. There is no such thing as maintaining status quo for any organization, so naturally new projects within individual departments will have started and others finished by the time the 'transformation' part of the programme is due to start. This means the final plan isn't even useful as a snapshot of current internal operations or objectives.

> I've seen big projects where tens of thousands of pounds have been spent
> on eighteen months of just writing the requirements, without actually having
> anything delivered that benefitted the business.
>
> **Interview with Stewart Atkins, Digital Transformation Consultant**
> **Former Head of Digital Strategy, British Medical Association, 2011–2015**

Third, and most important, none of what this plan contains is actually informed by the true needs of the company's customers, reflects any of the current behaviours or preferences, or takes into account the conditions of the market and sector the company operates in.

So, like the misguided ship captain, you're left with a plan that, when dark clouds gather on the horizon, is about as useful as a lifejacket made of spreadsheets.

The real solutions are outside your organization

The correct way for any company to start a digital transformation is to look outside.

In fact, your company's very need for digital transformation is evidence that gaps have formed that separate your company's current state internally, with the people it's meant to serve and the marketplace and sector it operates in. These gaps mean you lack the information internally to re-chart your company's course. To close them, you need to find out what your current and prospective customers want and expect, what technology exists to do it best and what business models and partnerships you could adopt to make the whole operation more sustainable.

Gaps like these are the root of any company's need for digital transformation, and the purpose of Stage 1: Bridge is to close them.

Closing these external and internal gaps will make you well informed about your customers, their changing behaviours and tastes, and the new technologies and business models that could better help you serve them.

It also makes it easier to gain consensus between leaders of a company by removing the ambiguity around decision making. Customer engagement and a shared knowledge of the market and its threats stops internal politics from taking over and allows decisions to be based directly on evidence that will lead to long-term success: meeting the needs of the customer faster, better, and more efficiently than anyone else.

I have a theory that most organizations today, even when they are trying to respond to the digital age or the formation of the new digital landscape, they still respond with an industrial model. We create and we design our organization with vertical towers, information gathering around those towers, KPIs pushing for vertical deliveries, every area has their own goals, and that is how we approach how we deliver to customers. We think innovation to ourselves and not innovation to what the customer needs. In this new era of digital and customer centricity, the customer sees all the touchpoints coming from the organization in a holistic way, beautifully, perfectly connected and what organizations do in general.

To deliver the new customer centricity, you need to have horizontal coordination of the digital presence, a horizontal coordination of the design of touchpoints and processes, and horizontal coordination of the information that is required to deliver the thing they're experiencing. 'Horizontality' is a question of fights, clashes and friction.

Interview with William Confalonieri, Chief Digital Officer, Deakin University

How to Bridge

This first section of BUILD shows you how to form bridges to the outside world, get your company's leadership teams and staff to understand what transformation is needed, and, most important, get everyone bought into why it's essential to your company's future success.

It also shows you how to make these bridges permanent to ensure ongoing engagement outside your company – especially with your target consumers – is part of your digital transformation.

Two types of gaps: External and internal

The changes brought about by digital, compounded by all these layers and systems of standardization, result in fundamental gaps that isolate the people in charge from what's happening at customer-facing levels of the business.

The voice of the customer gets farther from the decision makers, silos form within the business, resulting in leaders who struggle to make collective decisions quickly – if at all.

Sometimes looking up from your desk and out into the world can be a very difficult thing, particularly in jobs that are ever more busy and crowded. There are a number of things that allow great intelligence gathering from outside an organization. Something that worked really well at the British Heart Foundation was when we asked people to go on 'hunter gatherer' missions to interview, to find out, to report back. You can engage your own staff into expanding your organizational intelligence and knowledge, but also their own perspective, which is useful.

Most significant processes will also require some professional assistance, unless you're an organization that routinely goes through strategic change. At the Institute for Cancer Research, we sought some external expertise to do that through consultancy, but from people who really know our world. Getting consultants who understand your business but also have a really good world view is important.

Interview with Dr Charmaine Griffiths, Chief Operating Officer,
The Institute for Cancer Research
Former Executive Director of Strategy & Performance,
British Heart Foundation, 2013–2016

- **External gaps** between your company's decision makers, the people they're supposed to serve, and the markets you operate in.
- **Internal gaps** between your company's own business structures, its leadership groups, and everyone's understanding of the mission of the company overall.

These gaps wouldn't cause so many problems (and there are many) if it weren't for the speed of digital change requiring companies today to be more cohesive and manoeuvrable than ever before.

Bridging internal and external gaps

By forming connections with your customers, consumers, peers, and experts outside your organization, you can start to close the gaps between your company's leadership and the people it's meant to serve.

Your company's leaders also need to be aware of new technology and business models that could help them fulfil the company's mission in a better way than the processes created before those innovations were possible. And last, you need key leaders aligned, ready to implementing a shared vision of where transformation will take you.

To achieve the steps in Bridge, your company's leadership and select members of its staff need to form connections, gain insights, and establish ways of making these bridges permanent long after the stage itself is complete, otherwise the gaps will simply re-form.

The first section delves into how to bridge external gaps between your company, the needs it's meant to fulfil, and the conditions it operates in – namely the competitive landscape and technology available in it.

With external gaps identified and outside connections made to bridge them, the second section of Bridge addresses internal gaps within your company. A united internal team will give you a leadership team aligned to a shared vision, and a select group of sponsors primed to lead the second stage of digital transformation: Uncover.

Tips for success in Bridge

If you are new to the company, then you are the first bridge

If you've been hired because of your fresh insight from another sector or geography, you are the company's first bridge to the outside world. As you gather insights from customers and the competitive landscape, you also need to learn the inner workings of the company and develop relationships with people from across the business. Very few people tolerate the 'new kid' sharing suggestions before they've developed some trust and understanding within the business.

Giant companies need large internal bridges

You'll see many examples throughout this entire book from large and *very large* organizations because the challenges faced by them internally often take several rounds of the BUILD stages to tackle – in particular, building bridges internally between regions and/or departments. If you're part of a geographically dispersed organization with thousands of staff, you're in good company.

Embrace Bridge as an ongoing process

The world around you never stops changing. You'll never feel like this stage is done because it's never really meant to finish, so only take as long as needed to form a good starting point with your vision, align a few key leaders, and then get started on BUILD Stage 2: Uncover. The longer you take gathering insights and informing your vision, the greater the chance it will be out of date when you actually start any real transformation projects.

Get unbiased and expert help

If your company's leadership lack the headspace to think about big bold next steps, or don't have the time in their schedules to engage outside their usual obligations and networks, then get external help in the form of consultants and agencies. External help during Bridge can also make sure you get an unbiased view of your company's current performance and external opportunities. Just be sure to choose external help from those who specialize in gathering insights for digital transformation purposes, otherwise you'll end up with consultants guiding you on how to digitize your existing operations instead of how to innovate and become more aligned with the outside world. Also, don't delegate too much to outside help, otherwise once the consultants leave, the gaps they helped to close will all reappear.

Ask small (even if you're thinking big)

It's easy to scare people off – internally and externally – in Bridge, especially once you're armed with insights about how others are outpacing your company. Demanding too much time from peers or experts who have full agendas of their own is a tactic that won't grow your network and isn't necessary in the first place. Neither is making regular pronouncements about transformation starting internally – it only scares off the people you need on your side (and annoys the rest).

External Gaps

How external gaps form

Before you can bridge the gaps between your company and the outside world, it's important to understand how they formed in the first place. This requires stripping back the discussion to defining what it means to be any kind of organization in its most basic form:

1. **Every organization exists to serve external needs – not internal ones**

There is no such thing as an organization that exists to serve the people who staff and manage the organization itself – to do otherwise would make it a society or community.

This may sound obvious, but the longer an organization has been operating and the bigger it's grown, the easier it is to lose sight of this basic principle. There are many common examples, including:

- Publicly traded companies that make decisions based on pleasing investors instead of finding out what customers actually want.

- Prestigious universities that meet the needs of its senior academic staff over those of its students.

- Government bodies that structure services to earn praise for high-ranking officials instead of making life better for its citizens.

- Professional membership organizations that bend to meet the demands of their most senior members over those new to the profession and in need of the most support.

2.   Every organization has to align to external conditions beyond its control

Because every organization exists to meet some form of external need, it's also a fact that in meeting these needs, the organization needs to align to changes in external conditions that affect them.

These changing external conditions can include anything from:

- An airline selling seats, aligned to fluctuating fuel prices.

- A retailer selling clothes, aligned to fashion trends.

- A charity raising funds, aligned to changing needs for support.

- A finance firm managing investments, aligned with the economy.

But of course, the biggest external conditions now faced by every organization are those related to digital technology, either directly or indirectly. Taking the examples from above, consider these additional external conditions enabled by digital technology:

- An airline selling seats, aligned to changing behaviours from online booking and travel review sites.

- A retailer selling clothes, aligned to changing expectations from designers selling directly online.

- A charity raising funds, aligned to competition from social media enabling fundraising by charities of all types and sizes.

- A finance firm managing wealth, aligned to competition from sites that enable online investing and trading.

Failing to align to external conditions is not only unsustainable, in today's rapidly changing world, it's the root cause of any company's need for digital transformation.

Failing to align with the effects of digital

All organizations are faced with rapidly evolving external needs and conditions shaped by digital technology. Even when new digital innovations target us at home, the expectations they create quickly extend into our professional and consumer lives.

Table 1.1 *New expectations and the brands that shaped them*

New expectations	What it means for customers	Brands responsible for the shift
On demand	I can get what I want, when I want it.	Amazon
Real time	It's accurate up to the second.	Google
Unique	Only I get this exact experience.	Airbnb
Personal	It needs to match my lifestyle.	Netflix
Local	It's tailored to my specific area.	Uber
Effortless	No instructions. It just works.	Apple

Understanding the impact of digital technology on your customers is the key to identifying ways your organization needs to transform to meet those evolved expectations. For example, people who order from Amazon in their home lives will find a similar online ordering process preferable in their business transactions versus having to learn a business-to-business firm's own bespoke ordering system.

The significant ways most customer expectations have already shifted, regardless of age or sector, can be traced back to the original brands and the technologies they used to change them. Table 1.1 highlights the most commons of these shifts.

As a result of these and the many other expectations shaped by digital technology and the brands that created them, we all expect interactions with every organization to be more tailored to our individual preferences because the technology enables it so well. Features like personalization for individuals and localization for specific markets are not only possible, but also necessary.

If your organization needs to digitally transform, it's no longer meeting external needs in ways that are in line with these new expectations. What's crucial to understand in the first stage of transformation is no matter what state you find your company in today, your company did once align to the outside world. When it was first founded, your organization – like any others – would have had no choice but to align with external conditions and needs in order to survive its early stages.

The trick now, and the first stage of BUILD, is to identify and bridge the gaps that have caused this misalignment by returning to a founder's mindset and behaviours.

Before the gaps: A founder's mindset

Before a newly formed business can grow and scale into a competitive and stable company, its founders have to maintain close external connections to

> Before digital was so pervasive, if a customer wanted to buy something they normally had to buy it near where they lived, and the choice was therefore limited. With ecommerce and web, the choice now is global. The customers can come in and compare your prices, and if they have a bad experience they can shop somewhere else. All this has changed the dynamic. It's not the retailer that's in charge, it's the customer.
>
> Interview with Andy Massey, Director of Digital Transformation & Innovation,
> Lane Crawford

inform their decisions, track the impact of changes, and know when to alter their course at the first signs of trouble. These 'founder' behaviours include:

- engaging with customers to understand their behaviours and expectations;
- understanding the conditions of the marketplace;
- evaluating the competition's strengths and behaviours;
- experimenting with new technologies.

Compare these behaviours to those of your company's leaders today. How are major decisions triggered, made, and informed?

If your company hasn't completed the first stage of digital transformation, it's likely that internal politics, personal agendas, and the opinions of senior leaders have become the driving force for any change. It's also likely these leaders' decisions generally favour avoiding change – opting to maintain the status quo and 'wait out' the problem – long after the first clear indicators that it was time to act.

If these practices existed from day one, your business wouldn't have survived its first year. The reason it survives now is because it has the size and scale to absorb and offset losses suffered. This level of inefficiency can only last so long, especially if a fast-moving competitor encroaches on your territory, or your customers find new innovative alternatives for satisfying the needs you once fulfilled.

To bridge these external gaps, the next sections detail the activities you and key members of your staff and company leadership team can do to return to a founder's mindset.

Completing these tasks will give you the insights needed to inform your transformation, and you'll start to build the networks and establish the ways of working you'll need in order to ensure these bridges last long after the transformation programme is complete.

Many companies are pretty terrible internally because they are enormous, and so the people who work for them are very inward-facing. You just need to realign yourself with the world and become much more mindful of what's happening outside. Go backpacking for a few weeks. See how those problems are being addressed in other cultures, other places and for other demographics – see what the kids are going in Brazil or see how those problems are being solved in Kenya. If you don't have time to go or you don't have permission to go, then get someone to come in who has done it and can bring in that slice of the present.

Interview with Ben Hammersley, Futurist, BBC World Presenter
'Cybercrime, with Ben Hammersley' & WIRED Contributing Editor

Bridge the gaps: Customer and consumer needs

Because every organization is different in terms of its customer relationships and how services and products are offered, this section includes rules for conversing with customers, objectives, and key questions to answer, and suggested activities for a variety of sectors and organization types.

Using this format, you'll be able to see the purpose of each task, understand how to do it, and then choose the activities that will work best for your particular organization and customers.

At a glance: Bridging the gaps with customers and consumers

Who? Leaders and key staff from around your organization engage directly with current customers and target consumers.

Start with the customers and speak to them. It's usually very obvious what the gaps are but for various reasons, and it's usually cultural reasons, the business hasn't been able to meet those gaps or progress far in filling them.

Interview with Laura Scarlett, Data & Insight Director,
Guardian News & Media
Former Programme Director, Supporter Loyalty, National Trust, 2013–2015

What? Form meaningful connections with customers by engaging with them directly, immersing yourself in the experiences you're delivering to them, and experiencing first-hand what products, services, and innovations they value elsewhere.

Why? Give your company's people direct insights to what your customers expect, want and value, both from your organization and in their lives generally.

When? Allow enough time to engage along several points of the customer journey and lifecycle (this will vary by business and sector) but don't take too long or the insights will date and you'll lose momentum.

How? There are many methods but the first step should always be conversations with real customers, one-on-one in real environments.

Objectives

1 Investigate and prioritize unmet customer and consumer needs and pain points.
2 From your customers' needs, identify potential new business models and revenue streams.
3 Establish ongoing ways for staff and senior leadership to engage with customers and react to insights gained.

Questions to answer

- Does the current customer experience match what's being promised?
- Does your existing digital estate speak to the customer's actual needs?
- How have customer and consumer needs changed since you established your current processes and infrastructure?
- What experiences are preferred by your customers and consumers, both within your sector and outside it?
- How can you use the elements of those preferred experiences to deliver better value to your customers and your business?

Methods you can use

- Be a secret shopper of your own organization and your competitors.
- Interview or converse with customers at different stages of their experience.
- Host an event for customers to share feedback and suggestions in an open forum.

- Experience the digital products, services, and business innovations enjoyed by your customers.

- Recruit customers to record diaries of their end-to-end experiences with your company, noting where it succeeds and fails to meet their needs and expectations.

- Observe customers in your environment, the environment of the competition, and the ones enjoyed outside your sector.

- Provide questions for customer-facing staff to ask customers and facilitate the collection and analysis of responses.

- Spend time at the frontlines of customer-facing roles.

- Facilitate discussion groups between customers of similar segments.

- Pose questions for written responses on forums, social media, your digital estate, and in your physical sites using digital tools (e.g. tablets and touchscreens) or analogue ones (e.g. suggestion box).

Engaging customers and consumers for digital transformation

To bridge the gaps between your company and the needs of your customers, you first have to establish their true needs. Unlike years past, this doesn't start with looking at customer surveys, performance ratings, or metrics like a Net Promoters Score (Longworth 2015, Shevlin 2013, Systems 2017).

Let's say that you have a call centre and you want to create a tighter integration between the digital experience and the call centre experience, or you want to reassign some portion of the call centre because you're going to provide the direct service online. If you haven't spent the time with the people who are in the call centre taking the calls from the clients, you may misinterpret what the opportunity is. Your vision then gets shaped by those conversations. Once you've done that, you now have something that's informed by the facts on the ground, and of course there's an aspirational element to it.

Interview with Bryan VanDyke, Managing Director & Head of Digital,
Morgan Stanley

Instead, it starts with real conversations with customers and target consumers to understand how their expectations and behaviours have already changed due to digital technology and innovations. From these engagements, you can identify and experience first-hand the kind of products, services, and technology they understand and enjoy.

These are the insights your company can leverage to transform its own experiences and offerings, thereby attracting and retaining more customers with the innovation your customers already know and prefer.

This is true for every type of organization, but the difference will be in how you engage those customers and how many people to involve within your company. For example, leaders at a B2B financial firm can't simply walk up to consumers in the streets. Instead, they need to divide and conquer, strategically hosting discussions at several levels to cover the many people who make up one end 'customer'.

Depending on your sector and customer base, you can even turn these initial conversations into ongoing relationships by running specific ongoing engagements with customers as your transformation programme unfolds.

The rules of customer engagement

If you want to gather the right insights and build networks with these customers that can be used to trial new innovations as they're developed, how you have these conversations is crucial. From what might look like a normal conversation

---

When people hear 'customer research' or 'customer insights' they just think quantitative data, for example, how many people have clicked on something or purchased something. That's clearly an important part of your customer insights because it gives you an indicator of what's working and whether you're improving. But it doesn't tell you what else is possible, or whether you're actually missing the real expectation of the customer. Ethnographic and qualitative research is what I really espouse, but that took quite a lot of discussing within the business for people to understand why and what the difference was. For me it's taking a service design approach of understanding the whole customer journey, then working out where the pain points are as well as what you're doing well because you want to augment the things that work and fix the things that are broken.

Interview with Andy Massey,
Director of Digital Transformation & Innovation, Lane Crawford

on the surface, your goal is to create a carefully crafted interview with specific rules to follow.

For the purpose of informing digital transformation, the best practice for engaging customers starts with the following fundamentals:

1   When asking a question, don't lead the response by including your own opinions or assumptions as part of it.
2   When listening to the response, don't offer your opinion; instead ask another question to really understand the answer given.
3   If you spot a problem, never try to solve it – especially if you have the authority to make changes that people in customer-facing roles do not have or can't sustain.

It's very easy to miss out on these fundamental practices but, unfortunately, doing so invalidates any insights you might gather from the interaction.

Rule 1: Train your people to engage

Asking the right questions means the difference between getting real insights for how you need to transform your business and being given polite suggestions for how to make things moderately better.

The people in your company you involve in this stage will need some training, because asking completely non-leading and open-ended questions is not a natural way of conversing. This is especially true for senior leaders trying to engage at customer level. It's a big shock to their system because the purpose is one they're completely unaccustomed to: listening instead of advising, and collecting problems instead of solving them.

For example, working with many major universities, I've observed senior leaders 'engaging' with students in the following ways:

1   Asking loaded questions

Did you choose this course because of its high employability rates post-graduation or was it because of the quality of the research in the department?

This terrible question assumes the student chose the course at all versus, for example, being denied admission by another first-choice course. It also plants two great reasons right in the question so the easiest answer the student can give is 'yes' – especially if they know the person asking is senior administrator.

2   Ignoring the complexity of problems

In one instance, a senior administrator spoke to students in a long queue for ID cards and decided to get his staff to look into digital solutions to prevent queues in the future.

This is foolhardy in any major organization because just implementing a digital tool is never enough to solve a problem likely caused by multiple sources.

In that university, the long queue was actually the result of a process and communications failure by a different department that led students to think they had to collect their IDs all on the same day.

3   Attempting empathy or relatability

When my daughter was in university she really hated it when course material wasn't available online. Is there anything the university could do to improve your course experience?

Regardless of if it's a student or a customer, setting up a conversation like this sends the message 'I already know something about your situation' and that's awkward for the simple reason that it's just not true. Knowing someone who is like your customer, or having once been a customer yourself, doesn't mean you understand that specific person or the current context.

Rule 2: Assumption is the natural enemy of insight

The fact that your company needs to digitally transform is evidence that your current assumptions about external needs and conditions are likely incorrect. Because it's impossible to know which assumptions are right or wrong (and by how much), a good methodology is to state your assumptions upfront and specifically test them in your engagements. Be sure to also test the opposite of each, otherwise you'll miss out on insights your current assumptions are blinding you from seeing.

A government agency, for example, could assume its services are essential for its citizens and therefore only look to improve minor elements. In reality, there are many innovations that can replace or disrupt anything – and they can be uncovered by asking the right questions.

Here are just a few examples of services and products that governments once assumed could never be replaced or diminished:

- **Landline telephones:** Government-run telephone companies are disappearing. The now privately owned companies taking over operations consider themselves Internet service providers first and phone connection providers second (McCarthy 2015, Noam 1998).

- **Local libraries:** For the local libraries still in operation, the role has fundamentally changed from the only place to access knowledge (i.e. pre-Google) to the place offering special programmes and services for small children, new parents, job seekers, and a variety of other non-book-related community services (Bolt 2013, Warpole 2004).

- **Post offices:** Similar to libraries, the digital age has diminished the post office from being the only place to send and receive physical goods to a variety of services including selling insurance for travel, home, car, and contents (Postandparcel.info 2007, Titcomb 2015).

Rule 3: The real insights never sit at the surface

If you're familiar with 'lean' manufacturing procedures, you'll know about 'the five whys' (Ries 2010). It means literally asking 'why' five times to get to the real root of a problem. This is true for engagements with customers, too. The reason people do or say what they do is never at front of mind, because for most decisions and behaviours, many complex reasons and motivations are at play.

Because this principle is so important, here's a scenario we can all relate to as consumers.

Retail scenario: Transformation insights from one customer conversation

Imagine your company sells premium athletic equipment from a nation-wide chain of shops. Your company's mission and customer promise that distinguishes it from its many competitors is 'to maximize the athletic performance of every customer'.

As a senior leader of the company, you approach a man coming out of one of your stores with a box of new shoes and engage him in a conversation.

From the 'rules of engagement', you know already not to ask a leading question such as 'why did you choose that pair?' This is fortunate, because if you did ask, he'd respond with something like 'I saw the promotion in-store'. This would result in accolades going to your marketing team for creating the display – and this would be completely unjustified, as the customer's true motivations will reveal.

So instead you ask, 'why did you buy shoes today?' and, by asking follow-up questions and digging into his decision-making process, you uncover the following insights:

- He's buying shoes because he's replacing his favourite old pair that wore out during his marathon training.

- He was hoping to just buy the same pair again, and found your company's website because it had them at the best price.

- He wishes there was an easier way to track and replace his shoes when they wear out because he doesn't notice until they're causing him foot and knee pain.

- The shoes he wanted weren't available to order online, but the site let him search local shops that had his shoes in-stock, but when he arrived, the staff couldn't find the pair in the stockroom.

- He didn't get any further advice from the staff because they were too busy getting sizes for other customers.

- He chose his new shoes because he saw them in a big centre store display, but as a leader within the company, you know that model is designed for sprinting and not long-distance running, so they'll be less comfortable and wear out faster than his previous pair.

If the interaction had finished with 'why did you buy that pair?', none of these insights would be revealed and instead, your marketing team would just feel affirmed in its decision to promote its new lightweight running shoes with big in-store displays.

Instead, you have the answers and insights to investigate further with other customers and inform your company's transformation vision, including answers to the following questions.

1   Does the current customer experience match what's being promised?

The website attracted the customer with a low price and then failed to provide any services to help him find the perfect shoe online. This is the opposite of what's promised in the mission statement, which promises superior products with superior service, not low prices.

2   Does your existing digital estate deliver to the customer's actual needs?

The customer wanted to buy a specific pair of shoes online, and the site couldn't facilitate the purchase, even though the inventory was available in one of your stores.

3   What technology innovations could improve customer experience and decrease competitive threat?

The missing shoes in the store point to an obvious problem with your online inventory management and your shop inventory management.

There are also quick fix opportunities to use digital devices in-store so customers can self-serve and access personalized recommendations when staff are busy.

4   What business innovations could improve customer experience and decrease competitive threat?

There are opportunities to use digital innovation on the website and in physical stores to help customers find the perfect equipment for their specific needs. Digital innovation could also be used to help staff in stores provide better advice, and even ongoing support, for customers training for new sports.

There are business model opportunities as well. For example, a replacement shoe service that automatically sends the customer a new pair of shoes after they're reached a set number of miles, which can be tracked using software added to their existing fitness and personal devices.

What's next: Use conversations to create lasting bridges

By digging to uncover the real 'why', you find out not just the cause of the customer's decision to engage with you, you can also start forming networks with these customers to test new ideas.

In the shoe example, you could offer to refund the customer's purchase and give him the shoes he should be wearing for free, in exchange for sending photos and milestone feedback as he uses the shoes and agrees to be approached as a beta-test user of new digital services and products in the future.

Insights with customers and consumers are only the first half of the external gaps you need to close in Bridge.

The second half are found in the rapidly changing external conditions influenced by digital technology that your company must align to when meeting the needs of its customers.

The next section explains how to analyse and assess opportunities and threats in the external environment in relation to the competitive and technology landscape.

Bridge the gaps: Competitive and technology landscapes

The rift between you and your customers is the most important external gap to close in Bridge, though it's also important to seal the gaps between your organization and the external conditions it operates in. This means investigating the competition to see how well it's adapting (or not adapting) to the effects of digital and other changing external conditions. This will determine how urgently you need to transform, and by making connections with experts and suppliers in technology, you can be inspired with ways to accomplish it.

Like the previous section, every sector and organization faces its own unique blend of competitors, peers and technology that can either help or threaten its

I'm a big believer in user and behavioural research. Go out and meet with your customers where they are, and understand what the real-life use case for engagement with your product is. Quantitative research is vital for understanding the addressable market and competitive landscape. However, this doesn't obviate the need for taking a look at your buyers and seeing how they would actually use the technology – a step too often omitted by both large corporations (e.g. an internet-enabled eyewear product) and small start-ups (e.g. a cold-press juice company). Getting close to your users is another important way to assess product/market fit.

Interview with Perry Hewitt, Vice-President of Marketing, ITHAKA
Former Chief Digital Officer, Harvard University, 2011–2016

Many times, you hear 'But it's the way we've always done things' or 'I've been with the organization 10, 15, 20, 30 years' or just 'I don't know what's going on in the real world'. For us there was also this sort of malaise of 'well, we're the American Cancer Society, of course people want to give to us'. Well, in the last twenty years there are 1,000 other organizations that serve the same type of cause. They may be much smaller, not have our breadth and depth, but they're far more nimble and they're far more in the face of many of our potential donors and volunteers. I said we have got to allow people to fundraise on their own terms.

Interview with Jay Ferro, Executive Vice President, EarthLink
Former Chief Information Officer, American Cancer Society, 2012–2016

daily operations. As such, the same outline is provided below to guide the core objectives of bridging these gaps and questions to answer regardless of sector or organizations size. The suggested methods you can use can then inspire ways that will work for your own unique context.

At a glance: Bridge gaps with the technology and competitive landscape

Who? Leaders and key staff from around your organization engaging directly with peers in related companies and with experts and suppliers in relevant technology fields.

What? Form meaningful connections with peers, experts, and suppliers externally by engaging with them directly. This creates opportunities for collaborative working and skills exchange and allows you to experience first-hand what technologies and new digitally enabled ways of working are being used successfully.

Why? Your company's people receive direct insights to what's possible with digital transformation, and how urgently it needs to be accomplished.

When? Allow enough time for key members of staff and leadership to gain initial insights – technology and competition is always changing, so there's no such thing as knowing everything.

How? The best results come from finding ways to collaborate over short engagements with relevant peers, experts, and suppliers outside your organization.

Objectives

1 Gather evidence in the form of successful examples and case studies for why and how your company needs to transform.
2 Gather examples of technology that can help (e.g. decrease costs, improve quality) and technology that could threaten your business if adopted by a competitor.
3 Gather examples of new business models (e.g. subscription models, on-demand selling) and ways of working that could add business value or enhance customer experiences.
4 Benchmark your company against its competitors and peers, including those outside of sector that are appealing the same customer base with a related product or service.*

*Note: This is especially true for very conservative organizations that tend to only transform as much as their direct peers or competitors. This puts you at risk for when a competitor suddenly leaps forward, or when a new entrant to the sector suddenly steals a huge portion of the market share.

Questions to answer

- How have competitors and peers adapted to new conditions shaped by digital expectations?
- How are competitors or alternative choices in the marketplace meeting customer needs better than you?
- What technology innovations could add business value or enhance customer experiences?
- What new business models and ways of working are resonating with your target consumers that you could leverage through digital technology?

Methods you can use

- Speak at and attend conferences, seminars and events for digital professionals, start-ups, as well as events relevant to your sector but with innovation and digital as its focus.
- Connect senior leadership in your organization to their counterparts in more digitally adapted organizations, for example, CIO and CMO levels.
- Invite technology experts and peers in more advanced organizations to give talks and host working groups for relevant people in your organization.

I'm quite keen on using industry seminars and round tables. I use that for me and my senior team as a bit of a check that we're moving in the same direction as other people. That our vision is broadly aligned in tone and direction with the rest of the world. I look to retailers, charities and travel companies – people who know how to manage customer data at scale efficiently. What I'm going to try and do at the *Guardian* is to implement a loyalty model that's not one that's come from the publishing sector. I'm trying to transform with loyalty approaches learned from other verticals.

Interview with Laura Scarlett, Data & Insight Director,
Guardian News & Media
Former Programme Director, Supporter Loyalty, National Trust, 2013–2015

- Facilitate skills exchanges, temporary placements, and job shadowing for relevant people in your organization with more advanced peers and technology companies.
- Create small projects that allow collaboration between your organization's leaders with relevant peers, experts, and suppliers.
- Give preference to job candidates with technology and digital backgrounds for upcoming vacancies.

Engaging experts and suppliers for digital transformation

There is a plethora of digital technology available and you need to have a basic understanding of what can help you better fulfil your mission statement, improve operational efficiency, and fill gaps in your current experience in ways that can lead to new revenue, better collaboration and engagement.

Ultimately, what you're trying to assemble is a list of technology that can help (e.g. increase efficiency through automation) and technology that's a threat to your core business.

But because this will be very different depending on your company's sector and size, knowing where to start in bridging these gaps can be challenging. For example, if your company is relatively small and unknown, you'll have a much harder time attracting and building bridges with experts and suppliers than someone from a high-profile company whose reputation alone makes it an appealing candidate for collaboration.

Fortunately, there are ways to overcome these barriers, and they stem from the rules of engagement common to all organizations, regardless of size or budget, for connecting with experts, peers and suppliers.

How to write a good brief
During my career, regardless of whether it's been in an agency or at a global technology firm, I'm always surprised by the inconsistency of briefs written by clients looking for help with major projects. Even in situations where directly competing companies are requesting a price for the same service, one brief will be long, prescriptive, and with no room for suggestions or alternatives, while the other is as little as a few lines in an email.

In practice, both are terrible ways to write a brief, even down to the detail of them being sent in writing, instead of starting with a conversation.

When framing your brief for any expert or supplier, bear in mind the following guidelines:

1   **State your overall objective but also invite their input:** Always
    start with what your company is trying to achieve and why, but never
    prescribe how you think it should do it – not knowing how is the reason
    you're reaching out to them in the first place.
2   **Start small and be specific:** Suggest a first step (e.g. an invitation to
    discuss the opportunity) but also state the timeline you're working to and
    how you'd like to work with them.
3   **Set realistic expectations:** If you're approaching many suppliers and
    experts, state this upfront so there's no false expectation of exclusivity
    but with acknowledgement of their unique skills and strengths.

Internal Gaps

What are internal gaps?

If you're looking to digitally transform, it's likely your internal structures, processes, ways of working, and company culture aren't designed to leverage the full benefits of digital.

Like most companies, yours probably operates within a hierarchy and departmental structure, where people are measured by performance targets established long before the digital age, so there's little incentive to work harder to implement something that won't go towards a raise or promotion during year-end reviews.

It's also likely that digital skills in your company are sequestered in a centralized digital team or innovation lab, or sit with external agencies and contractors. This means it takes a long time for new technology to get onto management's radar, and even longer for the skills and expertise required to leverage it to reach all departments – if they ever do.

If this sounds like your situation, what you're actually facing are internal gaps within your organization between members of its own management and leadership, the objectives of its different departments, and the staff operating in functional silos within it.

Bridging internal gaps has already started in the previous section, by involving key leaders and staff in the activities needed to close the external gaps between your customers, consumers and the competitive and technology landscape.

The next step is to understand what caused your internal gaps to form in the first place and capture solutions in a shared vision for transformation. The shared vision is a succinct set of statements used to win support for transformation from the different leaders within your business and to begin the programme in earnest by gathering sponsors to guide and oversee the programme.

The final section is about setting up your own digital transformation leadership group for BUILD Stage 2: Uncover, when you start uncovering the barriers in your company's internal skills and resources to prioritize what projects to undertake first on your transformation journey versus those that need a bigger business case and investment.

By the end, you'll have the foundation needed to support a transformation programme that will have a profound and sustainable impact on your company, inside and out.

Bridging internal gaps

Who: Leaders and managers across selected functional areas and customer-facing staff across different areas and levels.

What: Articulate the reasons your company needs to do to transform and in what ways, by creating and presenting an evidenced shared vision for transformation.

Why: To win support and gain enough insight to start some initial activities and projects. Also to appoint transformation leadership duties to a small, select group of senior leaders as sponsors.

When: Only take as much time needed to align sufficient sponsorship to get one or two projects started. You will use the successful, incremental outcomes of these first projects to win further support and resources in BUILD Stage 4: Leverage.

By going around and dedicating time to understanding the activities in flight, how they add value and the activities that aren't being done, you do two things. First, you enrich your understanding of how the company works, which is essential if you are a transformation agent. Second, you build relationships. It creates a dialogue between the people who are doing the work and the people who are looking at the transformation needs. When you build up that communication then you start understanding the nuances of things that have been tried before and failed before. Then you understand the culture. If you know the business and you understand the workplace culture, then you've got two of the most important things you need to figure out if any initiative – digital or otherwise will work.

Interview with Bryan Van Dyke, Managing Director & Head of Digital,
Morgan Stanley

Objectives:

1 Identify gaps within your organization that are preventing you from adapting to changing external needs and conditions.
2 Identify answers to how your company should be delivering to those external needs and conditions if those gaps didn't exist and your company had been founded today.
3 Capture this 'before and after' state in an evidenced 'shared vision for transformation' that's succinct, aspirational, human, relatable, evidenced, and decisive.
4 Align selected leaders to support this shared vision by guiding the implementation of the digital transformation programme.

Questions to answer:

1 What would our company look like if it was founded today?
2 What relationships should exist between staff and departments to deliver to current customer needs?
3 What processes would need to be in place to react to changes in external needs and conditions?
4 What leaders across functional units of the business have the influence and power required to oversee the first projects needed to start the transformation programme?

> Executive sponsorship is critical. We could not have had the success we enjoyed at Harvard without the leadership's strong buy-in. That's absolutely critical and that's more than lip service and more than 'big bang' launch. That's someone who's going to be at your side when people are getting comfortable with being uncomfortable, and that's a really important space to get to and be in.
>
> Interview with Perry Hewitt, Vice-President of Marketing, ITHAKA
> Former Chief Digital Officer, Harvard University, 2011–2016

Tips for success

- Identify champions of digital transformation in your staff and leadership early and use their willingness and enthusiasm to influence others.

- Don't waste time trying to persuade others who aren't interested in change through discussion alone. Instead, find others to work with and start producing results you can leverage.

- Don't share the vision beyond the people whose support, power, and influence you need to start the programme. The time for publicity comes later when you have results to share.

A word of caution: Don't skip the shared vision

It might be tempting to skip this stage – especially if you've already been running a transformation programme and already have a vision for it – but this is a mistake. A shared transformation vision is very different from any other kind and for good reason.

The section on 'How to Create a Shared Vision for Transformation' addresses the real ingredients of a transformation vision that will:

1 Address the specific problems intrinsic to your entire company that, if not addressed, will simply cause you to fall behind again – even if initial attempts to modernize are successful.
2 Be specific enough in what it addresses to inspire the leaders across all of your existing infrastructure and operations that change isn't only possible, it's necessary.
3 Be open enough in how it can be achieved that you can identify and prioritize different routes to transformation in BUILD Stage 2: Uncover, and then use State 3: Iterate, to trial different solutions.

Most 'transformation visions' I come across aren't actually visions, they're a list of business goals or IT and marketing projects. Simply stating you want to increase your number of transactions, sales, engagement, or any other metric is not going to inspire anyone to change, or indicate the changes needed.

Neither will a list of major programmes or campaigns. In one example, a global financial and insurance firm invited me to run a session about digital transformation to its senior leaders. To prepare, I asked for a copy of any strategies they're currently working on, and I was told they had just crafted a digital transformation vision. To my dismay, the version I received included items: 'new CRM' and 'new customer facing website'.

Not only is this not a vision (it's a to-do list, at best), it gives no reason why these activities are required, or what change they are meant to achieve when complete.

If your vision is tied to a particular technology set, then in only a few years' time you'll be left with a software stack that's no longer good enough by competitive standards, and all the same external and internal gaps as before – but now compounded by years of inaction.

Where do internal gaps come from?

The best way to resolve internal gaps is to understand what causes them to form in the first place.

Probably the biggest learning about transformation for me in the several projects I've done over the last decade has been you need absolute clarity on ultimate project benefit: why are you doing it? You're not delivering a project for its own sake or a programme of its own sake for transformation. By holding on to that ultimate good, it will help you navigate the project better in my experience.

As for digital, I can't think of a single transformation project I've been involved in that didn't have a digital component. Digital can be a bit player, a sort of tool that helps facilitate a wider programme of organizational change, or a central programme or pillar of change that utterly revolutionizes your organization.

Interview with Dr Charmaine Griffiths, Chief Operating Officer,
The Institute for Cancer Research
Former Executive Director of Strategy & Performance,
British Heart Foundation, 2013–2016

The biggest and most universal reason for internal gaps within an organization actually stem from the traditional approach most companies take to achieve growth and scale.

It's this system of establishing hierarchies and trying to standardize processes and offerings across a mass scale that's fundamentally incompatible with today's pace of change and the digitally influenced consumer's expectation of more personalized and localized goods and services.

The problem with hierarchies: Inward facing company structures

For the last 100+ years, companies have created hierarchies, departments, and standardized offerings in order to scale and sustain growth. The longer a company is in business, the more layers of hierarchy and process are put in place to maintain centralized control. Once a good alignment with external needs and conditions was achieved by the company's founders, efforts would be made to standardize ways of delivering them.

The purpose of standardization is to predict and reduce cost to serve, while preserving the consistency of the brand and customer experience across bigger and more diverse markets – like McDonald's and its empire of nearly identical restaurants, no matter what country, city, or neighbourhood you visit. A company that's standardized has a second advantage: it's easier to grow, but for this you need hierarchies. Hierarchies let the people at the top maintain overall control. They're able to make decisions that affect the entire business, while delegating oversight and responsibility of individual parts of the business to individual leaders in those areas.

Within particularly large hierarchies, you'll also find hierarchies within each branch. Departments and regions form their own processes and structures and start to operate more autonomously to achieve their own (often competing) targets assigned by the global executive group.

The effectiveness of this traditional model to start, grow, and run a major company is based on three important assumptions:

1) The people at the top of the hierarchy are the most qualified and informed to make all important decisions.

2) Change can be assessed, then responses implemented across the entire organization, allowing for one big period of activity followed by a return to steady state.

3) Standardized offerings can meet the needs of all customers, with minor alterations only when significant factors demand them.

Unfortunately, for most businesses today, this model is invalidated by three major changes brought about by the ubiquity of digital technology:

1) Change happens too quickly for people at the top of a hierarchy to stay informed enough to make all important decisions.

2) Change doesn't happen evenly, so businesses must account for customers having differing needs, behaviours, and expectations within the same segments and regions.

3) Localization and personalization are easily facilitated through technology, so standardized offerings are failing to meet new customer expectations.

These problems are then compounded by:

1) The people in charge don't realize changes are needed until long after problems have appeared at customer level.

2) Multiple signs of trouble result in disagreement over the root cause of the problems and what approach should be taken to resolve it.

3) Not knowing where to start results in longer delays and more problems occurring, which only compounds the effects of inaction.

The silo effect: Internal gaps lead to disjointed companies

Hierarchical and standardized structures lead to gaps between areas with the business, resulting in a silo effect as individual leadership teams stop sharing objectives, insights, or even customer data.

For example, I work with a lot of major international charities, and it's not uncommon for the fundraising department to be completely separate from the campaigns department. One charity was so siloed that customers who ran sponsored races for them and then later donated money on the website were subsequently treated as two separate people: forever doomed to receive double of every future charity appeal because each department believed they were engaging with their own distinct customer base.

The winners today are the organizations who close internal gaps like this because it allows them to act as one company, anticipating and meeting the needs of its customers, in spite of the fact that those needs are always changing.

Even McDonald's, the business textbook example of standardization on a global scale, is being forced to change its ways. In 2015, the CEO of McDonald's publicly published a video (Peterson 2015) addressed to its stakeholders, explaining the company's poor performance over the last ten years is down to overly rigid hierarchies and processes across the company that were preventing innovation and the ability to adapt to the changing preferences of their customers.

An argument I often have at The Guardian is I say 'give the customers
what they value', then the response is 'ok so we should just produce cat
videos then'. It's very interesting for me because I came from a marketing
background, it was quite easy to be customer-centric because the more
customer-centric you are, the more you sell. But now I've broadened my
field and I'm working in whole company transformation rather than just the
marketing bit, these difficulties do come out.

Even if we did exactly what our Guardian readers wanted us to do, it
would be highly unlikely they'd want us to produce cat videos. The same at
the National Trust. The argument I used to get was 'Oh so our members want
an ice cream van in every field – is that what you want?' But of course, they
wouldn't actually or else they wouldn't be members of the National Trust,
they'd go to Lego Land instead. So there's a symbiotic relationship between
the brand values and the customer. There is so much opportunity, so much
can be accomplished with data and technology.

Interview with Laura Scarlett, Data & Insight Director,
Guardian News & Media
Former Programme Director, Supporter Loyalty, National Trust, 2013–2015

Since then, McDonald's has been working to 'digitally transform' through
launching new innovations in store, but more important, by closing the gaps
between McDonald's leadership, the people they're meant to serve, and the
markets they operate in.

Shared vision for transformation

A successful shared vision for transformation is one that inspires and excites
people in the same way an entrepreneur must pitch to investors for a new
business that hasn't yet been launched.

Traditionally, a business vision is a succinct and inspirational set of statements
that outline how a company will achieve its mission. This is also true of a 'shared
vision for transformation' but with two important distinctions.

A vision is transformational when it calls out what needs to change about the
current ways of operating based on changes externally. A vision is 'shared' when
it requires collaboration from all parts of the business in order to achieve it.

How to create your own transformation vision

Imagine you're founding your company today, and you're looking for senior leaders to join and investors to provide funding.

The vision you'd pitch wouldn't talk about operational models, products or services – it would outline what you're going to do and why, and it would spell out what everyone stands to gain long term for buying in.

Imagining your business being new is a very helpful analogy because unlike an improvement programme that takes a bit of time away from 'business as usual', a digital transformation programme is one that sets out to change the business' very definition.

This is one of the reasons leaders of younger companies have an easier time adapting to new technology. Even if they've built up infrastructure around particular products and services, they're still close enough to the founding principles of the company that they're not precious about preserving current operating models if the business needs to move in a new direction to continue delivering on the original promise and purpose.

Getting into the founder's mindset for your vision

To craft an inspiring shared vision, start by looking at the very reasons why your organization was founded and became successful in the first place. Ask yourself 'why does your company exist?'

Be careful how you respond, though; the longer your business has been operating, the less obvious the answer will be. Ask a typical employee of any long-

---

Sometimes the vision is clear and evident. Some external threats are obvious, making what you need to do especially clear. Sometimes you don't know. You just know that something's broken or that something has been missed. When that happens, you have to search for the opportunity and where there's receptivity to new ways of doing things.

My advice would be find the common ground that will allow you to understand the fastest and most valuable route to your digital destination, possibly before you even know what the destination is. Reaching a common ground and having interactions are the hallmarks of getting anything done.

Interview with Bryan VanDyke, Managing Director & Head of Digital,
Morgan Stanley

established business 'why' the company exists, and you'll hear a list of products and services offered and markets served. This is not the answer to 'why'.

The real answer to 'why' should be in your mission statement. If yours is a true mission statement, it will be wide reaching and ambitious – setting out the company's desire to solve a major problem, meet a major need, answer a universal question, or significantly enhance the lives of many people. It will also be timeless and general enough as to not define 'how' the mission will be met, which will maintain its relevance regardless of the year or state of the marketplace. Your mission statement will be independent from your current products, services, or assets, aspiring instead to fulfil a higher purpose that's bigger than the sum of its parts.

At a glance: Create your shared transformation vision

Who? Select members of your company's leadership collaborate to create a shared vision for transformation.

Why? To clearly state the changes needed to bring the organization back in line with customer needs and external conditions.

What? Succinct statements that outline the changes will enable the organization to continuously deliver meaningful value to your customers, while improving life inside the company as well.

When? As quickly as possible. Start with a draft and continue sharing and revising it. A transformation vision is meant to be a living document and communications tool, so don't delay progress by trying to perfect it.

The first thing companies have to do before they attempt digital transformation is actually define what it is that they do. The vast majority of companies I've worked with over the past few years have no idea what it is they actually do. For a business that's almost always solving a particular problem. Once you've got that reason, do what I call 'legacy-free reinvention'. Go away and work out how you would approach solving that problem if you were starting from scratch. That means saying, 'Ok, if I wasn't surrounded by these few thousand people and these processes and legacies, how would I approach solving this problem as a new modern business? If I had to start again, how would I solve the problems that my company is meant to be solving'.

Interview with Ben Hammersley, Futurist, BBC World Presenter
'Cybercrime, with Ben Hammersley' & WIRED Contributing Editor

Objectives:

- Describe your company's future approach to success in direct contrast to what it's doing today.

- Capture the biggest areas of change needed that are universal to your entire operation.

- Inspire people to address the internal and external gaps that have formed in the company.

Questions to answer:

1. If your company was founded today, how would it be set up to best meet external needs?
2. How is success currently measured for each area within your organization?
3. What are the common causes of failures, losses, and inefficiencies within each area?
4. What internal measures of success are at odds with the needs of customers?
5. How are decisions made and measured across the business?
6. What decision-making processes are at odds with the nature of changing external conditions?
7. Where are the natural crossover points in your company's internal operations where digital technology and new ways of working could lead to greater success externally?

Tips for success:

- To write a shared transformation vision that resonates across your organization, you'll need to understand the personal goals and motivations of each leader within it.

- Start with the most senior and influential people in your organization. Turn your shared vision into a short and impactful presentation and get them to help you shape it.

- Secure the endorsement of your company's most influential leaders first before you present more widely.

Informing and winning support for the shared vision

The biggest internal gaps are often the ones between the leaders of each area within your organization. By nature, leaders are competitive, so they'll look for

Everything is a business case, even in the non-profit sector; our existence depends on public trust and public trust is rooted in effective use of donor resources. So we can't on a whim make changes, they have to be rooted in an evidence-based approach and having a body of evidence that highlights the value of this shift is probably the number one starting point. Then it's working with people like the author of this book who help organizations with their change management and how to modernize and evolve various approaches.

You have to really start with the external landscape, see examples of why this kind of change is important, then slowly and incrementally implement that change institutionally within the organizational structures.

Interview with Zach Abraham, Director of Global Campaigns,
WWF International

ways to improve their own department's success before contributing to resources for the greater good of the organization.

Fail to align your senior executives, and internal politics or arguments over resources and priorities will prevent your digital transformation vision from being seen through to the end.

Where to start: Align influential leaders

Always start with the most influential and powerful of your company's senior leadership. That said, if the IT and marketing leadership in your company are among its most respected leaders, they will be a crucial ally for helping lead transformation.

If IT and marketing aren't respected or influential within your company, it's likely this is a direct contributor to your need for digital transformation. You'll still need to consult them because you can't digital transform without the cooperation of the people who manage and maintain current systems and external engagement channels. Just don't expect an undervalued IT or marketing manager to lead the transformation programme.

And whatever you do, don't talk about technology

You don't want your transformation programme turning into a vehicle for every division's pre-existing IT request that's only going to improve the state of business as usual. You want to transform ways of working, devise new revenue streams,

> At the National Trust I went for a practical approach, which was the new infrastructure would enable us to be more efficient at certain things. I've always tried to veer away from these big conceptual arguments and get on with the practical. So for example at the National Trust, the data system allowed us to identify people who were using old membership cards and nobody liked that. The medieval tapestry person and the marketing director both didn't like the fact that people were using old cards and basically defrauding the National Trust to the tune of about £5 million a year, so that was a great win.
>
> **Interview with Laura Scarlett, Data & Insight Director, Guardian News & Media Former Programme Director, Supporter Loyalty, National Trust, 2013–2015**

and open the company to collaborative working through external networks that grow value outside its traditional sources.

You'll find it very difficult to get 'big picture' thinking out of them – or even honest answers – if the senior leaders think the proposals they worked so hard to create for their areas might get backing if they can hitch it to your digital transformation programme.

The other very good reason for avoiding technology is it quickly becomes a barrier between you and the person you're speaking to.

It doesn't matter how technical a person is, there will always be a new development, product, or concept that they don't know about or haven't heard of but – and this is real kicker – there's something about technology that makes people afraid to admit when they don't know something.

For example, I've sat through meetings where senior executives have nodded along to technical recommendations by an IT specialist, only to receive surreptitious emails from the same execs afterwards asking me to explain the entire presentation.

How to craft a shared transformation vision

It's critical for the success of your transformation programme that the vision is understood and valued by everyone in the company.

The SHARED formula

Spelling the word 'shared' with the first letter of each descriptor, the most successful visions for transformation meet the following criteria:

Strategies that I would deploy normally, in terms of bringing experts in from the outside, spending time with people in off hours, taking them to different talks, giving them examples of other companies, we still do because we have to. Just because the CEO says it has to happen doesn't mean it's going to, but having that support makes a huge difference.

We've brought people in from other companies such as Disney and other hospitality businesses because you have to change out some of the leadership to get new thinking that's actually done this work. This is not the on-the-job thing that people can lead. You've either done it or you haven't. If you haven't, it's difficult to jump in and start it all by yourself.

Interview with Mike Giresi, Chief Information Officer,
Royal Caribbean Cruises
Former Chief Information Officer, Tory Burch, 2011–2015

1. Succinct

A good shared vision for transformation is pared back to the essentials only: 'why' change is needed, 'what' changes are needed, and the benefits they'll give to customers and the organization itself, and 'how' it can be started.

2. Human-centric

The focus isn't technology or business metrics. There are clear benefits to people – internally and externally. These benefits also aren't based on fads or current preferences, but relate to fundamental and ongoing needs and wants.

3. Aspirational

Complete transformation takes years, not months, so the vision needs to set high expectations that will continue to motivate people throughout the programme, and incentivize the work required to make big changes.

4. Relatable

The shared vision needs to be relatable to anyone within the organization, no matter the department or role. The easiest test for this is whether three people from different levels of seniority and different areas (e.g. the director of HR, a customer relations staff member, and the IT manager) can all see how the changes proposed in it would benefit them – either directly or indirectly – and therefore understand the vision, and its worth.

5. Evidence

Evidence that supports why change is needed and what benefits you'll get proves the practicality of the vision, but this can be difficult if the evidence you want isn't publicly available (e.g. the sales figures of your competitors following their transformations). This is where creative thinking comes in: insights gathered from customers, media coverage of competitors, measurable success of companies outside your sector that cater to the same audiences or face the same external conditions – all are excellent forms of evidence to support your need for change.

6. Decisive

Last, a shared vision for transformation is unambiguous about the changes needed. The best format for this is using a 'current state' versus 'future state' format, or 'before' and 'after'.

Inspiration for your shared vision for transformation

You can use the following questions to identify what your own vision should contain and determine how you need to frame it.

1. Why now?

What's different now that makes change necessary? For example:

- Evidence of problems and losses already happening (to your company or companies like it) due to internal and external gaps.

- Time-sensitive opportunities your company can pursue, evidenced by successes from other sectors and/or newly acquired insights from your customer base.

Get the vision well thought out and agreed before you embark on any technical implementation.

There are two sides to the vision: One is what does it do for the customer? How does it change the customer's life? So that took the form of various workshops at the National Trust about what a member experience is now and what we want a member to experience in the future.

The other side of the vision is how it changes people's jobs and work for the better, inside the organization. One's a strategic vision for the customer, and the other's a more practical 'how it improves people's lives in the building'.

Interview with Laura Scarlett, Data & Insight Director, Guardian News & Media
Former Programme Director, Supporter Loyalty, National Trust, 2013–2015

- Evidence that external conditions are about to change but the direction is unknown, so your company needs to be able to react faster than current operations allow.

- Examples of where the company has tried big changes in the past but failed, or were blocked from going further, and why now is different.

2. What's at stake?

What are the company-wide benefits you'll gain if the transformation goes well, which can equally be framed as losses or risks if the company fails to act? For example:

- Ways of increasing staff accountability, reducing bureaucracy, and making it easier to attract and retain top talent.

- Examples of how customer's lives can be improved through better and more personalized offerings and reducing the time and effort to get what they want.

3. How do we need to change?

A useful format for framing your vision generally, but especially for explaining the 'how' you need to transform, is in context of the current state versus the transformed state. For example:

- Comparisons of the company's actions today versus tomorrow, paired with specific examples and pieces of evidence that demonstrate the benefits.

- Describe the culture and decision-making styles of the company today versus tomorrow. This could be the difference between time lost in meetings versus not needing as many meetings thanks to collaborative working approaches.

Example vision: B2B financial firm

I once worked with a global finance firm because it was losing market share to a recently transformed competitor that was expertly adopting and using digital channels in ways unprecedented in the sector at the time.

The firm's main function is B2B, selling stock, bonds, and funds through independent financial advisors and wealth managers.

Like its competitors, one of the main jobs of the firm is to provide accurate and timely analysis of market changes as it relates to the financial products sold by the firm. This is critical to meeting external needs, because wealth managers and independent financial advisors depend on these analyses to advise their own clients and make informed portfolio decisions when the markets change.

You start by asking where do you see your organization in the next fifteen years? How does your mandate remain relevant? How does your mandate need to change to continue being relevant? Then you work back from that to identify the big change. At WWF, we have our core mission: Building a world where people and the planet can live in harmony. Our big change drivers are what that landscape is going to look like in 2030.

More often than not, organizations are scared to do that because that requires a different set of skills than those required for incremental and programmatic change. Particularly from the NGO world, we're very driven by doing what we do really well, and selling what we do today really well. Thinking about the areas we need to change our mandate around is really complex and scary, and often meets tons of resistance. You really have to reconceptualize large components of your brand. That is a terrifying value proposition for organizations when most employees don't stay in the same organization for twenty or thirty years, and so they want to define success in the short term.

Interview with Zach Abraham, Director of Global Campaigns, WWF International

Here is just one set of examples from the firm's shared vision for transformation, with the wording changed to protect anonymity:

Today:

- Our analysis of changes in the financial markets are of inconsistent quality, take hours to produce, and are viewed by fewer than half of their intended audiences.

- Our competitors are using new channels to reach greater audiences – including our customers – and they have streamlined their ways of working to produce analysis on the same topics within one hour of the market change.

Our shared vision for transformation is:

- To eliminate internal processes that cause duplication and barriers that impede collaboration.

- To use the best available technology to reach our customers in the format they prefer.

- To develop close connections with our customers to ensure the messages received are what they need to ensure their own financial success – especially when those needs change.

When I started as general director of the Rijksmuseum in 2008, in the middle of a very difficult building process, troubled by regulations, building authorities and local committees always against everything, I asked myself where do I begin, and where in fact does the museum start? I decided that a visit to the Rijksmuseum did not start in the galleries. Every visit to the Rijksmuseum starts in the head of the visitor. I wanted to make the visit to the Rijksmuseum the highlight of your day, or even your holiday. So, with that in mind, I decided to stretch the time of the visit to the max.

'Open' became my focus, and it became my main theme for the new Rijksmuseum. 'Open' to the Rijksmuseum is threefold: an open building, an open attitude and an open collection. The most radical change however we achieved was the opening up of our collection. The Rijksmuseum was the first cultural institution in the world to radically change its digital policy. We took the unusual step of offering high-resolution images from our collection, copyright-free for everybody to download at no cost. We gave unlimited access to over 200,000 works of the renowned collection, including all the masterworks by Rembrandt, Vermeer and Van Gogh. The Rijksmuseum believed that using the advantages of the Internet to share the collection, everyone could participate to bring art anywhere and in any which way into the public domain.

And this hasn't been proven wrong. Since the reopening of the Rijksmuseum and launch of the website in April 2013, the users of the digital Rijksmuseum triple the 'real' visitors to the museum building in Amsterdam. Millions of users took their advantage of the sheer endless new possibilities of the interactive tool Rijksstudio. T-shirts, car designs, coffee mugs, furniture, fashion and new paint decors originated from the rich Rijksstudio sources. And while the virtual museum is not a substitute for bricks and mortar, these figures clearly show that the actual museum nowadays is much more than just a building.

Interview with Wim Pijbes, Director, Stichting Droom en Daad
Former General Director, Rijksmuseum, 2008–2016

Leadership needed for transformation

With any major programme, you need a leadership group responsible for starting it, guiding it and ensuring its success.

This is especially true for a digital transformation programme – even one that's starting with a very small set of initial projects – because of the cross-functional nature of the work required.

In fact, the two most important jobs of any transformation leadership group when a programme starts is simply freeing up staff time and company resources from doing business as usual and removing barriers that are often caused by other senior leaders.

The anatomy of a transformation leadership group

Sponsors

The person or people with sufficient seniority, power, and resource to fund and propel transformation efforts. Ideally, this is the leader of the organization, though it can also be senior executives or board members, provided they have sufficient influence and budget control.

Champions

People in senior leadership and key influential roles who are also hungry for change and can contribute time, resource, and influence from their respective areas. These people are your programme advocates, and the areas of the business and markets they control are the perfect areas to trial new projects, ideas, and solutions.

The change agent

The person (or people) ultimately accountable and responsible for leading projects within the programme and achieving the shared vision for transformation. The change agent is the key decision maker, responsible for driving the digital transformation agenda. Their professional reputation rests on the transformation's success or failure.

Leading transformation: The role of the change agent

Change agent, programme director, or head of transformation: it doesn't matter what you call the person who does it, but every major programme needs a strong leader or set of leaders to align expectations, remove obstacles, and bring people together as the projects within the programme are implemented.

In the case of major digital innovation, this person doesn't have to be the most experienced in the technology either – in fact, many great change agents aren't.

Instead, this person must have the right level of seniority to effect change at the senior leadership level and be capable of inspiring others to invest their time and collaborate outside traditional structures in order to complete initiatives that could never be done by any one department alone.

Three key roles of the change agent

1. **The face of digital transformation:** Representing and answering for the programme at all important meetings and presentations.
2. **Remover of barriers:** Escalating and facilitating the removal of major barriers that individuals/departments can't overcome.
3. **Driver of transformation:** Advocating transformation and keeping it in the spotlight both internally and externally.

In truth, the ideal change agent is also the sponsor – in other words, the leader of the organization with ultimate power to make and enforce decisions about budgets, operations, objectives, and ways of working. However, it's rare for this to be the case.

In truth, even when the change agent is the CEO, there are still boards, stakeholders, and investors to answer to – and if your organization is part of a confederation, run by government, unionized, or in a highly regulated sector, then the power at the top is even more diluted.

Regardless of the seniority of the change agent, there are five characteristics all successful change agents possess: the five Cs of a successful change agent.

The five Cs of successful change agents

1. Compelling

Successful change agents have a strong presence and the ability to command attention, win hearts, and minds and inspire others to follow their lead down a high-risk and uncertain path.

The change agent of any programme will spend more time talking to groups and building consensus than any other activity.

2. Connected

Change agents need to know the right experts externally and all key players across an organization internally. If they're new, they'll get to know every key stakeholder quickly.

This starts at the top and takes the form of understanding what motivates each senior leader. Knowing the objective for each senior executive and how each person's success will be measured lets the change agent encourage agreement and collaboration from those departments.

3. Current

A great change agent is up-to-date on technology and what the competition and relevant other sectors are doing because this information is one of the best evidence bases for change within your own company.

4. Creative

It's not enough to be clever; the best change agents can solve big problems creatively.

As transformation programmes build momentum and more and more projects are added to the plans, change agents constantly face situations where the needed change directly conflicts with a process, way of working, product, or service the company currently values greatly. It could even be the only reason for a senior leadership position or entire department to exist.

This doesn't mean they should shy away from pushing to change it, but it does require a significant ability to think beyond the current operational set-up and devise brand new solutions.

5. Committed

There will be times when everything seems to go wrong and the best change agents are the calm, cool head in the face of the storm.

For successful change agents, one of the best methods for remaining committed when things go wrong is the process they use for assessing why a failure has occurred. This is covered in more detail in BUILD Stage 3: Iterate.

Commitment is also important because digital transformation programmes take years, not months. Change agents must be more committed to seeing the change through than anyone else in the company.

How to find a change agent

Every organization needs at least one person acting as change agent, at senior or mid-management level, leading and overseeing projects over the course of an entire programme. If you can't identify a person, or a combination of people, who possess the five Cs and enthusiastically align with and want to deliver the shared vision, then you'll need to hire externally.

You have to have someone lead who's adept at understanding and assessing the problem, identifying where gaps exist, can have those conversations with different parts of the business and understand what's working and what's not.

You may have a brilliant idea and you just want to move forward, but what matters in an organization is if the people agree to work on it. Because when it comes down to it, even in a highly digitized economy, there are no businesses that don't involve people. And every business that involves people means you have to engage, you have to inspire, and you have to motivate people to work in a certain way.

So, the person to lead your change must know how to connect with the different parts of the business, truly unearth the problems that exist that seem to relate to the digital capacities, such as competitors. If they don't know the technology, they need to get a partner who does understand it because you don't want to go down the road of 'solutioning' without someone who truly understands that domain. It's ok though if that partner isn't leading every charge.

Interview with Bryan VanDyke, Managing Director & Head of Digital,
Morgan Stanley

Three things to know when hiring change agents externally

1. **Pay for the best:** They need to be impressive and experienced enough to (a) know what they're doing and (b) compensate for lacking history in the company. For someone with impressive credentials and all the five Cs, expect to pay market rate or higher.
2. **Don't expect them to stay:** People great at leading change won't stay indefinitely, so make sure the role description includes leading the activities described in Stage 5 of BUILD: Disseminate, so there isn't a gap remaining when they leave. This includes upskilling and identifying capability gaps in your current company leadership.
3. **Anticipate passive sabotage from others:** Non-cooperation from leaders who feel threatened by an outsider brought in as change agent can derail an entire transformation programme, so proactively look for signs of this and mitigate it throughout.

If you talk about the characteristics of change agents, they are resilient, persistent and sometimes a maverick. Influence is sometimes being able to be brave enough to do something that everyone thinks is the wrong thing to do. In terms of digital transformation, no one wants to look like the fool who didn't know the answer.

There definitely are people who have been influenced in their tenure in the organization because of what we've done. But I fight and my team fights for what we believe are the best outcomes for the company, and we measure those outcomes to know we're not biased. So if it means that roles change, they have to change.

But the hardest thing and the thing we should all be good at as digital change agents is reinventing and repositioning our own mindset. You have to be prepared to let things go.

Interview with Ash Roots, Director of Digital, Direct Line Group

You've got your leadership group, now what?

Armed with your shared vision for transformation and your small leadership group, you can proceed to BUILD Stage 2: Uncover, where you'll prioritize the first projects the transformation programme should tackle.

Don't worry about finding major budgets or resources – the best transformation programmes start with a handful of carefully chosen projects whose successes prove the case for more investment.

Think of this next stage as scoping out the grounds for your new building site. Are you building on sandy soil or stone? Is the site south or north facing? Once you've ascertained the strengths and weaknesses of your current state, the projects you prioritize are the equivalent to pouring foundation and putting up a steel frame capable of supporting bigger transformation.

When I joined American Cancer Society in 2011, it had 10,000 employees in 900 locations, 3.5 million active volunteers and 77 million customers. So, you have this sprawling, very passionate user base, and technology plays a role in literally everything we do, whether it's fundraising, research, or the way that we deliver our patient services. We don't just raise money and then hand it off to somebody – and I say 'we' because I still serve on the board. We are the largest non-governmental funder of cancer research in the country here in the States.

There was this huge untapped opportunity to leverage digital technology, or just technology in general, to reach more patients, more people who were interested in finding out more about cancer, and in doing so provide a better consumer and constituent experience. But we couldn't do it. We weren't set-up to do it. We had thirteen different groups of IT people running in thirteen different directions. When they brought me in they said, 'you've done this at AIG and we want you to do it here because we're becoming one unified American Cancer Society'. My CEO at the time said, 'This is about building a world-class technology organisation that allows us to save more lives from cancer.' And I loved that because it was a recognition that technology specifically played a key role.

Interview with Jay Ferro, Executive Vice President, EarthLink
Former Chief Information Officer, American Cancer Society, 2012–2016

BUILD Stage 2: Uncover

Uncover your company's hidden barriers, useful assets, and needed resources to plan and prioritize its routes to transformation

Why Uncover?

Digital doesn't disguise problems, but it can help solve them

Since the global recession in 2008, companies have been looking to digital projects as magic bullets to solve a myriad of external business problems, from declining sales to increasing costs.

This results in an unpleasant surprise when these projects do more to highlight internal problems than solve external ones.

For example, imagine a struggling business investing in a new external website but doing nothing to first address its overly complicated product line, inconsistent brand identity, and many overlapping layers of old-fashioned management. The new website will act more like a magnifying glass than a miracle cure. Everything about the business will be condensed into web pages, providing a concentrated view of the company, warts, and all.

If you've been through a project like this already, you won't be surprised to know website redesign projects are the most common for triggering major business programmes – including complete rebranding work and the need for a digital transformation programme itself. Perhaps it's even the reason you've picked up this book.

The unfortunate reality is most business leaders either grossly underestimate or are completely unaware of many of their company's internal problems. In this way, don't be surprised if people in your company blame the need for digital transformation on changes in the outside world and not the company's own failure to keep up.

My job title for the vast majority of the time is 'futurist', but the vast majority of the work that I do is really 'present day-ist'. I'm not usually telling my big corporate, government or military clients about what's going to happen in 2025. What I'm usually telling them about is what happened last week. It's just that they themselves are situated in 2002.

A few weeks ago, I gave a talk about Artificial Intelligence where I demonstrated a whole load of capabilities and everyone in the audience was reeling with shock about the amazing possibilities and all the implications for their business. But the kicker was that I was demonstrating two-year-old capabilities from IBM and Amazon. None of this stuff requires any specialist access either – I just go on the Watson Developer site and read the developer docs.

The only way of doing it better is having from the beginning, a process where the learnings can be reapplied to the rest of the business as quickly as possible. But that is not a technology problem, it's a culture problem. The solution can't be technology because then the solution will change every eighteen months. The culture change is to transform your business into something that is capable of changing its processes, and changing the very nature of its business at the same pace digital technology is changing in the global context, the very context in which your business is operating.

Interview with Ben Hammersley, Futurist,
BBC World Presenter 'Cybercrime, with Ben Hammersley' &
WIRED Contributing Editor

The right way to put digital to work

To achieve your shared transformation vision, you first have to know what internal problems stand in its way, then choose the right fixes without detracting from your bigger goals.

While the worst mistake is ignoring internal problems altogether, coming in a close second is thinking you should use digital transformation to focus only on internal issues. As a company leader, you're looking for barriers to digital transformation lurking in your people, processes, and platforms.

Your company's shared vision will cover areas across your entire business – some requiring bigger projects to transform than others – but only so much time and resource can be diverted away from business as usual. Once you understand which of these have fallen most behind the curve, you'll prioritize the projects that will have the biggest impact on meeting customer needs in ways that will generate measurable business benefits.

Using this approach to uncover key barriers and prioritize the steps to transformation won't just increase your programme's success; your programme will become a repeatable and sustainable process for updating your company's roadmap on an ongoing basis.

What's happening at Royal is the concept of becoming a 'direct-to-consumer' business.

I was hired because of my direct-to-consumer and retail experience, including omnichannel. At the time I started, over 80 per cent of our business came through trade. We see them as a very important part of our value chain, but we weren't focusing on being a direct-to-consumer business. What I mean by that is not so much selling everything direct, but more about understanding who our guests were, what they liked, what they didn't like, and how we could talk to them to create a much more effective relationship with them by enabling what we're calling a 'frictionless vacation'.

In my first two weeks I went to the CEO and said, 'We have tremendous data that we're not leveraging properly in terms of how to talk effectively to our guests. We really haven't engaged the trade in any sort of collaborative planning and forecasting opportunity. I think there's a lot we can do with the product and I think what we need to do is really focus from the guest-and-ship-in versus shore-side-out, and start to think differently about our business'.

So we now have a project called Excalibur, which is in the formative stages, starting to develop and deploy solutions. It's a complete transformation of what we do in terms of how we support the business technically and also the operating model of the business itself.

Interview with Mike Giresi, Chief Information Officer, Royal Caribbean Cruises
Former Chief Information Officer, Tory Burch, 2011–2015

At a glance: How to Uncover

The Uncover stage shows you how to structure your transformation programme, starting with uncovering the barriers that stand between your company and its shared vision for transformation.

It can be incredibly hard to see internal problems within your company for the same reason a goldfish has a hard time seeing outside its bowl. 'Uncover' works by limiting the number of barriers you're looking for to the ones most likely to derail a transformation programme.

Tips for success in Uncover

Leave detailed planning for the next stage of BUILD

The important part about identifying routes to transformation is to identify top-level goals for each project but not to plan them upfront. The detailed planning and implementation of any project needs to take place at team level and must be done by an empowered and accountable cross-functional team, as will be discussed in Stage 3: Iterate.

Don't let ambition outstrip available assets

Taking on too much and failing to produce results can destroy all internal goodwill towards the digital transformation programme. Preventing this means balancing the number of projects with the availability of teams, space, and budget. If in doubt, start smaller than you think is needed and adhere strictly to the approach in Stage 3: Iterate. This will ensure your first project starts showing measurable successes quickly, enabling you to spin up more projects straight away.

Leverage your champions

Your most powerful asset is the support of people you identified during Stage 1, Bridge, as digital transformation champions. Uncovering huge barriers between your company and its shared transformation vision can be incredibly discouraging, but with the right support from key individuals, any company can begin a transformation programme. Even if you only have pockets of support and meagre assets, you can still find projects to quickly win more support and gradually break down the bigger barriers.

Barriers to Transformation

What are transformation barriers?

The first thing to understand about barriers to transformation is they're not the same as run-of-the-mill business problems.

Start with conversations with the key stakeholders to find out what they see is the important things within their business because digital transformation has to be grounded in the overall business strategy, or whatever that organization wants to achieve and what it's really about. You can almost define it as a sort of benchmark. Then look at how that current benchmark might compare with what's going on in the wider world.

Draw on as many and diverse examples as possible because you want to be thinking very laterally at this point. Also you might want to apply examples that might shake things up a bit and are a left field to gauge their propensity for taking risk, and to find out how aggressive they want their transformation to be.

You'll now have external parameters and benchmarks from the outside world to apply within. You can start to decide whether it's platforms, processes, whether it's culture or what are the key areas within the organization you need to be addressing. Once here, you have to identify the sponsors or advocates and champions versus those likely to be the people to oppose you. The decision then becomes how will you work around that opposition?

Interview with Stewart Atkins, Digital Transformation Consultant
Former Head of Digital Strategy, British Medical Association, 2011–2015

Every organization has its share of barriers to things like growth, profitability, and scale. But there are particular traits required for organizations to thrive in the changing environments driven by evolving digital technology.

In this sense, the barriers that prevent an organization from digitally transforming are also the barriers that hinder its ability to adapt to change. Identifying and mitigating these barriers is critical to your transformation programme's success.

It's also important to know that barriers to transformation are lurking in every organization – even advanced and innovative ones. This might sound discouraging, but there are unexpected positives which make barriers to transformation easier to mitigate.

First, transformation-specific barriers share commonalities across every sector, making them easy to identify. Second, and most reassuringly, identifying barriers to transformation is actually the most important part of mitigating them.

Just being aware of shortcomings and areas of difficulty means you'll be able to naturally plan around them or include extra steps to overcome them. It also

> There are so many barriers and hurdles that can be overcome by having face-to-face dialogue with different teams, understanding where those barriers are – whether it is about cost or whether it's about perceived challenges. It's only through dialogue that you can cut through those and find solutions, or realize that they don't really exist and that there are other ways of achieving the objective.
>
> Interview with Mike Walton, Chief of Section, Digital Engagement, United Nations High Commission for Refugees (UNHCR)

means you'll set goals and expectations that are realistic in the context and constraints of your organization.

Addressing barriers in digital transformation

All digital transformation programmes are actually many different concurrently running smaller projects, tied together with a shared digital transformation vision and guided by an overseeing leadership group.

This is in part to spread the effort required to transform. No company can afford to stop its business as usual completely – especially because transformation efforts require cross-departmental collaboration and significant changes to ways of working.

It's also because for every company, some parts of the business will need more 'transforming' than others. This is linked directly to the number of transformation barriers in place.

To begin this process of addressing your transformational barriers, start by breaking your organization down into one of four categories summarized below.

These categories aren't specific to transformation, but the classic barriers to transformation are found within each, so figuring out where your organization sits makes it easier to identify its barriers.

The four parts to every business

1. **People:** All things staff-related – from roles and responsibilities to company culture and management styles.
2. **Processes:** All aspects of operations – including all internal and external transactions, flows, rules, and ways of working.

3. **Platforms:** Everything relating to IT – from your company's technical equipment and networks to your entire digital presence.
4. **Partnerships:** Everything about your wider ecosystem – from your manufacturers and suppliers to joint venture relationships.

At a glance: Barriers to transformation

Who? Members of the transformation leadership group, under direction of the change agent.

Why? To ensure transformation plans include steps for eliminating barriers.

What? Identifying and prioritizing barriers in the four categories: people, partnerships, platform, and processes.

When? Depending on the size of the organization, it can be done in a workshop over a single day. For larger companies spread over multiple locations, time should still be limited to no longer than what's needed to reach an informed starting point.

Objectives

1. Identify the biggest barriers facing your organization from achieving the goals in your transformation vision.
2. Evaluate and score the barriers found in your organization's people, processes, platforms, and approach to partnerships.

Questions to answer

- Why hasn't your company evolved naturally to keep pace with its customers and environment?
- What are the current attitudes towards digital and innovation?
- What attempts to innovate have been made in the past? What succeeded and why?
- Why did certain attempts to innovate fail?
- What areas of the business present the greatest barriers?
- What areas of the business require the most transformation?

Tips for success

- Identifying barriers isn't about assigning blame. Most barriers are things in the business that already cause frustration.
- Start at the top of the organization and work your way down to customer-facing staff.

- Secure the endorsement of your company's most influential leaders before you present more widely.

Methods you can use

1. Attend team meetings and observe people working in various levels of the organization.
2. Question what you observe: Why are things being done in a certain way and if people had their way, how would they do them differently?
3. Consult members of management and senior leadership using materials gathered during 'Bridge' to act as conversation starters on how things can be done differently based on other organizations. Observe any pushback and ask for reasons why it can't work for your company.
4. Invite technology companies, agencies, and experts to present new ideas and gauge opinions and reactions from senior leadership, management, and staff.
5. Interview newly hired employees to discover what they find frustrating about your company compared to their last place of work and why.

Listening and trying to tune into the real signals and understand our USP and what really matters to our staff and scientists is important. If you get that early stage of listening right, you can generally flush out the big issues and have genuine engagement from the start with people.

Hearing what hurts your business, what slows you down, what causes pain either to your staff or customers, what your competitors are doing better and then articulating this at corporate level is sometimes difficult either because it's hard to criticize the organization you're in or as insiders we're being too optimistic. Sometimes creating space where you can critique, step back and be more objective and strategic is difficult. Creating safe spaces where people can diagnose the issue is critical.

Interview with Dr Charmaine Griffiths, Chief Operating Officer,
The Institute for Cancer Research
Former Executive Director of Strategy & Performance,
British Heart Foundation, 2013–2016

6. Host workshops with a cross-section of leadership and staff from areas around your business using your transformation vision to brainstorm ways the program could succeed or fail.

People barriers

People are the biggest barrier to transformation

Here's the good and bad news upfront: technology is not your biggest barrier to transformation.

Even if you're operating with stacks of outdated IT systems that will cost billions and take years to replace, the leaders and managers who allowed it get that way are the real source of the problem – they're also a lot harder to change.

Most of the international companies I work with grow through acquisition. This leads to a mishmash of legacy IT systems that can't be connected to one another, pockets of staff that operate with different processes and culture, and, depending on which part of the business you engage with, a completely disjointed customer experience.

If you focus on technology, you focus on process, you focus on many innovations, you are not going to get far. Always the big big big problem, the big issue where you need to dedicate most of your thinking is the people factor at the top level, at the cultural level, at the bottom level, or at the change management situation. The technology or the innovation is just an excuse.

In general, the most important barriers and obstacles are always of a political nature – different interests, agendas, missions. You need to be a political navigator to really push a programme like this. It is about winning some battles, losing some others and persistence, persistence, persistence. I lost many battles and I won a few others, and I have been loyal to my vision and never abandoned the plan.

Interview with William Confalonieri, Chief Digital Officer, Deakin University

You really need a CEO that actually has that vision. It doesn't need to be a younger person either. It can be an older person who's just got more vision.

I remember a time when I was working in the music industry back when they still used masters made of metal to create CDs. It was time to start the move to MP3s and I could have helped them move on it. I was talking with the CEO of one of the big business units about how they needed to digitize all of their back catalogue, but he said 'Oh, my customers will never buy online. This is just a trend'. Now we all know how that's played out, but I was having that conversation fifteen years ago and I could see it coming. He was convinced the customers would always want the CD in their hand, and this was someone who'd been through the transition from vinyl to A-track to cassette to CD, but he just couldn't see it.

Interview with Jan Babiak
Board of Directors, Walgreens Boots Alliance & Bank of Montreal

I often start working with these companies after they're already in the tail end of upgrading the technology, paying obscene sums for projects that take years to complete.

A new state-of-the-art platform can enable all sorts of transformative digital innovations, like connecting all the data across an entire supply chain to facilitate automatic personalization for each of its customers.

Yet by the time I start working with these companies, nothing's actually been done because its people problems still persist.

Staff don't know how to use the systems beyond what they were using them for originally. This is reinforced by management who don't think there was anything wrong with the company's ways of working before the upgrade, and because no one's job description has been updated to include using any of the advanced features.

As such, the platform might be new, connected, and capable of great things, but the people responsible for running it are ill-equipped and powerless to use it.

Top three ways people become barriers to transformation

The reasons people pose barriers to transformation can be summed up in three ways, starting with the first and most critical barrier.

1. Missing the innovation mindset

Not to be confused with missing skill sets, which can be hired in or provided through training, missing the innovation mindset is a much bigger barrier to transformation. It's also the most common reason for organizations and entire sectors to fall behind the technology curve.

The kind of mindset needed to support transformation is one that embraces change, rewards innovation, takes risks, learns quickly from mistakes, and is by nature collaborative and consensus building.

Compare this to the average traditional company that rewards and promotes individuals who practice sound judgement, adhere to hierarchies, make the fewest mistakes, take only the most measured risks, and work best in isolation and you'll understand how staff and leaders with an innovation mindset are scarce, if not missing entirely.

The nature of your sector can also exacerbate a lack of innovation. For example, in financial institutions, where strict regulation is a part of everyday life, a mindset that favours risk aversion and attention to detail is likely to be rewarded.

Helping to create more of the right mindset involves helping staff and management see the benefits of change. It coaxes them to take more risks, to be open to recognizing – and learning from – mistakes and to work more collaboratively.

If the innovation mindset is missing from your staff and management, even with the right technology in place, you wouldn't be able to use it to its full potential.

To change these risk-averse mindsets, introduce incentives to being more innovative. Construct environments and provide access to tools that are more conducive to collaborative working, experimentation, and sharing progress. This will be covered in more detail during Stage 3 of BUILD: Iterate.

2. Operating with false logic

If the right mindset is present but leadership and staff still underestimate or are ignorant to the need for change, it's usually because they're employing false or outdated logic to assess the current state.

Whenever you're building and going through digital transformation, you do need to question everything. You need to look at literally everything that you do in the space that you're re-evaluating and say, 'does this still apply? is this still right? What's the business case for this?'

Interview with Bryan VanDyke, Managing Director & Head of Digital,
Morgan Stanley

A good indicator of false logic running rampant in an organization is when you hear someone justify a disliked way of working with the rationale 'this is the way we've always done it so there must be a good reason'.

Fortunately, there's a great way to address the problem of false logic: trace it back to its original source, challenge it with direct evidence, and disprove it head on.

3. Poor accountability

The final way for people to stand in the way of transformation is when poor accountability exists between people's actions and the success of the organization.

This relates to one of the cornerstones of being a 'digital' organization. A transformed organization uses connected technology, collaboration between teams, and agile processes to make decisions based on up-to-date insights and data, instead of relying on old logic or poorly informed authority figures.

Poor accountability is likely a barrier for your organization if your staff and leadership's performance isn't judged on anything empirically measurable or observable, or if what's being measured doesn't relate directly to the organization's reason for existing.

Generally speaking, for a business to be efficient at serving its core purpose, people's work should be assessed by whether it contributes to that purpose. But this is especially true for an organization that needs to digitally transform.

If you're about to bring in new technology but there's no accountability for people to use it, or use it to a productive end, no one is going to put in the hard work needed for it to succeed. Instead, you'll have staff doing digital work as a 'box tick' exercise, or various leaders and departments investing huge amounts of time and resources into what are essentially vanity projects.

Poor accountability also removes any time-based urgency. I often encounter this working for wealthy organizations whose accountability is poor because staff and leaders don't necessarily have to work hard or well to keep revenue flowing in.

It's then exacerbated by the fact that the bigger these companies get, the more inward-focusing they become, creating their own means of measuring staff performance and deciding promotions that have nothing to do with delivering real external results.

How many high-profile meetings you attend, how well you're known by senior staff, how busy your schedule is – it's incredible the number of executives who are evaluated on these irrelevant metrics instead of by the direct impact their decisions have on what the company is supposed to achieve.

Support functions within a business, like accounting IT and HR, should also be just as accountable for the productivity they enable. Unfortunately, these functions are often where barriers first start to form.

It's very hard to find an equilibrium with stakeholders sometimes. On one hand, if everyone's agreeing it can mean compromise and consensus, which may mean you're not actually going to change anything. When everyone's happy, it's usually because you're keeping it as it is. The other end of the spectrum is you wait and pray for people to see the benefit. Some days I forge ahead because a solution is too important or sometimes the relationship's too important. It's one of the bits that's really stressful because when you get your end of year review you could be marked down because a particular unit said you weren't very collaborative with a particular item. But when that same thing you're championing becomes the thing that's then adopted two years later, what do you do? That can be a very challenging scenario.

Interview with Ash Roots, Director of Digital, Direct Line Group

When HR's performance is measured on metrics like cost savings and time efficiency, the first thing to take place is a standardization of all HR processes and a tightening down on exceptions to rules. This means the team with the innovative idea might not get the permission to carry it out because it doesn't fit standard process or procedure.

The same is true for IT functions in a business. If the accountability only extends to 'keeping things working' then there's no incentive to find better ways of facilitating people's work through better equipment or enabling better connectivity between systems and external partners. If an upgrade proposal is made, leaders reject it based on short-term cost implications because their accountability is to manage costs on a quarterly or single year basis – not factoring in the ever-increasing gap between what current systems are capable of and what the external needs and conditions already demand.

To increase accountability, demonstrate the value of empowering individuals to make decisions based on real insight and data, and create key performance indicators (KPIs) that link directly to the transformation vision and the organization's goals. BUILD Stage 3: Iterate details how to build the right kind of direct accountability into individual transformation projects.

How to uncover 'people' barriers

Reading the ways people become barriers to transformation has likely already triggered concerns about your company's culture and certain teams and individuals. To take preventative steps in planning your routes to transformation, you should take a score of the biggest problems you face.

First, assess the people in your organization according to the three traits below. Consider both individual job roles and team roles, departments, managers and leadership roles, and don't forget to include HR, IT and any other supportive functions.

With those categories in mind, read the traits below to determine which your organization's people either possess or lack. Consider the relevant people's level of importance in the company's current operations. The more important they are, the more you'll need to include them in BUILD stages 'Iterate' and 'Leverage' to win their support and change any counterproductive behaviours.

Traits to score 'people'

1. **Open:** Are influential people, managers, and decision makers receptive and optimistic towards change, including new technology and ways of working?
2. **Adaptable:** Do people of all levels cope well when changes do occur, including taking self-ownership over learning?
3. **Accountable:** Are people at all levels empowered and directly responsible for measurable or observable outputs that benefit the organization's success?

You have to have transformation in the first instance because of competition so you don't lose your place in the world. But you also need transformation because otherwise you risk losing people, because the very best people want to work in the best ways possible.

Most companies that don't transform have a blocking layer of middle management who don't want to embrace new technology. They become incredibly frustrating places to work for people in their late 20s and early 30s, so they just stay for five years and then go. That major loss of expertise and culture is another major existential threat to those sorts of corporations.

Digital transformation is the process you have to go through but you should call it 'contemporization'. It's about taking your organization and making it fit for the twenty-first century.

Interview with Ben Hammersley, Futurist,
BBC World Presenter 'Cybercrime, with Ben Hammersley' &
WIRED Contributing Editor

A note on outdated skill sets

If your staff haven't been introduced to any new technology for a while, and internal policies and structures have prohibited them from innovating regularly at team level, they'll lack the skills needed to adapt quickly when digital technology and new ways of working are introduced through any digital transformation efforts.

Fortunately, this is one of the easier people barriers to solve. We'll get into this in more detail with the approach outlined in BUILD Stage 3: Iterate.

Process barriers

Understanding Processes

To make the category 'Processes' easier to understand and evaluate in terms of barriers to transformation, it helps to divide them into three types. These types are applicable whether the process is external, like processes for transacting with customers, or internal, such as processes for managing a project or a supply chain.

Three process types

1. **Functional:** Processes that facilitate internal operations and external transactions.
2. **Decision making:** The rules and methods used to trigger and make decisions.
3. **Ways of working:** The approaches used to produce any business output.

Processes for governing transactions, decision making, and ways of working in a business are hugely varied and complex, sometimes differing completely depending on the time of year, geography, or department.

Culture underpins digital transformation. That's where organizational change comes in. For example with adopting Cloud, it's not about whether it exists or whether you can afford it or whether it's going to apply benefit. It's whether or not the organization is comfortable with a cultural shift in how it does things including it's not on premise or security is managed very differently, or that you can be a much faster organization. It is recognizing that the way you think may change.

Interview with Ash Roots, Director of Digital, Direct Line Group

---

Key Process barriers to transformation

1. Too much consultation

If a process requires input and consultation for every decision, it will naturally grind any quick progress to a halt.

This is found in all three types of process. For functional processes, there may be multiple reviews before one event can finish and another start. For decision making, there may be many senior stakeholders who need to 'sign off' before the decision can actually be carried out.

And last, for ways of working, it's measured by the number of unnecessary meetings that take place without any actions ever being completed as a direct result of having them.

2. Lack of automation

A lack of automation doesn't just slow things down; it can make certain activities impossible to measure accurately, which creates a vicious cycle: there's no way to know if something's working well or not, so people carry on doing it out of fear they'll disrupt a positive outcome.

Organizations that are used to paper-based systems, for example, are good candidates for this type of barrier. I worked with one university, for example, that would receive online applications from students, print them out, make comments by hand, then scan the documents to re-upload them to the server. This ludicrous lack of automation was easy to fix, but it persisted a long time because no one ever thought to evaluate or challenge it.

In ways of working, the lack of automation doesn't just slow things down, it diverts people's energy and brain power away from tasks that can't be replaced by a machine. For example, managing stock levels in a shop is a tedious and time-consuming process. Using salespeople in a shop to count items for inventory taking purposes doesn't just waste their time, it drains them of energy and enthusiasm to do the job they're good at.

The same applies to other routine and administrative tasks across an organization. An HR person having to track sick days and absenteeism, an IT person having to monitor times and purposes for support calls, or a charity worker having to track the number of donations for one campaign over another – all are examples where automation wouldn't just free the staff member to do something more valuable, but the data could also help them do their job better.

3. Too much internal competition

Companies often compare individuals and teams against one another – especially on a departmental basis. Unfortunately, this approach usually serves to hold back an organization from becoming innovative and fast moving for three reasons.

Nowadays, people are in each other's business. If you've grown up in an era where you're more comfortable with clear lines between roles, that's not the world we're living in now. To ready an organization for digital transformation, the culture has to be comfortable with being uncomfortable, has to learn to live with blurred lines, and has to develop ways for employees to interact and engage with one another that promotes understanding and productivity, and not territoriality and business unit politics.

Interview with Perry Hewitt, Vice-President of Marketing, ITHAKA
Former Chief Digital Officer, Harvard University, 2011–2016

First, the real metrics for measuring your company's success are external, not internal. Measuring teams and individual's performance against one another internally provides a false sense of security, and it teaches people within the organization to pay closer attention to their peers than to the customers whose needs your business is trying to fulfil.

Second, humans by nature seek the easiest path to fulfil their needs. This means that managers and staff alike will look for ways to achieve the best possible results with the least effort required. If you're measuring staff against each other, there's no reason to work harder or work better, providing you're still getting numbers that are average or higher than everyone else in your role. In extreme cases, it can even result in behaviours that are destructive for the business. For example, staff asking only feedback from happy customers to not skew their performance metrics.

Last, instilling a spirit of competition between parts of your business might seem like a good way to motivate people and build a sense of sportsman-like team spirit, but your whole company should be the team – not lots of teams fighting for a non-existent prize. Incentivizing people to beat others in similar roles encourages secrecy and destroys any chance of skill and knowledge sharing that could hugely benefit your company overall.

How to uncover process barriers

It's likely you're already thinking about the problematic processes in your organization just from reading the top three barriers. To make preventative steps in planning your routes to transformation, it's important to prioritize the biggest process barriers you face.

In the same way you scored people barriers, the following traits represent the characteristics of sound processes that do not pose barriers to transformation.

Because processes are so pervasive across organizations and because the lines between where one starts and other continues can overlap greatly, it helps to start with the processes most important to your company's bottom line. That's to say, the processes involved in the entire value chain – from acquiring products, staff to deliver services, or raw materials to turn into products, all the way through to delivering them to end customer.

Once major end-to-end processes like these have been scored, be sure to run a separate scoring for HR- and IT-related processes – such as performance reviews for staff and business processes for deciding software and hardware upgrades.

For each process type across your organization, review the traits and assess which of your important processes fall short of the attributes described. For processes that don't match these traits, consider the people involved, the historic rationale for the process, and the ultimate owners and their levels of importance and influence in the company. The more important the process and the people behind it, the more reason to include projects that challenge these ways of working and provide demonstrable evidence to start undoing these processes when you move onto BUILD Stage 3: Iterate of your digital transformation programme.

Follow the money. Find how are budgets getting created and what behaviours are being rewarded. In a large organization, you absolutely start with how do things get funded, what do initiatives look like. Then from there, figure out what's the job to be done.

I've been in a couple of organizations where the way things are budgeted for, there literally aren't line items for the way we buy software today, so that's a barrier. Let's say I want to buy Salesforce and the way that things are purchased today, there are budget lines for 'software license' and there are budget lines for 'amortization of software/hardware'. That is a great micro example of how a structure of organization hasn't kept pace with the way people need to transact and do business on a day to day basis. And you're going to do it on a larger scale in digital transformation.

Interview with Perry Hewitt, Vice-President of Marketing, ITHAKA
Former Chief Digital Officer, Harvard University, 2011–2016

Traits to score processes

- **Best practice:** Is the current process based on best ways of working as determined by independent and relevant experts?

- **Measurability:** Can all inputs and outputs of the process be observed and tracked to evaluate its performance?

- **Value:** Is the current process providing demonstrable benefits to all users in ways that directly relate to the core purpose and success of the organization?

Platform barriers

Understanding platform types

Technical barriers are the most overlooked and underestimated in the beginnings of a digital transformation programme. Even those that start with a technical project, such as replacing a website or CRM, often grossly underestimate the cost and timelines needed, giving a bad name to technology projects and all for easily avoidable reasons.

Often, these projects lack basic understanding of the constraints imposed by the company's current IT platforms. Too often, leaders don't want to understand technology at all (e.g. 'Don't give me the detail; just tell me when it's going to be up and running') or just don't want to acknowledge how far these elements are from being suitable to new ways of online working and integrations.

Knowing and understanding the restrictions upfront means not only will you plan achievable short-term goals while the old platform is still in place, but you can start to create an accurate IT roadmap with the right budget, time, and resource allocations from the start.

Transforming your IT and digital platform is critical to meet external demands and keep pace with changing technology. But there is a lot you can also do, while you're waiting for major IT infrastructure projects to take place.

Understanding the strengths and weaknesses of your current platform means you can plan around the barriers and start plotting a roadmap for overhauling what's out of date. To do this, it helps to first understand the core functions of any platform – whether it's the laptop on your desk, your company's website, its internal email servers, or the mainframe controlling your entire inventory and value chain.

The six core functions of platforms

First, to clear up any confusion over terminology, a 'platform' is an IT term to describe a group of technologies that are combined to act as a base for other applications, processes, or technologies to be built upon to perform useful

> The British Heart Foundation is an amazing organization with a huge ambition to fight heart disease. It was a real privilege to be involved in the iBHF programme, which was a multi-year, multi-million pound programme to transform the digital platforms that the BHF used to grow the business – right up to fundraising to contribute to the turnover of nearly £265 million last financial year.
>
> That was a huge programme that included input from literally thousands of people across the 30,000 staff and volunteer workforce. Its goal was to take an ailing platform and series of disconnected practices and processes and create something that was really a fantastic foundation for the organization to grow and to become digitally much more mature.
>
> Interview with Dr Charmaine Griffiths, Chief Operating Officer,
> The Institute for Cancer Research
> Former Executive Director of Strategy & Performance,
> British Heart Foundation, 2013–2016

functions. For example, your company's email platform includes a combination of software, systems, and databases to enable staff to send, receive, and store messages.

The best way to think about platforms is as the foundational layer for digital.

If you build the right foundation, it will enable you to do great, complex, and innovative things. If you build the wrong foundation, it will creak and break under the strain of too many things trying to run on top of it.

All platforms consist of combinations of the six core functions listed below. Where they differ hugely is in their size and complexity, and the speed with which they can perform these tasks. Another differentiator is how well a platform can integrate with other platforms to perform simultaneous and coordinated functions.

For example, another familiar kind of platform is your website. It's made up of core components that act as a foundational layer for building out other capabilities. For most websites, the core part of the platform is the content management system (CMS), which houses and organizes all the site's pages, content, and functionality. It can be connected to other platforms like your customer record management (CRM) system and your e-commerce platform to enable functions like customers putting products into a virtual basket, logging into their account, and inputting their credit card details in a secure payment gateway – all seemingly on your website, but in fact it's your website's platform bringing all these functions together from different platforms and applications.

This is why platforms are so important to understand and consider at the beginning of a digital transformation programme. Knowing the barriers you face today allows you to plan the right short-term projects to start immediately seeing results from your transformation, while also getting started on the bigger platform changes needed for achieving longer-term goals in your transformation vision.

Six core functions for thinking about platforms

1. **Sharing:** Displaying or sending any kind of output, whether between people through a user interface – like websites that display content – or between other systems or devices.
2. **Receiving:** Accepting any kind of input (e.g. computer code, messages, documents, data, media, signals).
3. **Analysing:** Processing, interpreting, and calculating any kind of input to produce a pre-determined output.
4. **Learning:** Weighing outputs from past analysis to anticipate and improve the accuracy of new analysis.
5. **Managing:** Controlling and monitoring of any process (e.g. triggering an automated system to stop, start, or run faster or slower).
6. **Storing:** Collecting any kind of input for future use (e.g. data in a database, documents in a knowledge management system, encrypted details in a hyper ledger).

Broadly speaking, you can classify platforms based on which of the six core functions are primary. In my experience, the platform types each come with their own common barriers to digital transformation.

Top four barriers to uncover in platforms

Grouped according to the three common platform types, Table 2.1 shows the top barriers likely hiding in your IT and digital infrastructure. Some will be easier to fix than others, but all pose equal threat to your efforts if not mitigated or at least planned around in these early stages.

Table 2.1 *Platform types and their common barriers*

Platform type	Primary functions	Common barriers
Systems of engagement	Sharing	**Inflexible:** Changes are difficult and result in breakages.
(e.g. internal and external websites)	Managing	**Incompatible:** Can't connect with other systems or work with newer technology.
		Non-user friendly: Even small changes require specialist skills.
Systems of record	Receiving	**Isolated:** Can't receive from other systems.
(e.g. company databases)	Storing	**Poor search-ability:** Errors and extraneous data can't be easily found or removed.
Systems of insight	Analysing	**Unintelligent:** Learning is flawed or absent.
(e.g. analytics platform)	Learning	**Unactionable:** Analysis doesn't produce the results needed for clear decision making.

1. Incompatibility with people or other systems

When it comes to IT, incompatibility covers a broad range of issues. If your platforms are hard to use by people (i.e. only your most experienced developers can make changes and even those changes take ages and often cause problems), it's likely your end users aren't having an easy time using them either.

Most terrible forms on a website, for example, are the result of technical limitations of the database it connects to, and not the company actually thinking that having a 40-field sign-up form where thirty of the fields are irrelevant is actually a good way of structuring a customer registration process.

Incompatibility also refers to a platform's inability to connect to or work with other systems, devices, or platforms. One retail brand I've worked with was stuck with a marketing offers platform that took a full twenty-four hours to update because it couldn't connect directly to the company's website or mobile app platforms. This resulted in complaints in-store from customers who were using their phones to log in during their shopping, only to realize the offer they just unlocked with their loyalty points couldn't be redeemed until the next day.

2. Slow to build on and slow to work

Slow to build on, slow to operate – a crawling platform is a killer of digital transformation.

Digital technologies elsewhere in our lives have given us all the attention spans of a gnat. Not only do customers no longer tolerate any kind of wait time – whether it's waiting for a page to load on a website or waiting for their package to arrive by Amazon Prime – staff within a company also get frustrated, lose interest, or start to distrust technology that takes too long to work.

You need platforms capable of fast operations, which can be quickly built upon and adapted. A large part of succeeding at digital transformation is your company's ability to react to change faster and more intelligently than anyone else in the marketplace.

3. Overly complicated and under-delivering

Sometimes the biggest barrier in platforms is that they're capable of doing too much and have never been properly configured to the particular needs of the business.

I see this a lot when companies upgrade to new content management systems (CMS) for their websites. Many made do with old systems for far too long, felt the sting of having an outdated system that's inflexible and hard to update, so made the big investment to upgrade to a platform so big and expansive that it will take a decade to outgrow – or so they think.

Instead, they find themselves with an enterprise CMS so complicated that none of their existing developers or web editors have a clue how to use it, and because the cost for the licence is so high, the business doesn't want to invest more in advanced set-up or training. In the end, the business limps along – treating the new platform like they did their old one, and ignoring all the feature sets that led them to buy it in the first place.

This leads to the second part of this barrier: under-delivering. If you have an analytics platform that gives you reams of stats and figures, but none of them directly enable you to make a business decision, that's an under-delivering platform.

The true purpose of any platform is to enable the core purpose of your business, either directly or indirectly. If you find your organization losing time to deal with platform delays, working to untangle conflicting outputs, or resolving complaints and problems it's created, you have an under-delivering platform, and it will throw a wrench in your digital transformation efforts in the same way it's already impeding the success of the organization itself.

4. Restricted in scope and scale

If your platforms are working perfectly for you right up until it's time to expand your operations or add a new set of capabilities, then your barrier is one of restricted scope and scale.

Restricted scope relates to the inability to cope with new capability demands. If your international company has its own internal phone platform and computer network but neither can facilitate video calling or virtual screen-sharing – despite many outside companies offering these capabilities for free – your company suffers from restricted scope.

Restricted scale refers to a platform's inability to cope with increased volume. For example, a fitness and lifestyle company I worked with ran into this barrier with its marketing and analytics platform. The platform wasn't incompatible with other systems, but it could only connect to a single Point of Sale (PoS) system. A PoS is the platform for handling sales transactions and typically includes all cash registers, the processing of payments, and management of shop inventory. This was a major barrier because, like many in the fitness sector, this company had grown through acquisition and inherited many of the acquired company's platforms – including a dozen different PoS systems. To have a complete picture of what's selling in order to decide what to promote and to which of its customers, the company had to replace the marketing platform, migrate all shop locations to a single PoS, or (and this was the option they chose) make a long-term investment into digital transformation and do both.

How to uncover platform barriers

It might sound easier to resolve platform barriers than barriers from people or processes because platforms can be replaced. Unfortunately, this isn't the case. Replacing a platform involves changes in people and processes and can be incredibly disruptive, costly, and time-consuming.

To decide which platforms to tackle first, consider first the ones most directly related to serving external customer needs. Next, tackle the internal platforms.

It's really hard to 'transform digitally' when you have 95 per cent technical debt and only 5 per cent free capacity to do anything. Saying ok, well, Project X over here isn't sexy, but when it goes away I'm going to recoup $2 million of OpX that can I either deploy to either research or lifesaving projects, or I can reinvest in the business. It's a digital transformation enabler. Getting people to understand that all of these things need to work in harmony to be successful with digital transformation.

Work hard to retire your technical debt so you have more ability to innovate and transform. Go in, start small, get your victories, earn credibility, start with a small project and execute the hell out of it. I promise you the next you go back they're going to be like 'hell, you hit a homerun then, let's give him a bigger one'.

Interview with Jay Ferro, Executive Vice President, EarthLink
Former Chief Information Officer, American Cancer Society, 2012–2016

Then, score your platforms against the traits below to determine the FACE value of each – an acronym I came up with for simplifying platform discussions with my own clients. For the platforms missing the attributes described, start consulting external IT experts to weigh options and investigate costs for upgrading or replacing key platforms.

While you're waiting for major IT infrastructure projects to take place, gather external experts from digital agencies and tech firms to find out low-cost digital technologies and channels you can use to turn into short-term digital transformation successes. You can do this by generating real results and using these short-term projects as a test bed for cross-collaboration and agile working styles within your organization.

Traits to score platforms (determining the FACE value)

- **Fast:** Can the platform perform its functions quickly, and can your staff customize, change, or upgrade it quickly when needed?

- **Accessible:** Is the platform easy to use by all parties – external and internal? Do you have to have specialist training or technical skills to perform basic functions?

- **Clever:** Is the platform capable of reliably collecting and analysing data to produce insights and outputs that are consistent and actionable?

- **Extendible:** Is the platform capable of connecting to relevant systems, devices, and networks, with the capacity to add more as needed?

Most companies just want to meet short-term objectives, for example, to keep shareholders happy and show they're making progress. But a lot of this work around digital transformation is so seismic, that you're never going to get it done well if you try to deliver all of it in just a three- to six-month period. There will be projects that need to be longer than that and require much more investment, in both time and budget to have the quality and be sustainable. So, you really need to make a judgement: is this about sustainability, or is this about getting it to market as quickly as possible? The ideal of course, is to do both at the same time but it can be difficult to strike that balance, especially at the beginning.

Interview with Andy Massey, Director of Transformation & Innovation,
Lane Crawford

Partnership barriers

The importance of partnerships in digital transformation

The future is less predictable now than in any previous decade or century. Technological environmental, and political aspects are changing too quickly and to such extremes that the next necessary innovation is nearly impossible to predict. With change itself as the only predictable outcome, the organization that succeeds and thrives is the one that can handle change externally and internally. I've already addressed the need for internal change: being more agile and coordinated with decision making and being able to act as one company rather than a collection of competing departments. Now it's time to address the need for external agility, and this is done through partnerships.

Transformed companies have their fingers in lots of pies. They work well with others and can move quickly when a new opportunity presents itself. Compare that to your company today and you probably cringe at the lengthy processes you'd have to go through to partner with another firm – the legal hoops to jump through, the IT upgrades to allow your systems to pass internal data easily to an external one, and the difficult mindset shift to get your directors and managers thinking about how to make the transaction benefit the partnering company instead of their own division.

If you've been in business for a long time, chances are you've built up a significant physical presence in the form of buildings and staff across one or many geographic areas. While it's easy to overlook this when considering your future digital asset inventory, having physical infrastructure to pair with a previously pure-digital one is a lucrative prospect to younger companies who haven't built up their real-world presence.

For example, Walgreens in the US has introduced application programme interfaces (APIs) to give the creators of photo editing mobile apps the ability to create a feature within the app to connect to Walgreen's own digital platform and let the app users send their photo directly from the app to any one of over 8,000 Walgreens locations for printing (Hoffelder 2012, Photo.walgreens.com n.d.).

Types of partnerships for digital transformation

When it comes to digital transformation, there are three partnership types to consider when planning your organization's routes to transformation.

Timely and short term

These are partnerships that are formed when a market opportunity presents itself and two or more companies come together quickly and temporarily to capitalize on it.

Digital transformation comes from short-term partners contributing unique assets or capabilities to create an entirely new proposition that benefits all parties and most important, the end customer. There are more examples of these partnerships now than ever before: grocery stores partnering with bicycle delivery companies to provide one-hour delivery to customers in a two-mile radius (e.g. Sainsbury's in the UK and Chop Chop (Butler 2016)); car companies partnering with fuel delivery start-ups to offer their customers on-demand fuelling (e.g. Bentley and Filld (Cunningham 2016)); or hotel chains partnering with fashion rental companies to offer in-room wardrobes for hire during the guest's stay (e.g. W Hotel and Girl Meets Dress (Conroy 2015)).

The best part about these partnerships is they're only around for as long as both parties see return on investment. As soon as demand dies down, the partnership dissolves and both companies go back to business as usual.

The challenge for most companies to run these partnerships though is two-fold. First, it's usually not anyone's job in the organization to look for opportunities like these and start these conversations. That's why the activities in BUILD Stage 1: Bridge are so important to maintain long after formal digital transformation efforts have been complete. It's also why it's so important to address people barriers such as poor accountability, ensuring that roles such as identifying and maintaining external partnerships are formally assigned, maintained, and tracked.

Most organizations in need of digital transformation are not set up for quick and easy partnerships. Instead, the only partnerships they'll know how to run are the ones that involve endless negotiations, teams of lawyers, and contracts of five years or more. If this sounds like the way your organization approaches partnerships, then prioritizing your partnership barriers and addressing them in the next section 'Routes to transformation' will be critical to your programme's success.

Capability building

A capability-building partnership is a partner brought in to help an organization develop a missing capability. This is often how big consultancies or digital agencies are used – they start full time on a new project or large programme of work, then decrease the number of consultants and specialist contractors as the client organization hires and builds internal teams of its own.

Capability building is essential for most organizations needing digital transformation, but these partnerships are notoriously tricky to get right. It's easy for the partner to become so bedded in the client organization that, before anyone realizes it, the partner becomes responsible for an integral part of the client's business and can hold the organization to ransom if it so chooses.

It's also easy for the partnership to go sour for the opposite reason. The partner is brought in to build the client's capability in a new skill set, such as digital marketing, but because the client is so worried about the partner taking advantage of the relationship, the client treats the partner more like a supplier than a real partner. This puts the agency or consultancy at a major disadvantage by blocking it from accessing the right level of staff and information to provide the best quality advice and services, and as such the relationship sees diminishing value the longer it lasts: the partner can't provide the best quality services and the client feels they're not getting their money's worth.

This is another scenario addressed in the top three partnership barriers, and its mitigation is included in the ways of working detailed in BUILD Stage 3: Iterate.

Long term, value adding

Long-term partnerships are possibly the most common for any organization because they are the most traditional: two companies agree to mutually benefit from a shared value exchange over a period of many years.

Where it crosses into the territory of digital transformation is when the purpose of the partnership is to advance an organization's technology capabilities on a scale that would be impractical or impossible to achieve on its own.

Before you decide to outsource digital capabilities rather than build them internally, remember the fate of companies who did the same and later paid a steep price.

> External people are here to break the back of the project, not to run it on an ongoing basis in the future. Part of any successful programme is ensuring that you have nurtured the capability in-house, if that's the objective of the programme. What should be happening in an organization is the programme strategy should almost be becoming BAU [business as usual], so by the time you get to the end of an eighteen-month programme, there shouldn't be a massive gap between BAU and programme.
>
> Interview with Laura Scarlett, Data & Insight Director,
> Guardian News & Media
> Former Programme Director, Supporter Loyalty, National Trust, 2013–2015

Toys R Us, for example, made the mistake of outsourcing its e-commerce functions to Amazon for years before realizing it should have been building that capability internally all along. When the partnership ended, Toys R Us found itself significantly behind the competition in digital maturity and struggled with low profits and a steep learning curve for years in a scrambled effort to catch up (Stone 2013).

As a rule, even if something seems like it should never be part of your company's core business, evaluate and question that decision constantly. At best, you'll keep your eyes and ears open to better deals or arrangements elsewhere and at worse, you'll spend extra effort double-checking for the reward of peace of mind that you're not letting the false comfort of complacency obscure reality.

Top three barriers to uncover in Partnerships

The following barriers are common to all three partnership types, whether it's a short-term opportunistic partnership, a capability building one, or a partnership that's supposed to build value in the long term.

The reason they're so pervasive is because of the traditional approach too many companies take. For innovation to flourish, it takes openness about business goals, transparent ways of working, and flexibility around outputs and deliverables.

Until then, review top three barriers to transformation lurking in your company's approach to partnerships so they can be prioritized and mitigated in BUILD Stage 3: Iterate.

One of the things we launched this year was with a high street bank. Outside of it being a technical platform, we put home insurance into stores and online so you buy our home insurance via the website. We've put an interface into branch, which means that when store staff are selling a mortgage they can add home insurance on via our website. And we've added extra functionality, checks and balances that mean all Compliance is 100 per cent managed. When we launched, it showed the amount of time it took to complete a home insurance purchase in branch was faster and easier because of our interface. It was an amazing thing we did because it encapsulated new technology, a platform change, increasing speed, making it better for customers – you name it.

Interview with Ash Roots, Director of Digital, Direct Line Group

1. Too many partners, no clear oversight

Having too many agencies, consultants, and partner projects happening at once without any clear leadership or coordination is a common barrier in large companies and for organizations that have already started a piecemeal approach to digital transformation.

Typically, there are many people internally who are 'responsible' for one or more of the relationships, but because of the project nature of the work, there isn't anyone senior enough whose job description includes looking at all the projects happening, whose doing what, and bringing them all together to work in a more coordinated way. Or, if that person does exist, there are too many historical or political reasons that prevent the leader from having a clear picture of what's happening across the many projects.

For example, I've worked with CIOs and CMOs who get handed this responsibility once several projects have already been running without proper oversight for many years. They are then in the difficult position of deciding which contracts and partnerships to keep when the project is perhaps no longer in line with the company's long-term transformation vision, but the work being done is only one year away from completion after three years of work and millions spent doing it.

Unfortunately, situations where there are too many partners and not enough oversight or leadership can create another common barrier: unproductive and unhealthy competition between partners.

2. Pitting partners against each other

Whether it's in a contract negotiation or midway through a relationship, pitting potential partners against each other might temporarily drive the price down, but at a much bigger cost to the quality of work and the levels of trust.

As anyone who has ever faced redundancy or termination knows that you don't produce your best work when you're stressed. Worse than affecting creative output, keeping partners in direct competition with each other produces the same detrimental effects for digital transformation as having too much internal competition between employees or departments.

To be able to react quickly to changes in external needs or conditions, companies need to leverage insights and the full capability set of its available resources and this includes its partners.

If those partners feel their territory or livelihood is in anyway threatened, you can almost guarantee that full transparency will be replaced with holding back insights and ideas in order to provide themselves an 'ace up the sleeve' advantage.

One major travel brand even hosted a 'Dragon's Den'–style procurement day for its top tech partners, where each had only ten minutes to pitch to the entirety of that location's staff, plus the CEO and executive board. The result was a lot of frenzied presentations with little substance, fried nerves, and diminished trust from all the partners. The clients were forced to choose one of the lacklustre ideas but only with a fraction of the time needed to actually deliver results – which leads nicely to the next barrier to transformation in partnerships: not incentivizing the right outputs.

3. Focusing on deliverables instead of outcomes

When companies put more onus on the timescales and budget of a project than what it's supposed to deliver in terms of business results, it's often a sign of old-fashioned project management and procurement mindsets.

It's also closely linked to the previous barriers for partnerships, whereby the organization's leaders think that the only way to avoid overpaying and to keep partners motivated is to hide the company's real objectives and keep the threat of competition constantly in front of mind.

I've come across companies that try to procure digital agencies in the same way they would a supplier for office stationery. I once even led a contract negotiation with an organization to rebuild its new digital platform, and the legal team were trying to insist on using the same boilerplate contract they would for IT equipment, like the leasing and maintenance of photocopiers.

What these poorly mistaken company leaders don't realize is the difference between a digital transformation partner and a regular supplier, and that agencies, consulting firms, and tech companies want to see real results as much as they do.

Projects in the digital transformation space should never be fixed-price and fixed-scope, and BUILD Stage 3: Iterate explains how in more detail.

Just like any business, it's a cut-throat competitive environment for digital companies of any size, so being able to fill a portfolio with examples of real returns on investment that you've achieved for your clients is what's going to win you your next job – especially in today's digital age where news about poorly executed work travels fast.

BUILD Stage 4: Leverage specifically delves into the benefits of sharing progress on digital transformation projects as they're happening. That means for the partners involved, there's added incentive to deliver real results quickly.

How to uncover partnership barriers

The best and most realistic way to overcome the barriers lurking in your company's existing approach to partnerships is to ensure you're establishing new partnerships with the right approach and mindset.

For partners you're already working with and where these problems are already pervasive, it's never too late to try and reopen the channels of transparency and

> If you're a good collaborator, it drives your learning and it drives your relationships. It also drives coming up with a better answer. You can stem that all the way to paired programming or just good cross-functional working. If you're not collaborative, your culture will not change and that's normally quite a negative culture or at least a very protective one. What companies are really trying to do in their corporate culture is replicate what the internet has done globally.
>
> **Interview with Ash Roots, Director of Digital, Direct Line Group**

honesty. Changing contract terms is likely not possible, but simply by sharing information more openly – especially about long-term goals – and being willing to invest longer term, it's possible to undo some of the damage done by previous barriers that impeded more collaborative working.

If the partnership is no longer the right fit based on the new direction of the digital transformation vision, cutting loses earlier is a much better approach than seeing a project through to the end only because of concerns over sunk costs. The wrong fit is always more expensive and harder to reverse long term.

To help decide which partnerships in your organization pose the biggest barriers, consider the ones currently in place to help deliver core functions of the business – in particular, those that fulfil objectives around meeting external needs and adapting to new market conditions, including digital.

Rate these partnerships against the traits below to determine which existing partnerships need replacing or mending as part of the next section where you'll plot your routes to transformation.

In BUILD Stage 3: Iterate, you'll also find ways to construct projects in ways that facilitate partnerships and support digital transformation.

Traits to score partnerships

- **Flexible:** Is the partnership changeable and renegotiable when circumstances change and needs dictate?
- **Transparent:** Is the partner sharing relevant information and resources to enable mutual benefits and trust between all parties?
- **Open:** Are you and the partner permitted to partner with others as well, bringing relevant ideas and opportunities from external sources?

There were many people who were against our vision because they thought if you make your treasures accessible in the highest quality available via the web, no one will ever go to your physical museum anymore. I've learned that is not the case. Digital can never replace the real thing. It can get close. Maybe even so close that you can't see with your naked eye the difference. But the difference is there's only one original and to see The Night Watch or the Mona Lisa, you have to go to that specific physical place to see the real thing. That argument worked because museums are doing very well world-wide simply because there is a high demand for the original thing.

The other thing is you enter the field of copyright. My argument was that we take care of the national collection in the public domain so why should somebody pay at all because this collection is public domain. So the answer to the question 'Who owns the Night Watch'? The answer is: the whole world. If you agree with that point, it's ridiculous to ask for a fee if you use it even for commercial use.

Interview with Wim Pijbes, Director, Stichting Droom en Daad
Former General Director, Rijksmuseum, 2008–2016

Before you move on

You're now well aware of the barriers you face and the next stage is prioritizing and deciding outcomes needed to overcome them. Before you do though, take a moment to reflect again on your vision. Remember why this transformation is important – to your company, its people, and to yourself. It's easy to get discouraged by the barriers but they're a natural part of getting to what in the end will be a hugely gratifying set of achievement.

Hold that 'why' in your mind as you boldly go to the next part, defining the 'what'.

Routes to Transformation

What are routes to transformation?

Routes to transformation are the major outcomes your individual projects will need to deliver to achieve your shared transformation vision.

Unlike a strategic roadmap or implementation plan, routes to transformation don't dictate the order of projects or prescribe how the outcomes will be reached.

This is important because by its very nature, the path to digital transformation is full of unknowns. There may be hundreds of ways to accomplish the same goals. Finding the right method that suits the dynamics of your organization can be a major undertaking in itself. Identifying routes to transformation means you can run multiple projects to trial different solutions, technologies and partners. This allows you to find the fixes that best deliver the outcomes your company needs.

In this way, routes to transformation also find the best ways to overcome fears of change, build digital capability, and demystify technology to those who still consider it a separate skill set from their daily work.

How to identify routes to transformation

The good news is you've already done most of the hard work in identifying your routes to transformation. The step that's left is combining what you've accumulated so far.

In BUILD Stage 1: Bridge, you identified the gaps between your business, its customers, and the competitive environment you operate in, and prioritized them in a shared vision for transformation.

Then in 'Uncover barriers to transformation', you identified and prioritized barriers in your people, processes, platforms, and partnerships that have to be mitigated in order to achieve the vision.

Now combine the objectives in your vision with the barriers you need to resolve, and these become your routes to transformation, framed as outcomes for individual projects to achieve in BUILD Stage 3: Iterate.

For example, the transformation vision for a financial organization I once worked with included the objective 'Be faster at responding externally following major global financial events as a voice of authority and reassurance'.

Within the organization, there were many barriers to achieving this objective, including outdated platforms and a very competitive and fragmented culture – both of which made any kind of communications slow and laborious.

For the organization, the routes to transformation for that one vision became: 'facilitate real-time communication' and the projects they launched as a result was re-platforming and redesigning the website, using new social channels, and trying new third-party software.

These options were enough of a starting point to launch the digital transformation programme. It started small with a few projects that let the company test each option until it found the projects worth scaling into finished solutions.

Digital transformation at UNHCR is about putting digital first, and how that can change the way we communicate and engage with our audiences more effectively to deliver positive impacts for refugees. That includes everything from the amount that's been raised for the refugee crisis digitally. But equally, we've seen a shift in how refugees use connectivity and digital engagement to help them on their journey to safety, and that's been a major feature in the last two or three years.

When we started digital transformation, we started with a premise of how can a central team of digital expertise, work across the different business needs of the organization? So rather than having one fraction of a digital team dealing with online fundraising, or one team that was dealing with communications with refugees, we were asking if you have one team that is there to stimulate change across the organization, how could they then engage with different business units and open up the conversation about how digital can transform the way that they communicate.

Rather than work as an isolated digital silo we sit with each of the different audience owners and talk about how they communicate now and how they could communicate in the future. It is reaching out to different teams and helping them understand what digital can do and then understanding from them what their needs and objectives are. It wasn't about getting people to understand the technology, but talk about principles that were close to their hearts This might include understanding the needs of staff in order to develop a compelling digital workplace experience or working with the digital Private sector to develop e-learning and connected access projects for refugees.

Interview with Mike Walton, Chief of Section, Digital Engagement,
United Nations High Commission for Refugees (UNHCR)

When do routes turn into plans?

Unlike any other kind of programme, digital transformation can't be achieved by doing a lot of planning upfront, soldiering through each project, and having

To overcome the barriers, really ground those observations in customer insight and behaviour, then make a really simple and clear plan of action. In my experience, a really simple plan with very clear goals and intent and very simple execution often work the best.

With innovation, sometimes it's allowing people freedom to fail. With any new transformation process, it's going to be imperfect, it's going to bruise people, it's going to break processes – otherwise it's not really disruption. To a certain extent you can plan for the majority of that but you have to try things that you know only a small percentage of will succeed, just because otherwise you're not pushing yourselves or the organization enough. Being open to failure as part of the learning process is really important.

Interview with Dr Charmaine Griffiths, Chief Operating Officer,
The Institute of Cancer Research
Former Executive Director of Strategy & Performance,
British Heart Foundation, 2013–2016

to wait months or years after completion to know if it's achieving its desired outcomes. Instead, digital transformation is planned and achieved incrementally, through the cumulative successes of many projects developing results using an iterative approach.

In these smaller projects, each has measurable goals determined by the leadership group, but are planned and implemented by a collaborative and cross-functional team. The leadership group use the results achieved by the incremental development of the smaller projects to inform decisions and seize new opportunities as they're uncovered.

Results happen regularly so there's no 'wait and see' worry for the leadership group, and because the people responsible for doing the work are also empowered to make decisions to ensure its success, they're more motivated to produce the best possible results early on.

The best way to learn how to plan routes to transformation is by understanding the difference between this new iterative approach, and the old ways of project management.

BUILD Stage 3: Iterate goes into more detail on how this approach works and why it's right for digital transformation success.

At a glance: Uncovering the routes to transformation

1. **Who?** Transformation leadership group, leaders from key business areas such as IT, and external experts in digital and technology.
2. **What?** Determine the outcomes needed to achieve the shared transformation vision, then prioritize options for achieving each outcome, weighing factors such as cost, time, and difficulty against the potential return on investment (ROI).
3. **Why?** To provide flexible options rather than a prescribed path, allowing project teams find the best approach based on technology, tools, skills, and partners available.
4. **When?** Start projects as quickly as possible using the incremental and results-focused approach detailed in BUILD Stage 3: Iterate.
5. **How?** Prioritize your organization's biggest opportunities for transforming its customer experience and factor in its biggest barriers in people, process, platforms, and partnerships.

Objectives

1. Identify the first projects to kick-start digital transformation by improving customer experience.

Open the building, open the institution, open the collection. That was the three-fold transformation of the Rijksmuseum. I had to open the building, of course because it was closed. I had to open the institution because it was a top-down institution like a big national museum. To do this I changed the behaviour and the attitude of the people. The third thing I wanted to open was the collection online and share it with the world. It's never been done before and thanks to the Internet we could do that. So while others were busy with the renovation and the physical transformation of the building, the curators and some other departments had time to make the highest resolution, quality photographs possible of the collection.

This three-fold plan came during the process. It wasn't the original plan. The original plan was to rebuild the physical building because it was old. The building closed in 2003 to adapt to new fire regulations and add needed facilities. These were the very practical reasons to make a very big renovation project. Doing that started in 2003 before the iPhone and WiFi and didn't finish until 2013. Over the ten years in total, the world was changing.

In 2003, the original plan was to have desktop computers to explore the galleries. I mean can you imagine, desktop computers? But that was really state-of-the-art in 2003. Later the iPhone arrived and the world was getting mobile. Overnight the whole concept of adding computers in a museum seemed ridiculous. Nowadays you read on the iPad or you read it at home, but you're not going to a museum to sit at a desktop computer and read. Gallery space is supposed to be the most beautiful spaces in the museum to install and to present art, not a computer screen.

So we decided a very radical step to kick out anything that was electric or digital from the galleries. That included any projection, any electronic device, and anything with a plug. We decided that everything in the physical museum should be authentic. At the same time we decided the collection should be shared with the world. So we wanted to make the best website, the best accessible collection online in the world. Now the vision is that the physical museum is authentic and the web should be the best website of any museum in the world.

Interview with Wim Pijbes, Director, Stichting Droom en Daad
Former General Director, Rijksmuseum, 2008–2016

2. Determine where on your transformation journey you should tackle major improvements and transformations for areas of people, process, platforms, and partnerships.
3. Identify people from across the organization with the right enthusiasm for transformation and cross-section of skill sets to form the first project teams.

Questions to answer

- What digital opportunities exist to transform your current customer experience?
- What are the critical and major barriers to achieving your digital transformation vision?
- What are the immediate digital opportunities to start transforming your current customer experience?
- What skills, capabilities, and resources are you missing to be able to undertake transformation efforts?

- What assets can you use to start transformation efforts, even if it's short term and on a smaller scale?

- What are the costs, risks, and potential payoffs for each transformation effort?

- What do you need to get started on your first projects?

Methods you can use

- Start with digital-only channels as your programme's initial focus (e.g. website, mobile app) to reduce the impact of existing internal barriers.

- Evaluate and score your organization's current customer experience to prioritize areas of transformation and improvement.

- Invite pitches from potential partners and suppliers to see how they'd approach each route to transformation.

What The Guardian's doing at the moment is transforming into more of a membership business. As I'm sure you know, the publishing model of advertising revenue supporting the paper is completely broken and most of the publishers have gone towards a paywall model. The Guardian is trying not to do that; we're trying to have a membership model where we get to know and build a deep relationship with our loyal customers and they pay us to be a member of The Guardian.

I'm from a CRM background so I'm approaching the transformation challenge of 'customer relevance'. The main difference for me is between anonymous and personal data because I'm a data person, and I don't think you can have a relationship with a cookie. We've got an 'anonymous to known strategy' that I'm spearheading. It's really about finding out what loyal customers value from us, and it's really quite varied and quite different. I do wonder if we're going to end up with a very personalized model here where both you and I are Guardian members but we get things of value and different experiences. That's very possible to make that happen, but it's quite a different way of thinking for the publishers. The message I'm trying to get our journalists and editors to hear is there's just so much content now that a single individual simply cannot consume it. What personalization does well is to prioritize things according to what a person gets value out of.

Interview with Laura Scarlett, Data & Insight Director, Guardian News & Media
Former Programme Director, Supporter Loyalty, National Trust, 2013–2015

Transform your customer experience

The primary route to transformation: Customer experience

Real digital transformation isn't about adding new technologies or making products or processes more connected or automated. Real transformation targets the fundamental drivers of your organization's sustainability: your customers – the people whose needs your organization is meant to serve. The transformation's success is measured by metrics like increased revenue, market share, engagement, and impact, or reduced cost, effort and waste.

For this reason, the primary goal of any route to digital transformation should be laser focused on better aligning to those customers and the environments in which they work and live.

This might sound obvious but it's incredible the number of digital transformation programmes that decide to start with back-end system upgrades, taking months or years before tackling anything visible to the end users.

Part of the reason for this is often down to ignorance over how many gaps exist between the organization's products and services, and the true needs of existing and prospective customers. BUILD Stage 1: Bridge was entirely about shedding light on this issue.

The other big reason comes down to a lack of imagination around what needs could be better filled, or which new needs could be met with the company's existing assets and skill sets with a bit of digital innovation and ingenuity.

There are countless examples of businesses, especially Internet start-ups, coming up with creative new ways to gain market share and keep customers loyal. In addition to sharing specific examples, the following is meant to act as useful framework for brainstorming your own routes to transforming customer experience.

What is customer experience?

The term 'customer experience' refers to every point of interaction your users have with your organization, online and offline, directly and indirectly, across their entire history with you.

When your company was first founded, every point of the customer experience would be carefully crafted to align with the customer's needs. Over time, gaps formed and, with the advent of technological change, new channels emerged to make the customer journey more varied and complex. This is where more gaps form but also where opportunities lie to transform the experience – especially using digital technology, as it's lower-cost and lower-risk than making complex changes to staff or infrastructure.

I saw a tremendous amount of technical debt we needed to retire, and we were looking at opportunities for quick-wins and short-, medium- and long-term wins as well.

For example, we have programme called 'Road to Recovery'. Our volunteers and our staff provide millions and millions of rides over the years to patients who need to access lifesaving cancer treatments and therapies either because they're too sick to drive or they just don't have access to an automobile.

We were managing that thirteen different ways, most of which were on spreadsheet or using pen and paper. So, we came up with the idea of 'Uber' for our patient services.

We built a technology where we said 'I want a core technology and I don't care what the service is we're providing'. Ultimately the goal for this platform is to really be engine behind all the services we provide, and we called it 'Service Match' because it took that service and then matched it with people, like Uber does. We started with Road to Recovery, where the 'service' was a ride to and from treatment.

So, for example, you want to volunteer to the American Cancer Society and you're free Tuesday and Thursday afternoons from twelve o'clock to six. You'll create an account. We do a background check and make sure you have a driver's license and insurance. You'll have a secure profile online and a mobile app and you'll be able to see your schedule and reschedule. The patient on the other hand, would see who's picking them up at 2 o'clock, their photo and where you're going to meet. We even integrated Google Maps technology.

It transformed everything. Suddenly our ability to give rides went up by 25 per cent. We gave more rides, got more volunteers, and we attracted more millennials. So, Service Match was a huge success, and a prime example of digital transformation because the reality is it transformed our business model. We had a new organizational process for doing things and were able to centralize our support versus having it in thirteen different ways. That means we're able to roll-out mobile technology to attract and recruit a whole different segment of volunteers, which was very, very exciting.

Most importantly though, we were literally impacting more lives. Those are more people now who can get to the life-saving chemotherapy, radiation, surgeries and consultations they need. To me that's an example of technology literally saving lives, which is pretty cool.

Interview with Jay Ferro, Executive Vice President, EarthLink
Former Chief Information Officer, American Cancer Society, 2012–2016

For example, here are all the phases and possible points of interaction for a student that make up the entire customer experience for a university:

- **Potential student:** Looking at the university website, receiving a brochure in the mail, speaking to an advisor on the phone, attending an Open Day, chatting on university-related forums and social media.

- **New student:** Applying online, receiving an acceptance letter in the mail, registering online, paying for campus housing, buying books, moving into residence, attending welcome sessions, switching classes, and applying for campus jobs.

- **Existing student:** Attending classes, taking exams, joining study groups, accessing counselling services, joining clubs, running for Student Union roles, attending sports and social events, renting a cap and gown, attending graduation, receiving a diploma by mail.

- **Long-time student:** Getting employment advice, making alumni contributions, mentoring students, researching post-graduate study options, attending alumni events, hiring university services for business needs, forming business partnerships with the university.

You can see from this one example how many different complex interactions can exist in a single customer stage, let alone across the entire customer experience. There are also many different ways digital technology and new ways of working could start transforming the student experience to help the university increase revenue, engagement and impact on any one of those interaction points.

Many of the universities are still thinking of the technology first and then trying to complete the journey, well that is completely wrong from my perspective. This is not about technology, it's about premium user experience. When you've designed the experience you want and you pay attention to that, you can build back to the technology decisions but it's not the other way around.

Here in the State of Victoria, for seven years in a row we have been first in student satisfaction based on the government survey on all the students in the country. So it's not an accident that we decided premium experiences, in particular premium digital experiences, are the key to this journey.

Interview with William Confalonieri, Chief Digital Officer, Deakin University

Needs common to all customers: Surviving and thriving

The challenge for most is not knowing where to start or how to prioritize. The common question raised is 'what do my customers really want?' The good news is, that answer is same for everyone; no matter the sector, geography, or scale of the business, there is one thing everyone's customers have in common: they're all human beings. Humans are motivated by only two types of need: things we all need to survive and things we all need to thrive.

By using these two camps of human need as a framework for targeting your transformation efforts, you can easily prioritize which routes to transformation will have the biggest impact on your organization's divers of success.

1. 'Surviving' needs

To survive, all humans need health, wealth, and security. To identify routes to transformation that target survival needs, look for ways your organization – including its products, people, and assets – can increase your customer's financial success, physical and mental well-being, and sense of safety.

For example, health insurance companies are now regularly letting customers save money on premiums when they connect their wearable devices to insurance company apps that automatically track activity goals like number of steps taken and heart rate. Customers benefit by saving money and are motivated to exercise more, which is good for their health. The insurance companies build loyalty and gather useful data on the behaviours and habits of their customers, which helps them improve the accuracy of their insurance risk forecasts.

2. 'Thriving' needs

To thrive, all humans need freedom, social status, and mental stimulation. These are the higher-level human needs that are also the most powerful to target because they appeal to us on a much more emotional level.

To create routes to transformation that target thriving-related needs, look for ways to increase your customers' sense of self, including ways to make them more respected by peers and more knowledgeable. You can also find ways to save them time and mental energy, allowing them to focus only on what matters most in their interactions with you.

There are great examples of companies meeting thriving needs everywhere. It's the entire premise behind every single social network and loyalty scheme. It's also the big driver behind companies changing their business models to offer subscriptions to products and services that used to be bought outright. Companies like Amazon offer hassle-free ordering and super-fast delivery, and create 'premium' versions of services that only paying subscribers are able to access.

If you think about it from commercial standpoint, it's whether you want to become that bleeding edge or leading edge, or fast follower, or whether you can discern what's actually just going to be a fad. So it's actually not just being adaptive to technology, but actually making good commercial decisions about what's going to be transformative to the customer experience.

Interview with Jan Babiak Board of Directors,
Walgreens Boots Alliance & Bank of Montreal

Top three routes to transform customer experience

With the two types of needs in mind, there are three common routes to transforming customer experience. Starting from the easiest, these paths show how traditional organizations are transforming to meet the needs of customers today, and how start-ups and new entrants are winning market share away from the companies who ignore them.

1. Solve pain points

Solving problems and pain points is the easiest and most effective way to gain traction and start showing results in any digital transformation programme.

Not only is there a tangible before and after state to compare and showcase results, but you can also take benchmarking measurements before any project starts to be able to track improvements when new results start coming in.

The best approach is to focus on pain points that are easy to measure and valuable to the customer. For example, making a service or turnaround time faster by digitizing steps within it, or making a product or offering easier to understand and use by communicating better through digital channels.

The routes to solving pain points can be a simple solution (e.g. redesigning a section of the website) or big and complex (e.g. introducing an entirely new digital service).

Whatever path you take, make sure you can link it to a business metric and to filling one of your customer's thriving or surviving needs.

2. Enable a lifestyle

When deciding how to transform your organization, start by thinking how it might transform the lives of its customers. Sometimes the customer experience you currently offer is too limiting in this regard and you have to look beyond the existing points of interaction and consider the interactions your customers have before, after, and in between.

Digital innovations and new ways of working can help you support parts of the customer's life that your current products and services don't reach. Thinking about the full range of your customers' thriving and surviving needs, decide how you can fit into and enable the lifestyle they aspire to.

Often this requires introducing new technologies to facilitate services outside the traditional spaces, or forming partnerships. For these paths to transformation, the evidence you gather can be extremely compelling internally, proving an excellent case for further change.

We do 'Relay for Life' which is an amazing event. We do 5,000 of them in twenty-four countries and three million people participate. It's a huge fundraiser for us and it raises hundreds of millions of dollars. But in many cases Millennials and Gen X want to fundraise on their own terms. We say 'here's a relay' and they say 'well no, I just wanted to have a bikeathon'. We'd stare back and say 'ok well we can't really help you with any digital tools … but give us the money when you're done'. Those people are going to go find a charity who can actually give them a hand.

So, we built a combination of two different technologies. We built a mobile app that allows you to not only create an event and take secure payment via credit card. You can either type it in or scan it through a partnership with PayPal. It also allows you to scan cheques. This was big because when you're at a big fundraising event one of the big things you always see is 'bank night' because you've received 200 cheques. That means you've got to bundle them, you've got to put them in a spreadsheet, and you've got to send them all in. We eliminated that business process. What's more exciting about is it started to allow people to fundraise on their own terms. If you say 'I want to do a bikeathon', we can say 'well you're going to need a team website, so here's a digital presence for you. You get to control the content, you can use our brand, here's a number for support, and here are some apps for you to use'.

Suddenly we had incremental income growth almost immediately out of the box, and from people we never would have reached before. To me that's a perfect example of digital transformation because we changed our business model. It is all about our volunteers and constituents. It is not about us.

Interview with Jay Ferro, Executive Vice President, EarthLink
Former Chief Information Officer, American Cancer Society, 2012–2016

When measuring results from projects that try to serve more of the customer's lifestyle, be sure to factor in the set-up and scaling costs should the innovation take off beyond the pilot stage. It's easy for leaders to get attached to early successes without understanding the full cost of adding new staff or permanently diverting resources from business as usual, especially in organizations where return on investment and accountability aren't carefully tracked.

3. Facilitate long-term goals

Every company has a view of where it wants to be in five to ten years – but what about your customers? Facilitating long-term goals for your customers means rewarding people for sticking with you and helping your business achieve its long-term goals.

This can be the most challenging area to tackle because it can take a long time to show positive results. The secret is to pick multiple paths that fulfil the customer's same thriving and surviving need. These routes are then tracked simultaneously to determine which should be enhanced and scaled up.

Just be sure to avoid the traditional traps – for example, introducing a point-based loyalty scheme where customers earn discounts through regular purchases is not digital transformation.

The information you gathered about your customers during BUILD Stage 1: Bridge will tell you the kind of long-term value they seek in their lives. You'll get inspiration from other organizations and technologies currently fulfilling needs outside the ones you provide.

Now it's time to start putting these great ideas to use in BUILD Stage 3: Iterate, where the routes to transformation become individual projects working towards individual goals but a common vision: achieving your digital transformation.

We have a very ambitious 'Smart Campus' programme where physical locations respond to you. We have self-service screens all over our campus and when you walk by, the screen can respond to you and show information that's relevant to where you're going and what you need to do. We have the location of every single person across all our campuses, and we provide 'Near Me' services, so when a student wants to see where their friends are, that student can see it on a map on their mobile. We understand when a student needs to step in a classroom, and we can push to their devices the notes they need for that class. The campus really responds to your presence.

Interview with William Confalonieri, Chief Digital Officer, Deakin University

What you'll need to start projects

Skills, transparency, and empowerment

There are three elements needed to create routes to transformation and to make sure they stay up-to-date and informed as the programme runs.

1. The right skills at leadership level

Digital transformation involves a lot of different skill sets across a broad range of topics.

To lead major projects, you need people with relevant expertise across your organization's locations, offerings, and customer base, as well as individuals to take personal responsibility for the success of individual projects running within the programme.

You'll also need people with expertise in technology and innovation, but this can be supplemented where needed with external partners.

The iBHF was one of the biggest projects in many years, and by biggest I mean it involved people from every aspect of the organization from the back-end to the nurses helping heart patients. It involved volunteers who worked a couple of hours a week, right up to people in the digital team who are immersed in platforms and digital technology itself. So, in that case it was a full-blown programme management approach with a dedicated programme manager, full steering group, working groups, sub-groups. That gave the programme enough structure to function. It was also in keeping with the culture of the organization too. It used a Waterfall approach but it had some Agile elements. The people structure side, who drove it, and how it worked was the making of the programme because it gave responsibilities, relationships and the purpose real clarity.

We had very strong governance but I feel that term doesn't do it justice. It's around ownership of the programme and that felt very clear. We were then able to navigate both the changes between moving through Waterfall and Agile, and between some of the challenges we came up against, I felt that helped keep the project going at certain points internally.

Interview with Dr Charmaine Griffiths, Chief Operating Officer,
The Institute for Cancer Research
Former Executive Director of Strategy & Performance,
British Heart Foundation, 2013–2016

The number of leaders and the exact split of roles and responsibilities will differ greatly depending on the skills possessed in your digital transformation leadership group, including the strengths of your change agent. It will also depend on the size and sector of your organization and the scale of the project you want to undertake.

I've worked with clients who kept a large leadership group to oversee the transformation programme that met monthly as a panel. This included assigning individual project leadership tasks to over ten senior staff members who acted as project owners and points of contact across the business.

In other organizations, programme leadership is small but each member takes full-time responsibility for project leadership, with multiple projects running in parallel.

The right skills at project level

The right skills become very diverse at project level, where each stage of the transformation requires a blend of expertise and capabilities across a wide range of subjects. These skills are the ones unlikely to be found entirely within your organization, and can be supplemented with partners like digital agencies.

When staffing from across your organization, be sure to pull a diverse cross-section of people. The best way to make transformation sustainable is to change mindsets and ways of working across your business, and it won't happen if only one department or team is doing all the eye-opening and innovative work.

Depending on the size of organization and the nature of the project, you may have multiple roles fulfilled by a single person or multiple people in a single role working full-time or split between many different projects.

Rather than get bogged down in job titles, these are the areas of responsibility you'll want to make sure are covered – even for very small digital transformation projects:

- **DevOps**: Building the solutions, mapping how new elements will integrate and work with existing systems and IT infrastructure, and ensuring security, performance, and speed across the testing, launching, and running of solutions.

- **Customer experience:** Deciding how to seize opportunities and stay aligned with external needs throughout the project.

- **Design:** Creating visuals and user flows for new digital tools, channels, and products for high usability and brand alignment.

- **Insights:** Ensuring digital outputs meet customer needs in real-world and high-demand scenarios and that results captured are relevant to the goals and transformation vision, and are tracked as KPIs (key performance indicators) throughout.

Nothing promotes collaboration more than an exchange of hostages. I find it very helpful for there to be cross-team assignments. For example, if you work in IT and I work in Marketing and we have a project together, maybe ten of your people report to me for the first six months of the project and ten of my people report to you for the year you need to get it off the ground. That cross-team assignment tends to really sharpen one's focus on the end result rather than on local politics.

Interview with Perry Hewitt, Vice-President of Marketing, ITHAKA
Former Chief Digital Officer, Harvard University, 2011–2016

2. Systems for ensuring transparency

The best way to build trust in the programme and its new ways of working is to ensure transparency between projects and across all stakeholder groups. This means keeping relevant people informed of important updates and progress, and allowing access to more detail when it's requested. That said, if you're relying on making these updates in person through meetings and presentations, your progress will slow down and, in busy periods, grind to a complete halt.

Conflicting schedules, people in different locations, and team members and leaders trying to work across multiple roles or projects mean transparency has to be facilitated through automated means, or you risk spending more trying to coordinate diaries than actually doing anything transformational.

Facilitating transparency doesn't have to be complicated. It can mean adding relevant stakeholders to project management software and letting them log in to see progress and workflows online. It's also a good idea to create an online space for the project teams to post key updates, examples of work in progress, and milestones reached. The hardest part, in reality, is getting this type of system going. Like any change, it takes patience and incentives to get people to change their normal ways.

Another way to ensure transparency is to use online collaboration software for tasks like design and development. This makes it easier for team members from different geographies to work collaboratively remotely, and it prevents knowledge being locked up in one person or team. With online design collaboration tools, designers can divide work easily, stakeholders can see and approve outputs, project managers can track progress, and developers can access the most up-to-date designs without having to request it from the designers.

Depending on the size of your company, you might be able to get away with systems that are free and simple to use, but more likely you'll want to invest in a tool that's robust and scalable so you can add layers of governance. Investing in proper systems for ensuring transparency also makes it more likely to gain widespread use across the company over time, which in turn makes digital transformation itself more sustainable.

If you choose the enterprise software route, make sure you spend time and money training people on its use – you want good practices followed from day one to prevent it from becoming a blocker in the future. With this investment in place, be sure to motivate and enforce 100 per cent adoption and regular use of the tool – if half of the process is managed outside the system that will become the sure point of failure as the programme gets larger and more complex.

3. Governance to empower the right people

Empowering the right people at the right levels of a digital transformation programme is what makes the difference between success and failure. Many companies overlook the crucial importance of empowering people when adopting new methodologies like Agile, Lean, or Design Thinking described in BUILD Stage 3: Iterate. Empowered teams are what enable the quick decision making and solutioning that are fundamental to each of these innovation fuelling practices.

When looking at empowerment, there are two levels to consider: team level for project-related planning and decisions and leadership level for goal setting and decisions relating to routes to transformation.

Project team empowerment

Team members need to be empowered at project level to be able to use their relevant expertise and skills to plan the best approach, spot and solve problems, and seize opportunities as they arise.

The best form of governance to facilitate this involves senior leadership setting goals and objectives for project teams to meet, rather than prescribing how the teams should achieve them. It also requires transparency and regular updates to senior leadership, especially when new information is revealed that requires a decision requiring more time, budget, or resource.

To be able to produce regular results worthy of sharing with senior leadership, empowering project teams also requires working in shorter cycles to produce products incrementally. Agile methodology, for example, typically operates in two-week cycles (called sprints) so there is work to demonstrate biweekly. Key principles of Agile and another method of working and showing results faster will be covered in more detail in BUILD Stage 3: Iterate.

Allowing teams to make their own decisions makes sense not just because they're the ones with the relevant skill sets but also because giving them control over making the project successful builds motivation and starts establishing a new precedent for accountability. Both attributes add to the sustainability of your company's digital transformation long after individual projects are complete.

You've got to have the right people on your team, first and foremost. What I mean by that is people who are transformative in their mindset, they're willing to think about things differently not have all the answers. And if you know in your heart of hearts they're not going to be the change agents that you need, change people. Make sure you have the right crew with you because there are going to bullets a blazing at times when you're talking about changing the way an organization is doing business.

Interview with Jay Ferro, Executive Vice President, EarthLink
Former Chief Information Officer, American Cancer Society, 2012–2016

Empowering leadership

Empowered teams can only innovate so far before a decision beyond the scope of the project needs to be made. Prioritizing which transformations occur and to what extent are decisions for the people in the transformation leadership group. These leaders need to be empowered to make calls on whether to add more resources, stay the course, or change track altogether – and they need to be able to do it quickly or progress will slow, teams will lose momentum, and stakeholders will lose interest.

To facilitate empowerment at leadership level, the most important factor has already been touched upon. It starts with needing the right skill sets on the teams, and in the leadership group itself, to make sure decisions are best informed. Beyond this though, you need to establish trust and respect because it's paramount for senior leaders to have faith in the capabilities of the project teams.

During a mobile app project for a global retail client, I chose project team members specifically for their extensive experience in mobile technology. When senior leaders questioned decisions about the app's design, functionality, or build, they received well-informed rationale directly from relevant members of the team. The trust this built freed senior leadership to focus on decisions around making the app more profitable from a business perspective, and let the team carry on troubleshooting and enhancing the app from a customer perspective.

The second important factor in empowering leadership is through delivering timely and relevant information. At the start of any project, the approach needs to be designed to meet the goals set by the transformation leadership group and keep them informed of developments and insights gathered as the programme develops.

BUILD Stage 3: Iterate goes into more detail about how to structure a project that shows progress on a regular basis, and tracks the right sort of metrics to enable leaders to make important business decisions quickly.

With this structure in place, the leadership team will be able to update the routes to transformation on a regular basis, and it starts to embed real-time decision making based on external insights and data as a sustainable practice beyond the programme itself.

One thing is to make sure you have the right people on those teams. The team has to be a cross-functional business team that happens to have technology people as a part of it.

You have to identify a sponsor, who is ultimately the leader of that team who has the most to gain and quite frankly, the most to lose. You need to empower that person by enabling them to make a number of decisions on a day-to-day basis.

Empowerment comes from having one integrated team that owns the delivery of that product. In other words, they deliver the whole solution. So it is about getting a cross-functional set of people who have the capability and competency to deliver. Cross-functional teams are so motivated working together versus working in separate silos.

Interview with Mike Giresi, Chief Information Officer,
Royal Caribbean Cruises
Former Chief Information Officer, Tory Burch, 2011–2015

BUILD Stage 3: Iterate

Iterate in short cycles, test with real users, and improve as you go to know which innovations should be scaled

Why Iterate?

The wrong ways to manage transformation

Managing a digital transformation programme can be incredibly stressful and there are two incorrect, but unfortunately common, approaches leaders take to cope with the pressure.

The first is to turn to traditional management techniques. Leaders who opt for this approach try to calculate things like each project's potential return on investment (ROI), but they quickly find there are too many unknowns to confidently plug numbers into an equation or apply figures to a scoring system. Because the numbers are based on best guesses, no one has real confidence in them, which shows when tough decisions need to be made.

Despite all the upfront work, the traditional management method quickly deteriorates into the second common type of approach, which is to forgo the use of any formal management process at all.

Leaders pick projects that sound exciting and look good on paper. The outcomes succeed in engaging people but aren't measurably tied to the direct drivers of the business' success. In these cases, digital transformation often gets a bad reputation for being all show and no substance, and because there are no hard metrics to prove otherwise, enthusiasm and funding wane.

The right way to manage digital transformation

Fortunately, there is a way to manage a digital transformation programme that ensures measurable results that are directly linked to your business' success

You've got to own it and have some skin in the game. To me, when you start breaking into uncharted territory, there are certain assumptions you need to make, whether it's a market analysis or a pilot or a proof of concept that you're leaning on saying 'well we funded this for ninety days, let's see how it goes'. You're going to get hand grenade close, you're not going to get dialled in plus or minus 10 per cent on many of these things, if you're breaking new ground.

Now on more incremental digital transformation, I think you can have a much more solid business case. Today I can only reach 10,000 constituents, tomorrow I can reach 100,000. Well, that translates into lives saved, which translates into more donations. The business case or the payback or the ROI is very similar in a non-profit as it is in a for-profit. The additional dimension that we get is lives impacted whether its research grants funded, the number of rides that we give, the number of stays in a Hope Lodge, the number of events that we can run, the number of donations that we take, the number of calls we can take from all around the world and just about every country. If I can roll out new technology, whether it's chat technology or a mobile chat experience to go from 1 million to 1.5 million calls or interactions a year, that's 500,000 people more who literally have asked us for help and we did it on their terms. I measured things in that way.

Creating a culture where failure is allowed so long as it's fast and productive is key. Most companies aren't willing to do that. They plan 'innovation' or 'digital transformation' as part of their normal budget cycle and say 'well, we'll plan for it next year'.

Interview with Jay Ferro, Executive Vice President, EarthLink
Former Chief Information Officer, American Cancer Society, 2012–2016

metrics and allow you to prioritize resources and make fast and informed decisions throughout.

It requires a more modern approach to running projects, including how the teams are structured, what work is produced and when, and how decisions are made as products are developed.

This section is entirely devoted to this new way of working, called the iterative project approach. It starts with an overview of how iterative projects can be governed by leadership in a single process; then it details how each project needs to run in order to deliver measurable and relevant results.

When I first started, the team said we have to rewrite the entire reservation system and it has to be done in two years. I said 'why'? They said 'because it doesn't work and because it's not Agile and we can't go fast enough'. But when you really look at the architecture of the reservation system, it's not just the reservation system itself. It's a payment gateway, a guest profile system, a property management system, a pricing system, and a promotion bundling system. This system has almost 9 billion lines of code, so you are talking about a very complicated system. No one in the world makes a system that does all the things this does, so why should we start to rewrite it. Instead, you can take a few things out of it and start to decouple some of the services that become manageable. We can then, in theory, rewrite and/or purchase the right solution to allow us to scale. You start small because starting big like rewriting the entire reservation system is a huge mistake.

Interview with Mike Giresi, Chief Information Officer, Royal Caribbean Cruises
Former Chief Information Officer, Tory Burch, 2011–2015

Within this section, you'll see references to proven methodologies such as Agile and Design Thinking, but learning these specific methods is not the goal. Instead, I want to give you the principles and core ingredients needed to craft your own organization's approach to digital transformation, using the components that have been proven by countless successful transformation stories.

At a glance: How to Iterate

Who? The transformation leadership group and self-directing project teams that are staffed based on the needs of the project with the right blend of skill sets to build, test, and learn in iterative cycles.

Why? To prevent the organization from completing a project customers don't want or need and to enable truly innovative solutions that have the power to transform the business.

What? Run many iterative projects and evaluate their progress against predefined goals so decisions can be made quickly and based on measurable and observable evidence.

How? Projects use a blend of Agile and Design Thinking methods to engage customers, creatively solve problems, spot opportunities, and test and improve solutions as they increase in scale and complexity.

You can't tell people what the gaps are. If you sit across from someone and say 'I've got a whole list of examples of how we could do things better', it's really hard to influence that person.

My one approach out of all the learnings of what failed for us and what succeeded, is you show not tell. For example, I was trying to convince people internally that we could save more money. When you get in a room though and one person is talking about one solution and the other person wants another, how do you prove who's right? You can't, you just end up in an argument. The only way to do it to show your solution.

Interview with Ash Roots, Director of Digital, Direct Line Group

Tips for success in Iterate:

- If the organization is concerned about damage to its brand by showing customers 'unfinished' or experimental work, early testing and customer engagement can be done under different brand names or by third parties until ideas are proven successful.

- When getting started, providing teams with an environment away from their usual space can help encourage innovative thinking and reinforce the organization's commitment to the digital transformation programme.

- Be ready to amend the shared vision and the routes to transformation as you go – they are intended to be living constructs that will be informed throughout the programme by the innovation and progress you're about to start making.

Leading the Programme

How to iterate

The key element to leading digital transformation and achieving success through innovation is with cross-functional teams working in iterative project cycles.

From completing BUILD Stage 2: Uncover, you'll have a prioritized list of routes to transformation as a set of outcomes projects need to achieve to complete the vision. Rather than planning how each project will achieve those outcomes from beginning to end, this is the opportunity for your organization to experiment with different approaches and solutions, produce real results quickly, all while learning new and better ways of working.

The iterative approach follows a cycle of build, test, learn, improve, and repeat. This replaces the traditional project approach, which follows a linear process of plan, build, test, and launch. The focus of the iterative approach is on building and testing quickly to learn from the results and improve the product or service in repeated cycles.

The rationale is to prevent companies from wasting effort completing a project from start to finish, only to find out at the end that its customers don't value it, its staff can't manage it, or that it doesn't create any real return on investment. Also, because changes in the world never stop happening, products and services developed through an iterative approach never go out of date. Its cyclical nature ensures gradual improvements are always taking place, allowing offerings to evolve in pace with the needs and wants of customers, negating the need for another 'transformation' in the future.

Where I've seen these projects go terribly wrong is when someone, often an agency, comes in with a 50-page PowerPoint deck that's the most beautiful thing that you've ever seen but they've taken the idea so far down the road to sell the vision. Show me a working prototype, show me how you expect people to engage with this. One ended up being a $1.2 million project that got flushed a year later. That's the biggest danger is when you've got the slick agency or smart marketers who tell this story that is so compelling, but they haven't done the quick prototyping that shows 'Is this reasonable? Would people really use this?'

Always go back to the user and their actual behaviour. Would an actual person do this? Find me that human and walk me through that use case. Because it's so easy in a boardroom with the aromatic tang of expensive coffee in the air for people to just absolutely lose sight of what normal humans want and need to do in a typical day – you know, 'Maslow's hierarchy of internet needs' – and it very rarely involves clicking on the $4 million visualization the agency sold you.

Interview with Perry Hewitt, Vice-President of Marketing, ITHAKA
Former Chief Digital Officer, Harvard University, 2011–2016

Labs, accelerators, and internal start-ups

For some organizations, getting even one cross-functional team together to try an iterative approach is too far from the current culture, or the right skill sets are in too short supply across the company. In these instances, there are different organizational models you can use to kick-start your transformation programme. These models can also apply to organizations where digital engagement and technology is still far enough outside the core business of the company to not yet require those capabilities decentralized and embedded across the structure.

Innovation labs, hubs, and accelerators

An innovation 'lab', 'hub', and 'accelerator' are somewhat interchangeable terms used to describe a centralized group of people in a specially equipped space dedicated to digital, innovation, and transformational activities.

These models are commonly used when it's not possible or practical to hire or upskill enough people across the organization to have sufficient digital capabilities in every unit or department. For some businesses, these models are an efficient way to cluster your best equipment and most highly skilled people, assigning them to work with other areas of the company to jointly tackle problems and opportunities.

To differentiate between the three, the following distinctions have gained recognition across various sectors.

- **Innovation Lab:** Tasked with tackling big opportunities like generating new revenue streams, rather than solving pain points or improving efficiency. Labs are generally expected to produce the most cutting-edge work of the three models and, therefore, will have the most specialist equipment, space, and staffing needs.

- **Digital Hub:** Sometimes also called a 'centre for excellence'. Follows a 'hub and spoke' model (Dhar 2015) and is responsible for all manner of digital activities, generally used when trying to upskill existing staff and digitize existing parts of the business, rather than spark radical change and major innovations.

- **Accelerator:** Often used in very conservative organizations where people are change-averse, sector regulations are strict, and digital skill levels are low. They are often entirely staffed by an external partner organization (e.g. a digital agency) or brand new staff. Accelerators are often created when the barriers to transformation are too great to form a Digital Hub.

The team is structured at the moment to include expertise in digital tech, design, and marketing – this means there's an appropriate resource for people to call upon for most digital projects. The model we are basing it on is a hybrid model of central and individual team digital expertise , working with individual teams and building digital expertise in them. Eventually you may say we no longer need to be in existence because every team has become so digitally transformed that it's part of the DNA of how they work.

Interview with Mike Walton, Chief of Section, Digital Engagement,
United Nations High Commission for Refugees (UNHCR)

These definitions aren't standard, and what these special units are called in an organization can sometimes depend more on what term gets the most traction with the senior leadership team (e.g. some prefer 'lab' because it sounds more state-of-the-art than 'hub').

All three models can be hosted either on- or off-site – in either specially provisioned space or one owned by the partner company (e.g. the agency's studio). Hosting off-site is often the preferred choice when the organization is particularly conservative, corporate, or restrictive on how space is used. Taking the unit off-site lets the transformation team have a more modern workspace with breakout areas, better equipment, and other perks to keep staff happy as they work long hours on tough problems.

Regardless of the model you choose: A word of caution

It's very easy for any kind of centralized team to become its own silo, which means transformation and innovation won't scale and your organization will still be at risk of future disruption.

For any of these interim models to work as a step towards enabling wider transformation, following the iterative project approach outlined in this section is crucial to ensure cross-collaborative working and skills-exchange with people from across the business at all times. The final stage of BUILD Stage 5: Disseminate also details the steps for how to incrementally scale models like these beyond the confines of the hub, lab, or accelerator.

> Accelerators are good because you can get people from IT and from the business units, and often from the customer or supplier standpoints as well, take them off their day jobs, put them in one room, and give them the target for a couple of months to do something really meaningful. I find those are good ways to make sure you get the buy-in by having multi-dimensional and diverse teams. Too frequently teams are only the people interested in the latest and greatest, but you also have to put in some people to be devil's advocate in these things.
>
> Interview with Jan Babiak
> Board of Directors, Walgreens Boots Alliance and Bank of Montreal

Internal start-ups and external joint ventures

Some companies opt for a much more arm's length approach to innovation teams and create them as separate entities either in or outside the business.

Internal start-ups are generally given a seed of investment money and treated like a separate business running inside the company. This means the team is free to create entirely new platforms, processes, and partnerships free from the parent company's barriers to transformation. It also gives the people on the team greater job security than working on a real start-up, where their livelihoods are at risk if the new business fails. Company leaders often opt for internal start-ups when there are such significant barriers to transformation that a success is needed to prove the business case for the major investments needed to resolve them.

External joint ventures (Murray 2016), on the other hand, are like those used in a normal business context, just with digital innovation as the means for generating the new revenue streams. This approach is usually chosen when two or more companies want to urgently respond to a major direct threat or massive opportunity, but don't have the right assets or access to market to do it alone.

In choosing either of these models, company leaders may also want to dissociate the main company brand from the new business venture, and the risk that comes with it, if it fails.

That said, these models are much more difficult to transition into sustainable, company-wide transformation than labs, hubs, and accelerators, so proceed with extreme caution if this is your company's only route.

The most important thing to not do, and to me is the symptom of imminent doom, is to have anything with the word 'lab' in it that's in a separate office, totally cut off from the main business. Anything that is produced there will never filter out of that building. This because the reality is you don't transform a business by creating a new completely isolated business. 'Labs' like these only demonstrate that the transformative process is a career dead end because if it was really going to happen, the main business would be doing it.

Interview with Ben Hammersley, Futurist,
BBC World Presenter 'Cybercrime, with Ben Hammersley' &
WIRED Contributing Editor

How to start a digital transformation programme

The critical principle that allows the iterative approach to work is the onus it puts on testing and measurable goals. Each goal is based on a business metric and testing is conducted on a pass or fail basis to remove any doubt. Anything that fails to meet the minimum success criteria is either replaced or improved using the customer's feedback until it's capable of passing. The sections 'Iterative Project Approach' and 'Goals, Minimum Success Criteria and Testing' go into more detail on the specifics and methods you can use for each.

Before getting into specifics, it's important to understand how an entire programme of digitally transformative projects should be led and managed,

We said we're going to borrow some of the key best practices out there. We created an innovation cross-functional team that wasn't too big. They all had ownership, so when we piloted new technologies and look at these things, they were voice for those particular functions.

You know the old mantra: there are business successes and IT failures. We flipped the script on that one. There are no IT failures because there are no IT projects. Every project is a business project.

Interview with Jay Ferro, Executive Vice President, EarthLink
Former Chief Information Officer, American Cancer Society, 2012–2016

including the answers to core questions like how do you balance resource between projects, and how many projects do you take on at one time? I'm not going to prescribe a specific approach, but instead relate the important principles and a framework so you can create your own version that best fits your company's needs.

1. Maximize your project count (and expect it to fluctuate)

The first principle when running a digital transformation programme is to run as many projects as your resources allow because when you use the iterative approach, you'll only scale the ones that demonstrate real business results.

The whole point of innovation is to experiment and try bold, new ideas – if you only pick a handful, there's a high likelihood they won't pan out, and having so few will make it harder to kill them off even when they aren't successful. This principle, however, is entirely dependent on following the iterative approach to projects, which includes multiple rounds of building and testing, followed by evaluation points.

If you attempt this using a traditional project approach, you'll likely exceed your resources halfway through when it's not clear which project to continue, resulting in nothing being able to finish or scale. The other risk in a traditional approach is you take on the right number of projects, but maintaining oversight of them takes too much time from senior leadership, which causes delays or results in attention being diverted from other important activities outside the transformation programme.

2. Keep projects on short cycles

Keeping your iterative cycles short (e.g. weeks, not months) for all projects allows you to start and run multiple projects at once with low upfront costs and minimum risk because it only takes one cycle of 'build, test, learn, and improve' to gather measurable and meaningful results. Even major IT projects can run on short cycles, developing parts feature by feature for continuous testing and improvement.

These results let you compare which projects are succeeding, which ones need significant improving, and which ones should be culled or replaced completely.

Running short cycles can be hard to adapt to, so prepare for a steep learning curve if most projects in your organization last a minimum of eighteen months before being expected to show results. You'll also need to plan around internal timetables – for example, if a major project needs board-level approvals, and the board meets only once a quarter.

It's also incredibly helpful to stick to the same project rhythm, or cadence, for all the work that's being developed. In the section 'Running an Iterative Project', you'll find out more about Agile methodology and how the two-week cadence of projects helps to not only give a predictable pattern of working and producing to project teams, but also makes it easier to schedule regular reviews with all your concurrently running projects since everyone has results to show at the same time intervals.

3. Set goals for project teams and stick to them

The number one killer of innovation is when staff feel they don't have the freedom to fail. What goes hand-in-hand is when people don't clearly know what success or failure even looks like.

'Shifting goal posts' is a term used to describe nightmarish projects where senior leadership change their minds about a project's priorities and expectations. For an iterative project team, this is especially devastating because the approach is completely designed around each iteration either passing or failing, and then learning from a round of testing constructed against the project's goals. Passes or failures are acceptable in a cycle, providing the learnings from a failure can be applied to the next new attempt to reach the goal. If the goal is unclear or changes midway through, then what could have been useful learning is now just random data.

The section 'Goals and Minimum Success Criteria' goes into this principle in more detail, including the importance of setting minimum success criteria to be able to decide immediately whether to continue a project based on its results at any stage.

4. No one's opinion matters more than the customer

In digital transformation, goals are constructed and projects designed to improve the metrics that drive your organization's success. There is only one group with the power to either sustain your business or drive it into extinction, and it's made up from the people whose needs your organization exists to serve: your customers.

Your senior leadership must adhere to this principle throughout, or else the measurable and meaningful results gathered during testing risk being overruled by the highest paid person in the group. The next sections cover the decision-making process in more detail, and how the four principles factor across the entire life of the programme.

5. Criteria for evaluating transformation projects

Evaluating projects in a digital transformation programme comes down to your leadership group's ability to make fast and informed decisions, and to do this you need criteria that are trusted, testable, and relevant to your business' success.

These criteria require systematic and consistent application so evaluation doesn't become a full-time job in itself, and so teams working on projects can strive to produce results that fit the decision-making criteria.

For any organization, there are five categories of decision-making criteria to consider when evaluating a project's viability in a digital transformation programme.

Bake in measurement from the very beginning. I'm committed to a lean start-up and Agile development approach, where you have project that have quick wins built in, regular touchpoints, and rapid cycles of measurement so you can refine as you go. That means cross-functional groups where you have say, four developers sitting with two designers, sitting with one content strategist, sitting with one marketer. And then you have these quick four- to six-week cycles where you're churning out products and ideas, and delivering and measuring quickly.

Interview with Perry Hewitt, Vice-President of Marketing, ITHAKA
Former Chief Digital Officer, Harvard University, 2011–2016

1. Customer value: Do customers value the project's output enough to be worth the investment?

This requires looking at the customer behaviours that drive the success of your organization and evaluating a project's ability to positively impact one or more objective (e.g. buying or spending more, using more of your services, choosing you over others, and referring others to you).

2. Competitive advantage: Is it offered elsewhere and how will ours stack up?

First, you want to know how competitive the product's output will be when it's released, especially if it's a saturated marketplace and the competition's version is already very advanced.

Second, you want to determine how likely a project's output will be to attract new competitors, especially ones who will be willing to invest more and quickly outpace you. This doesn't mean a project likely to attract new competition should be cancelled, but it does mean making a decision on how much long-term investment to offer it (e.g. hoping for a short-term pay-off from a burst of upfront investment versus planning for a longer-term play with major ongoing investment).

3. Business impact: Can the business enable and support it long term?

Business impact relates to your organization's ability to resource the project's output once complete, such as providing staff, space, and equipment. It also needs to consider the impact the new innovation will have on existing business.

That said, the fear of cannibalization should never be used as a reason not to innovate. Instead, evaluating business impact is more to ensure the cost and effort for redistributing resources, retraining staff, and communicating changes to existing customers are all factored into investment decisions.

4. Technical feasibility: What's the cost and what's the impact to existing systems?

Technical feasibility is evaluating one-off costs like equipment as well as ongoing costs like licensing fees and hosting once the project's outputs are complete. Technical feasibility and business impact have a natural cross-over with evaluation criteria because new technology may create the need to train, hire, or reallocate staff, as well as make changes to incompatible existing systems.

5. Scalability: Can it be customized and is it applicable across the business?

Scalability can be controversial as evaluation criteria because it's often viewed as an all-or-nothing decision: Either the project's outputs can be applied across every geography and customer segment the company serves, or it's too niche and not worth developing further.

This of course is a mistake, as it's often this generic approach to meeting customers' needs that makes organizations susceptible to swift moving niche competitors and puts them in need digital transformation in the first place. However, it's also true that some standardization is needed to make innovation scalable across a large enough number of customers to prevent the company from becoming too fragmented and incapable of growth.

The best approach to scalability, therefore, is to evaluate a project's outputs on the basis of how easy it is to adapt to another set of needs or conditions, and whether the customers and markets it does suit are big enough to be worth the investment. For more on scalability, BUILD Stage 5: Disseminate details ways to scale and improve the standardization of innovations across different customer segments and geographies.

The right way to evaluate projects

Right now, you probably have dozens of projects you would like to run based on the outcomes you revealed in BUILD Stage 2: Uncover ranging from small projects to large, safe bets to experimental gambles. You need a way to quickly evaluate the outputs of these projects against one another, improve the ones that show promise, and learn from the ones that don't pan out so you can apply those learnings to the rest.

A good analogy for how projects, goals, and project evaluation criteria all hang together in a digital transformation programme is to imagine each of your projects as a group of new army recruits. You don't know which new recruits will make good soldiers, or will turn out to have specialist skills. Also, because they're all new and lacking any basic training, you don't just want to test them –

Digital often plays into organizational ignorance where we count quantity over the quality of engagement. Ultimately our legacy is in the change we achieve, not the number of people we reach. I will still take one deep engagement over reaching a 100,000 people if that one is the one that I need to make the difference that we set out to achieve.

If you ask me if I could have 10 million people from around the globe or 500,000 from the country in which I was trying to affect the change, I would take the 500,000 depending on the country and context. In some countries, having millions of signatures from outside of their country would be offensive and would force them to dig their heels in against the issue because they don't want to be told what to do by the rest of the world. Having their own people challenge them would mean more.

Interview with Zach Abraham, Director of Global Campaigns,
WWF International

you want to give them the opportunity to get better, faster, and stronger as part of the testing process.

Think of the five evaluation criteria as different obstacles on a military fitness course. Each obstacle evaluates the recruits against your selection criteria, with the combined purpose of determining which one are worth continued investment. Goals are purposefully set high to emphasize overperformers, whereas minimum success criteria are set as a cut-off point by placing a baseline for the lowest results allowable to stay in the running.

Before going into this detail, the next part of managing digital transformation programmes is understanding the three major project stages that will allow projects to grow as they prove their worth through increasingly complex tests.

Common stages to trigger project evaluations

In addition to needing decision-making criteria to determine which of your projects to progress and which to cut, you need project stages to ensure the risk and cost are minimized throughout the programme.

You're likely already familiar with the following project stages in an IT context for developing and releasing a new product or service. Each stage is crucial because it allows the decision-making criteria to be applied at each, as well as allowing projects to scale incrementally starting from a simple prototype and finishing as a completed product/service in beta release, waiting for final launch.

In terms of how you measure the success of each one of our projects, it's very important you measure impact rather than just performance. We've got performance statistics, which are your run of the mill digital metrics, but then we've got our impact measurements on top of that. Impact measurements might include 'has brand awareness changed?' or 'have attitudes to refugees changed positively?' or 'have more people supported the advocacy campaign and has that supported real change?' It has to be driven by that final purpose of what the end objective is, rather than perhaps looking at these less-meaningful statistics of engagement like likes and shares. Once we're clear on that, we move towards this impact based way of measuring. That makes it much easier to produce that change because it's much easier to make the case for it internally as well.

Interview with Mike Walton, Chief of Section, Digital Engagement,
United Nations High Commission for Refugees (UNHCR)

Stage 1: Prototype and/or proof of concept

A prototype or proof of concept is a simple version of a proposed new product/ service designed to test customer and competitive value, as well as give early indications of business impact, technical feasibility, and scalability. A prototype is used to test customer behaviour with the new product or service, whereas a proof of concept is used to test the viability of the new product or service from a technical and business perspective.

For example, in a project trying to create a simple and fast way to pay for shop items with a mobile app, the prototype would be a designed version of the app loaded onto a phone that looks real but doesn't actually do anything when the buttons are tapped. The proof of concept for the same project could be a developer sending and receiving a dummy packet of encrypted data from the app's backend system to the store's electronic point of sale (EPoS) to prove the app can interact with the store on a technical level.

The section 'How to Run an Iterative Project' goes into more detail on what makes a good prototype or proof of concept for testing purposes, as well as tips for constructing good testing processes.

Stage 2: Alpha

Alpha, named after the first letter of the Greek alphabet, is a more developed version of the prototype or proof of concept that is released to a closed group of customers and staff.

For example, the mobile payment app's prototype had no integrations with external systems and the proof of concept had no user interface, so the Alpha version would combine the two. This would allow the designed version of the app to exchange data with the store's EPoS, making the test scenario more real and complex.

Like the prototype, the Alpha versions are tested goals within the five decision-making criteria, but with more emphasis on business value, technical impact, and scalability, since the test is able to include more users and more staff to see how each reacts and what impact it has on external systems. Testing an Alpha version also looks for ways to improve the new product or service on practical levels such as its speed, security, performance, as well as identifying opportunities for enhancement. This is also discussed in more detail in 'Running an Iterative Project'.

Stage 3: Beta

Beta, named after the second letter in the Greek alphabet, is a complete version of the new product/service that's released to a statistically representative proportion of the audience as a final test of the decision-making criteria.

In the mobile payment app example, the Beta could be released to the Apple and Google app stores but without any marketing or promotions. Instead, the company would invite a cross-section of its high-value customers to use the apps and share their feedback in exchange for a small incentive. It's also common for Beta versions to have limited geographical release, so it could be that only a small number of stores, or only stores in a particular city are able to use the Beta version of the app.

In addition to final testing and resolving any final performance issues, the Beta stage allows work to start on scaling the new product or service (e.g. identifying and doing iterative testing on customizations for other markets or segments) and is also used to build excitement and/or familiarity with staff and customers before launch.

Beyond Beta stage

Following the three stages means that in prototype and proof of concept stage, the first iterative cycles of the project are small, low-risk, and low-cost. As the new product or service achieves its goals, or at least meets the minimum success criteria, it can get bigger without introducing unnecessary risk, while still undergoing tests to prove its value.

The final point to note about the three stages is that each one can result in new projects spinning up off the back of testing results. For example, the company might identify ways to enhance the mobile payment app during Alpha stage that warrants a new prototype to be created with its own goals and minimum success criteria. The same project team can take on this spin-off project, or it could require its own team if the enhancements apply to a new customer type or geographic area than the original.

We encouraged 'tinker time' or dedicated time in app dev and in other groups to tinker on new opportunities. That is really how our mobile app came about. Internally people just couldn't get their head around why it would be valuable, so we built it and we showed it to them. It was three architects and a developer, meeting with my VP of app dev and myself. We just whiteboarded and sat around a table. They would go home over the weekend and tinker with it. They brought up a Proof of Concept, so we struck a deal with PayPal to at least pilot it at no charge to us to use their credit card scanning APIs. We built the first prototype and we brought it to the CMO. They all stared at each other, stared at us and said, 'when the hell did you guys build this?' and we said the last few weeks. It was like the clouds parted and the light went on.

That approach did two things. First, it encouraged my team that whether we have approval or not from the company, we're doing it. Second, our credibility went through the roof. Suddenly everyone understood: 'Hey, you do get what we're talking about, you do get our challenges, and you do understand our business.' And we were like 'Yes, and we've been trying to tell you this for a year.'

Interview with Jay Ferro, Executive Vice President, EarthLink
Former Chief Information Officer, American Cancer Society, 2012–2016

Setting Goals and Measuring Success

The right goals are the keys to success

The entire process of managing and evaluating your organization's digital transformation comes down to setting very clear and testable goals for each of your routes to transformation. If your routes to transformation include solving customer pain points to improve the customer journey, you'll need to define what success looks like before any individual project can attempt to achieve it.

How to structure goals so they work across all these areas is part science and part creative solutioning, and this section is going to take you through the principles of both so you can craft your own. Before getting into principles of what makes good goals and testing processes, it's worth dispelling a few commonly made mistakes.

> Most business units know what their metrics are so most organizations, whether they use balance scorecards or KPIs, will have a set of deliverables as a sign of success for a healthy organization. So, at a macro level, it's often too simple to say this is what great looks like and this is what the transformation should achieve.
>
> When setting your metrics at a more granular team level, my experience in digital is it can get a bit too inwards focused rather than on your user experience. My personal learning is it's really important to hold onto the fact that you're thinking of the organization as a whole, rather than a series of silos – that's critical. In fact, the very process of going through digital transformation will alter how teams think and work together.
>
> Interview with Dr Charmaine Griffiths, Chief Operating Officer,
> The Institute for Cancer Research
> Former Executive Director of Strategy & Performance,
> British Heart Foundation, 2013–2016

Top three mistakes in creating goals

1. Getting distracted by vanity metrics

Vanity metrics refer to the kind of metrics that might seem important at first glance, but have nothing to do with the project's success or the business' goals (Ries 2010). When it comes to digital-related work, there is a lot of data that can be captured, but very little of it is useful unless you know what you're looking for and how to apply it.

For example, in a digital marketing project for a retail brand, a common goal based on vanity metrics would be to 'increase number of website visitors'. It's a vanity metric because the retail brand doesn't make its money from people visiting its website – it makes money from selling things. A true metric of success could therefore be 'increase the number of qualified leads' or 'increase the number of conversions'. Otherwise the people responsible for implementing the project can call it a success just for getting random people to click through on ads or search results that have nothing to do with what the brand offers.

Other vanity metrics to watch out for are goals that go too granular and distract teams from more meaningful objectives. For example, a large university could set a goal for its Open Days, a critically important recruitment event for prospective students, to reduce the amount of time people spend navigating the massive campus. This might sound like a noble goal because no one likes getting lost, but reducing travel time isn't as important to the university's success as improving the quality of the visit – especially when students have a huge range of talks, exhibits, and things to do available all day across many different buildings.

With the vanity metric of reducing time, a project could be successful simply for adding a campus map to the university's mobile app – hardly digital transformation when they could have come up with ways for students to get personalized recommendations to plan their day, as well as custom alerts tailored to their location at the time they happen to be nearby.

2. Not establishing a benchmark

Goals must be measurable in a digital transformation programme to know which of your innovations are making a tangible difference to your company's success. To know if you've increased or decreased a success metric, you have to know what the starting point was before the innovation was introduced. This involves either taking existing data or creating tests and taking measurements of what's currently in place so you can have benchmarks later.

This is a hugely overlooked area for most digital transformation programmes. Everyone gets excited and wants to start innovating right away, finding themselves midway through various projects and not knowing if the numbers they're getting in testing are an improvement on the current state.

Not only are benchmark figures essential for informing decision making during the programme as multiple projects start to compete for more than equal share of resources, it's also critical for growing the programme itself when it's time to increase transformation efforts, scale new innovations, and grow the profile of the organization as you'll see in BUILD Stage 4: Leverage.

The exception to this rule is when an innovation is so new that there is nothing in the current state to directly compare it to. In these instances, creative solutioning for your goal creation comes in. For example, if a charity is trialling a new way for shoppers to donate by tapping a phone with Apple Pay or Android Pay enabled against an attention-grabbing shop display, the goal could be that the new method generates 40 per cent more donations and with an average donation amount 20 per cent higher in a 24-hour period than employing a charity fundraiser with a money pot to approach people.

3. Being untestable or open to interpretation

The worst thing you can do in crafting goals for digital transformation projects is leave any room for people to doubt, question, or incorrectly interpret the results. As a rule, no goal should rely on trying to quantify human feelings because it's impossible to do consistently or accurately. Instead, goals should allow teams to create tests that measure clear pass or fail results.

For example, goals such as 'customers must find the new website fun and engaging' would require tests that must resort to methods like a Likert scale, where participants are asked to rate things on a scale from 1 to 5. Tests like these are impossible to interpret accurately because human thoughts and feelings don't really translate into a number, and because people's methods for doing so will vary hugely depending on personality type and personal beliefs.

Some customer treat Likert scales like a 'yes' or 'no' test, only choosing 1 or 5 because it's faster and requires less guesswork. Others refuse to score anything a 1 or 5 because they view it as too extreme. Mixed results like these do more to cast doubt and invite personal opinions from internal stakeholders into the evaluation process, instead of proving where the project is on the right track versus where it needs improvements in the next iteration.

Common mistakes in leading iterative projects

1. Not testing with real, high-value customers

For test results to inform major decisions, there can't be any doubt as to their veracity. This is especially the case in organizations where hierarchies are strictly adhered to and people at the top are used to having their opinions overrule all others.

A common mistake is to save testing with customers until later in the project when outputs are more refined and complete – this is especially the case for high-value customers, for example, an airline not wanting to test early prototypes

---

I know too many organizations are still counting things like 'likes', shares and pageviews and these things aren't always indicator of quality engagement. What is the change you're trying to achieve? What are the levers that need pulling to achieve that change? If you're looking for creating champions or, advocates who will take your message forward, you might not need the 'twitter storm' and all the tools we're trying to currently use and overuse to put a momentary spotlight on an issue.

Change isn't measured in increment, it's measured in impact. If you start looking at measuring things with that more blunt approach of did the change we set out to make happen, then everything else is secondary. If you've achieved the change you're really setting out to achieve, that's your headline.

Interview with Zach Abraham, Director of Global Campaigns,
WWF International

with frequent flyers or business class customers for fear of irritating them or damaging their perception of the brand.

Not only does this mean projects miss out on the opinions and feedback of these valuable users, but it also increases the chance of senior leadership interfering during early stages because the evidence gathered isn't compelling enough, disempowering the project teams and undermining the entire iterative approach.

There are many ways to organize and conduct testing in ways that protect the brand and ensure customers aren't irritated by being approached. Tips and recommended approaches for testing with high-value customers from all sectors and segments are included in the section 'Running iterative projects'.

2. Testing with biased participants or in false environments

Sometimes companies understand the importance of testing with real customers but forget how influenceable we all are as people.

If you test regularly with the same panel or groups of customers, it's highly probable they know too much about your brand to be representative of a typical customer. It's also highly likely their willingness to participate in a regular panel or consultation process is a sign of ulterior motivations.

For example, I've encountered panel member customers who secretly wanted a job with the company, and thought being on the panel would improve their desirability as a candidate. The results from customers like these have to go straight in the trash because there's no chance they'll say anything negative out of fear it will impact their hiring prospects.

The same sort of bias can come from conducting the testing in false or contextually inappropriate environments. People are highly influenceable, and it's easy to overlook the effect of surroundings and the test set-up on our perceptions and actions. This refers to both the testing device (e.g. a prototype for an app needs to be tested on a phone and not a computer) and the testing environment (e.g. testing a retail innovation in a lab environment won't produce as accurate of results as testing it in a shop).

The section 'Running an Iterative Project' includes tips for reducing environmental and test bias, as well as guidelines for when it's appropriate to test less realistic settings.

3. Testing too many people at each stage

Iterative projects use what's called 'cohort analysis' to gather test results, where 'cohort' simply means people with similar characteristics. The number of people needed to make up a useful sample size within a cohort is no more than five individuals (Nielsen 2000). This might sound like a shockingly low number, but there are two reasons why each test should be limited to only five people.

First, people within a cohort are matched by shared characteristics, which means they act as a representative sample of a larger population. If you test an innovation and three out of the five people fail to complete the assigned tasks, it would be foolish to test with more people – you already know you have a failure rate greater than 50 per cent and your innovation needs improving.

The same is true with positive results; if all five people per customer segment pass the test then testing further people will only produce repeat results. This is why iterative projects have three stages of increasing complexity – after a successful test cycle, you have to move on to the next project stage in order to test it at a higher level of complexity.

This leads into the second reason for limiting cohorts to five people. It takes a lot of time and resource to conduct testing – especially to recruit and incentivize participants. The more time you spend confirming results, the less you'll have later in the project for unexpected problems or for adding enhancements based on user feedback.

I worked with an athletics organization to develop software for tracking people's training against specific sports and fitness goals. The prototype passed easily because the designs were intuitive and customers from all segments liked the concept. The Alpha version, on the other hand, took many rounds of testing and iterative improvements to pass (testing with five individuals per segment for each round) because once connected to external systems, the application was too slow and repeatedly failed to update in real time.

If the company had insisted on testing the prototype on more people per segment at prototype stage, it would have only confirmed what was already known after five. This would have delayed timescales and increased costs

---

Testing is vital. It's important to get a product out for testing in an early stage while there's still "wet cement" to work with, both technologically and culturally. Use testing to stop wrong directions in their tracks, and to refine the features and flow of your product.

One note of caution: testing can't become an end in and of itself. There's always more data that you can capture, another customer to test. You don't test to find your strategy. You test to refine and implement your strategy.

Interview with Perry Hewitt, Vice-President of Marketing, ITHAKA
Former Chief Digital Officer, Harvard University, 2011–2016

exponentially before even getting to the Alpha version, which was where the real time and effort was needed.

The section 'Running Iterative Projects' includes advice for constructing cohorts and ensuring tests are conducted to get the most accurate results from this cohort analysis in an iterative project cycle.

Goals checklist for digital transformation projects

Setting the right goals for the project in your programme is just as important as setting the right vision for digital transformation itself. Think of it as plotting the directions for long journey. If your shared vision is your destination and your routes to transformation are the major stops along the way, your individual project goals are the actual roads you choose to take over other options, as well as how fast you decide to travel.

In other words, fail to set the right goals for your projects and your path to transformation will be a long and meandering one.

The following checklist for crafting the right goals for each route to transformation will keep your journey on track and efficient, and let you make fast decisions along the way.

1. Are the goals mapped to your shared transformation vision?

There should never be a goal that isn't relatable back to your shared transformation vision. This relationship is important not just to ensure you stay the course and keep everyone motivated towards achieving your vision, but it also prevents unimportant goals from creeping in that distract and divert resources away from more important objectives.

Too frequently organizations treat digital as an outcome unto itself, not as a tactic to achieve lasting impact. I was a bit seduced by this in the very beginning like a lot of us are. Using the tool is almost the objective in itself. Nobody wants to be seen as behind the times, so you latch onto Twitter or Facebook without actually thinking about 'how does this tool help us achieve our objective?' We think we need to use the tool so you can almost shoehorn the objective retroactively into the application of the tool. A lot of people tried to use a hammer when they really needed a scalpel, just because everyone else was reaching for the hammer.

Interview with Zach Abraham, Director of Global Campaigns, WWF International

2. Are the goals linked to drivers of your organization's success?

Goals should always be based on metrics that actually matter to your business' success and long-term sustainability. The best way to start is to answer the question: 'what's the biggest influencer of revenue or loss for my business right now?' Examples include attracting new consumers, retaining existing customers, increasing the value from existing customers, decreasing waste/spoilage, decreasing staff turnover, and attracting high-quality staff.

3. Can the goals be measured against the five points of evaluation criteria?

The goals should be applicable to the five criteria for evaluating projects: customer value, competitive advantage, business impact, technical feasibility, and scalability. This ensures project teams gather evidence that cover each of these categories, making programme-level decision making easier at review points.

4. Can the goals be applied at all three project stages and beyond?

Good goals are as applicable in prototype stage as they are in Alpha and Beta testing because they link directly to drivers of the organization's success, as opposed to being specific to what's being tested.

Using this approach, goals also become the benchmark to beat after the project launches. For example, if during testing, a project meets its goal of raising the average shopping basket amount from $35 to $40 by suggesting

---

Measure what you treasure. Spotting what really matters to your business and making sure you're measuring the right things can take some careful thought but once you've got that, it's so easy to get instant data in many cases. There's almost no excuse not to keep an eye on the data these days.

Insight, having great editorial judgement and having really good smart people who understand use of digital tools and technology was definitely something critical for the BHF project. So, that balance of brilliant data and blending that with really good instincts and experience from people was crucial.

Interview with Dr Charmaine Griffiths, Chief Operating Officer,
The Institute for Cancer Research
Former Executive Director of Strategy & Performance,
British Heart Foundation, 2013–2016

better last-minute products during check-out, the new benchmark for any future innovations to beat is £40.

5. Are they measurable and empirically testable?

Like in a science experiment where the aim is to prove or disprove a hypothesis, each project needs to be able to prove or disprove its potential solution for achieving each goal. For the results to be trustworthy and reproducible, goals must be based on quantifiable criteria that can be observed and measured.

6. Do they leave the 'how' open for the cross-functional team to decide?

Neither the route nor the goals within it should prescribe how each should be achieved – this is up to the self-directing project teams who'll have the right subject matter experts to devise and test different approaches. I've worked with many companies whose leadership decide they need a smartphone app to fulfil various transformation goals. Very few goals can be achieved through an app, because apps require customers to go out of their way to download them, remember to use them, and so on. Better options require specialist knowledge about technology and digital marketing that reside at project team level, and not within the average senior leadership team.

Establishing minimum success criteria

Each route to transformation needs goals to aspire to, but it also needs minimum success criteria to set the baseline for what's acceptable to continue. Minimum success criteria tell project teams what constraints they have to work within, and for transformation leadership, it provides an easy baseline for deciding which projects in the programme are worth iterating to improve further versus those where investment could be spent better elsewhere.

> Our focus was on digital efficiency and consistency of communication and brand. How can we avoid running seventy different web systems and the cost that's incurred from that? How can we avoid seventy different training exercises? How do we ensure that a different version of the same web story is kept up to date across multiple markets? And therefore, how can we work more efficiently and have a more consistent image and communications with external audiences while still not over investing in technology.
>
> Interview with Mike Walton, Chief of Section, Digital Engagement,
> United Nations High Commission for Refugees (UNHCR)

For every goal you set, you need to have accompanying minimum success criteria to answer the following questions.

1. What's the lowest pass rate allowed?

The lowest pass rate is the cut-off point where the business benefits of the solution aren't enough to justify the investment in the project, or the ongoing resources it will require once complete. Good minimum success criteria allow for different variations of lowest pass rate, based on other metrics. For example, if your goal is to increase online sales by 30 per cent, the minimum success criteria could be 20 per cent if one full-time staff is required to run it, or 5 per cent if it can be completely automated.

2. What's the maximum resource allowed?

The maximum resource allowed should include the project budget for reaching each project stage. More important though, it also needs to include the costs and changes needed to existing operations to set up and fund the project's outputs on an ongoing basis.

For example, you could cap a project's budget to $40k for prototype stage, $50k for Alpha, and $100k for Beta. These maximum budgets would need to cover the costs for all project activities and resources, including specialist skills needed on the team, space to house the project, and incentives to pay test participants.

3. What are all the known constraints?

Constraints include conditions outside the organization's control, as well as known barriers within the organization that can't be addressed by individual projects. Conditions outside the organization's control depend on the nature of the organization, and the seniority and influence of the leaders themselves. Financial organizations, for example, have to comply with all sorts of regulatory restrictions, and these must be stated upfront as minimum success criteria. Failing to do so can result in innovations that can never be implemented, or that fail customer testing at the end of a project because of legally required content.

If a company has just signed a five-year licence agreement for a major digital platform, part of the minimum success criteria is that proposed solutions must not require a new platform, or that required changes to the existing platform cannot exceed a specified cost within the five-year term.

Running Iterative Projects

How to run an iterative project

The goal of any digital transformation programme is to be faster and better at dealing with change. To do this, you must create and establish a new way of working, collaboration, and iterative improvement to replace the old, less flexible and more siloed approach that's grown up over time.

This section provides guidance and best practice for how to run an iterative project including:

- Gathering and vetting ideas
- Building testable prototypes
- Creating and running tests with customers
- Interpreting test results and applying changes
- Running Alpha and Beta stage testing
- Gathering and prioritizing ideas for enhancements along the way

Before getting into the details, it's worth laying out the fundamental characteristics of an iterative project approach versus traditional project management styles.

Everyone wants to rally behind something that feels big, feels new, feels different, but sometimes people think about creativity as if it's something that only occurs without boundaries. True creativity would mean total freedom to do anything. In fact, the richest creativity requires boundaries because creativity is by definition, coming up with unexpected and new ways to work out a problem. If you have no limits to how to do a problem, why and how are you going to come up with something totally new? In the same way coming up with a product, solution or with a new way of operating in the business is not about dreaming up something no one has ever done before. It is about working within your constraints, whether they're regulatory or based on your business. Doing it in a way that people don't expect is where the most creative and best ideas come into play.

Interview with Bryan VanDyke, Managing Director & Head of Digital,
Morgan Stanley

Digital transformation versus traditional project management

Project stages	Traditional project approach	Iterative project approach
Planning	Detailed requirements are gathered over many months. Senior leadership approve the budget, timescales, and deliverables.	Subject matter experts (internal and external) collaborate to determine the best way to reach the desired strategic outcomes defined by senior leadership.
	Senior staff or external vendors are given a detailed brief to quote against. They respond only to their portion of the work, and won't be able to amend it once work commences, except in cases of extreme unmitigable issues.	They put forth an approach and quote for the first iterative cycle, with performance-based targets to meet at the agreed review point.
Delivery	The project is developed in linear stages by different isolated teams, doing only their part of the work before handing over to the next team or department.	The project is completed in iterative cycles by the cross-functional team composed of people from across the business and external specialists.
	Because each stage produces an incomplete product, there is nothing to test or demonstrate results until the very end of the project.	The entire team is accountable for producing a complete and testable solution in each cycle to measure against goals and learn from.
Project Management	Project managers track risks, timescales, and costs and report them to the senior leadership at regular intervals. They check teams are working to the agreed plans, and record tasks that are falling behind to notify leadership.	In addition to tracking risks, timescales, and costs, project managers also work closely with the team to identify and escalate barriers for senior leadership to mitigate the moment they're identified.
	Once problems grow big enough, decisions for how to correct them are made by senior leadership and handed down to the teams responsible for carrying them out.	Decisions are made at team level when new information indicates a need to change the overall approach and are presented for approval by senior leadership.

Project stages	Traditional project approach	Iterative project approach
Testing	Testing or quality checking is done at the end, resulting in an extra phase of required fixes.	Testing, quality checking, and bug fixing is done throughout.
	The project isn't released publicly until it's been completely tested and signed off internally.	Incremental public releases (e.g. Alpha and Beta) are done regularly as part of testing in real-world conditions to identify opportunities for improvement and strategic enhancements.
Launch	The project publicly launches and starts gathering results. The launch also reveals problems that weren't replicable in the testing scenarios.	The project is already mostly released when the final parts are completed, with the team having been tracking results and making improvements throughout the entire process.
	The teams involved are already working on other projects, so they have to focus only on critical fixes.	
Evaluation	The project is deemed complete by senior leadership, and the teams involved are rewarded against project metrics such as completing all deliverables within the budget and timescale that was originally estimated.	The now-live solution continues into its next phase of enhancements based on the continuous gathering of test results and new insights. Team members involved in the first phase are rewarded against business metrics such as increasing the company's sales.

We had to bring in some people who understood DevOps and help educate others who didn't. We had to show the value of it to the organization so people got excited about it versus just reading it and saying 'oh sounds interesting, not sure the value'. So we took a couple of new programmes that were kind of more tailor made to DevOps, treated them differently than the projects currently underway, and we started to deploy them.

Then after that, we've got all these enterprise systems, why do we need to treat them like waterfall? Why can't we treat them iteratively also? People started to see that we actually could. The way we did that was I took some of the key people in the organization and went to visit companies who are doing that. AT&T for example, they have Agile and DevOps on their phone purchasing system. It's a 30-year-old system and they're doing DevOps on it so I said if they can do that, and think about how many orders they're processing, why can't we do it for our reservation system. People started to see this isn't impossible and started to believe.

Interview with Mike Giresi, Chief Information Officer,
Royal Caribbean Cruises
Former Chief Information Officer, Tory Burch, 2011–2015

Rules for self-directing project teams

1. Never plan in detail what you can build and test instead.
The people sitting around a planning or boardroom table aren't the drivers of your business' success – your customers are. Creating a detailed plan only invites criticism and input from people within your company and not from your customers. The longer you delay putting ideas in front of customers in ways they can understand it and test it, the more time you're potentially wasting on refining an idea no one in the real world wants.

You're also not just testing ideas; you're testing the team's ability to deliver them. If your idea is valid and valued by the customer, but your internal team isn't equipped to deliver it, that's a costly way to find out. It also deprives you of the chance to form a solution that is the right fit for your company and its existing resources.

The section 'Proven Project Methodologies' will help you decide the complexity needed for accurate testing of each project stage: prototype, Alpha, and Beta. This helps keep each iterative cycle informative without having to commit more than needed in terms of build time and resources at any one stage.

2. Teams should consist only of the specialist skill sets the project needs.
One of the biggest differences between an iterative project and a traditional one is that complete versions of the final product are produced throughout the project. This is in stark contrast to a traditional project, which doesn't produce a complete version of the final output until the very end of the project.

To produce complete versions on a repeating basis without taking years to do it, the team needs to be tightly aligned, have the right specialist skills for the nature of the project, and be small enough to work collaboratively without needing extra layers of project management and governance just to facilitate communication or workflows between members.

The other reason to limit teams to only the best specialists available is that in an iterative approach, it's the team that decides how to achieve the goals set by senior leadership. This high level of accountability requires a team of individuals from the right blend of skill sets to create the best approach and instil confidence in leadership that it's the right one to take. If you have people with the wrong skills or too many people trying to contribute to key messages, this confidence will be quickly lost.

This rule is hard to follow though for many organizations because by nature of needing digital transformation, there is likely a shortage of people internally with skills in technology, strategy, design, and other digital specialist disciplines. The answer to this is to limit the complexity of the project to the skills you have in-house, which means also limiting the ambition of its outputs. The much better approach is to supplement missing skill sets with external help. Digital agencies, consultants, and contractors can provide staff or entire teams with missing skills – just be sure to follow the next rule about bringing in external help.

3. People of different skill sets need to work collaboratively at every project stage.
Having a cross-functional team that works collaboratively at every stage enables quick decision making about what approach to take and how to improve results with each test cycle. It also means the people needed to build the product have informed the approach and can do the work straight away. This won't come naturally for most organizations, however, so be prepared to actively nurture this new way of working.

Working in close collaboration with people of completely different skill sets is an especially alien concept to specialists accustomed to working independently and doing handovers when their part of the work is complete. It will also be against normal ways of working with external parties for organizations that are used to keeping 'suppliers' as separate as possible from internal teams and operations.

It's critical to enforce this rule though, because handovers have no place in an iterative project approach. Handovers between teams, individuals, or

> The inclusiveness of the approach and the ownership of the end product by a different team is critical. We have no desire to be seen as the ones who have done all the work. We want to be the ones who enabled it and facilitated it, but those different teams own it.
>
> Interview with Mike Walton, Chief of Section, Digital Engagement, United Nations High Commission for Refugees (UNHCR)

suppliers don't just slow things down as everyone needs briefing on what's been done so far; they can introduce major problems when the people receiving the work don't understand the decision making or intentions of what came before.

This is especially true for any project involving major digital or software outputs, where having the right technical skill set from day one is the most critical component of the cross-functional team. The last thing you want is for an idea or concept to be beloved by customers and approved by senior leadership, only to discover it's not actually feasible from a technical perspective.

Having the right technical people collaborating from the start with other specialists does more than prevent these problems; it lets everybody fully understand the broader ambitions of the work, assume accountability for its technical success, and continuously input better ways of achieving goals throughout each stage.

4. Be strict about capturing all insights and findings so they can be applied elsewhere.

One of the biggest benefits of the iterative approach is how much insight is gained through repeatedly testing with customers and trialling lots of implementations. All this learning must be systematically recorded, however, if other projects in the transformation programme and the leadership team itself can benefit from it, and avoid repeating the same work elsewhere. The strict capturing of results is also needed in case the project's outputs are challenged or questioned at a future stage of the transformation programme. You'll see in BUILD Stage 4: Leverage how carefully recorded outcomes don't just fend off criticism but can actually result in more buy-in and greater resources following the first few project successes.

Capturing results and insights as well as the approach used and the rationale for why certain decisions were made saves huge amount of time when training new team members or starting entirely new teams later in the transformation

Giving content strategy a seat at the Agile table is really important. The idea that when you're building experiences and applications for the customers, you have a content strategist in there who's saying 'what should be on this button?' 'does this make sense?' 'how does this flow work?'. There's a lot of focus on colour, workflow and interaction with less on explanatory text, in-line help which are guideposts. When you think of how much energy goes into the planning of signage and traffic lights in a city. I live in Manhattan so I spend a lot of time thinking about this. What are all the wayfinding tools we put in so that people can get through life without actually physically killing each other or understanding where to go on a subway overpass. That's what content strategists do on the web, and it's too often an afterthought in that important customer interaction user testing phase.

Interview with Perry Hewitt, Vice-President of Marketing, ITHAKA
Former Chief Digital Officer, Harvard University, 2011–2016

programme. BUILD Stage 5: Disseminate explains how the records you make now can be used later to transition 'digital transformation' from being a special programme to your organization's standard way of working.

Starting an iterative project

Checklist for starting a new project

Before any iterative process can start, certain elements must be in place to ensure the project and team's success.

1. Does the project have a sponsor at senior leadership level that can empower the team?

Projects that fall under the remit of digital transformation need ownership at the senior leadership level, otherwise the barriers identified in Uncover will pose immovable obstacles to the project teams. For major projects, such as entire website redesigns, the senior leader will need to be available to project team on a regular basis, joining them for multiple days a week to make executive decisions, approve extra resources, and help remove blockers as they arise.

On smaller projects, the role of the sponsor can be less time consuming, but should still involve taking accountability, empowering the team, and supporting the project across the organization.

2. Do the team members understand and agree with the goals and minimum success criteria?

Goals and minimum success criteria are developed by senior leadership, but should never be set until the project team meant to achieve them has had a chance for input. Failing to do so is an instant way to drop team morale and remove any sense of team empowerment before the project has even started, since the senior leadership team lacks the specialist skills of the project team. This means the project team can advise where goals are unrealistic or inapplicable to the approach they want to take with the solution.

3. Have the format and timescales for project reviews and decision making been agreed?

It is an unfortunately common misconception that iterative projects don't or can't have defined deadlines. There absolutely should be fixed deadlines for iterative projects to prevent overspend or unnecessary rounds of iterations to perfect the solution before formally launching it. The difference between fixes dates in an iterative project versus a traditional one is they're designed to act as stopping points to review and make major decisions on how to proceed, rather than arbitrary cut-offs for completing a particular stage of work.

Insurance is a bit different to retail because a lot of the effort we put in is before you even talk about selling a product. To make a sale in insurance is easier if the price is right, but to get someone to complete a quote is hard. You're getting someone to type in all of their personal details to request a quote, so how do you reduce the number of things they have to type in before they can get a price? So the challenge for me is you've got to make it enjoyable and easy to drive the conversion.

All our metrics are all funnel related. Can we get them to complete the form? Can we get them to actually convert? These things are fundamentally important to the business, but also reflect that we're doing a good job for the customer because they're willing to give their details and they're willing to make that purchase.

The team creates problem statements, do testing, create hypotheses, and speak to customers, but sometimes they just try something because they think it's a good idea.

Interview with Ash Roots, Director of Digital, Direct Line Group

The project team need to know these dates upfront so they can work backwards from them in planning their approach. They also need input into these schedules in case enough time hasn't been allocated to a particular stage.

More than just the dates themselves, the team also needs to know how they'll be expected to share the results gathered. Details such as whether they will have an in-person presentation or a conference call will make a difference in how results need to be prepared.

4. Are team members properly equipped to fulfil their roles?

At minimum, any iterative team needs access to functioning office equipment and communications devices. This might sound obvious but it's shocking how common basics for a project team aren't in place. I've been brought into client organizations where developers are struggling to perform basic tasks because their computers lack adequate processing power, designers are working from tiny laptop screens because they were denied the request for external monitors, or the office phones are impossible for hosting conference calls because anyone on the line sounds like they're shouting from the bottom of a tin-lined well.

Beyond the minimum, team members should be equipped with what they each need to ensure the project's success. This can include specialist tools like digital drawing pads for designers, test environments for developers, and a range of digital devices for user experience practitioners to run tests with customers.

5. Is the team equipped with adequate space or technology to facilitate daily collaboration?

Proper space for the team to work collaboratively together is just as important as giving team members the right equipment. Moreover, creating a project space can act as a great promotion tool within the company, showcasing new ways of working and allowing staff and managers from outside the digital transformation programme to learn about the new work. BUILD Stage 4: Leverage explains how collaborative working spaces can further digital transformation efforts by demystifying the approach and enticing senior managers outside the programme to want to join.

If space for collocated teams isn't possible in your organization because of real estate limitations or team members in different countries, it is possible to work around it, providing you invest in really good video conferencing and online collaboration tools. This, however, also requires a project manager who's committed to getting the team speaking on a daily basis, and individual team members communicating online or by phone multiple times per day. These practices won't come naturally if staff aren't used to cross-functional working, so will need regular encouragement and enforcement.

Ideal spaces get team members together in one collaborative working area and are equipped with large tables and whiteboards, wall space for displaying status updates, and a large screen with video conferencing equipment for hosting daily meetings, demonstrations, and review sessions.

No workspace set-up is prescriptive though, and it's the team members themselves who are best placed to decide what they need to ensure their own success. To prevent teams from going overboard with requests (e.g. catered lunches and a pool table), make sure the overall budget allocated to the project sits at team level with personal incentives in place for achieving the goals. Project funds that go towards set-up and tools means less available if new needs arise midway through the project. If more resources are needed later on, the team has to be willing to take on bigger goals in exchange, or complete the original goals in fewer iterative cycles.

6. Is the team personally motivated to achieve the goals?

Ensuring accountability at team level means making sure there's personal incentive for each team member to achieve the project goals. Depending on the nature of the origination, this might not need to be a specified reward. In some organizations, just being part of something new and exciting, or that will address long-standing frustrations felt by staff, is enough reward to stay committed. For agencies and suppliers, the incentive can be having a new portfolio piece to demonstrate their effectiveness, as well as opportunities to promote the work alongside the company through conference talks and other events.

For some companies, especially those who need to combat lowered morale, the motivation for the team members may require more specific incentives. Examples of this include being considered for a prestigious company award, personal recognition from the senior executive group, and of course, cash bonuses that correspond to the levels achieved within each set goal. This is discussed further in BUILD Stage 5: Disseminate.

7. Does the team have access to needed stakeholders and experts?

To be fast and efficient, an iterative team needs to be collaborative, cross-functional and as small as possible. This means there will inevitably be skill sets and areas of knowledge missing from the team that should be supplemented on an as-and-when-needed basis.

Depending on the nature of the project and the complexities of your organization, these experts and stakeholders can be internal or external and may include people to advise on:

- The current IT infrastructure
- Your company's markets and sector (present and historical)

- Competitors and their movements
- Complimentary technology
- Internal operations
- Safety and legal policies
- Recruiting customers for testing
- Engaging with staff in different areas of the business

The project sponsor on the senior leadership team is the first port of call for any of these information and advisory requests. As such, it's in the leader's best interest to have as many of these people named and on hand at the start of the project to reduce the time spent later trying to track them down once the iterative cycles have started.

What to do when failures occur

There are two types of failure in iterative projects. The first type of failure is one that needs to be encouraged and embraced, which is trying an idea that doesn't succeed. This is a natural part of innovating and if your project teams aren't regularly coming up with ideas and solutions that don't pass customer testing, they're either not testing correctly or they're playing it too safe (e.g. making improvements to existing offerings instead of coming up with new solutions or addressing new needs) (Thrasyvoulou, X. and PeoplePerH 2014).

I usually have a Programme Board that consists of a few analysts and technical people, but also really importantly, an HR person, an internal communications person and a finance person. The HR person would deal with the people and process change. That's very important because you can change technology but that isn't what makes the difference. The difference is the way you use technology and especially around seeing the customer as one entity horizontally across different departments. That often means quite a radical change in process and the way we do things.

Interview with Laura Scarlett, Data & Insight Director,
Guardian News & Media
Former Programme Director, Supporter Loyalty,
National Trust, 2013–2015

The second type of failure is more important and needs a new way of working to address correctly. These types include breakdowns in communication or process, errors made in delivery or execution, and general system failures.

Traditionally on projects, the response to either type of failure is to determine the party responsible so they can be held accountable for fixing the issue, or, if it's a supplier, recompensing the client. This approach has no place in a digital transformation programme because if teams feel they'll be blamed for errors, they'll take fewer risks and risks are essential in innovation. Moreover, assigning blame on any project is counterintuitive because rarely is one person or a group of people solely responsible.

Instead, the first important part of dealing with failure is to understand its root cause. That's to say, what were the circumstances, barriers, and shortcomings that prevented people on the team from doing what they needed to do to achieve success? As a rule, it won't ever be just one thing. Projects that are technically complex and require lots of people, process, and other moving parts to achieve success are prone to accumulations of minor misunderstandings and other seemingly trivial oversights that on their own wouldn't cause a failure but together can cause catastrophes.

To determine the cause of a failure, get everyone together to unpick the steps that preceded it.

The 'five whys' in Lean manufacturing, mentioned in 'Uncover' for identifying the root causes of organizational barriers, relate to identifying the root cause of any failure. The idea is that asking why a failure occurred once only puts blame on the people most directly involved. By asking 'why' four more times, you'll unpick how circumstances materialized that led to the failure, therefore revealing its true cause (Corporation 2006, Toyota Production System n.d.). Taking this approach, however, requires the project's owner and any other relevant senior leaders to

---

Innovation comes from failure. One of the things I like seeing is a celebration of failure. In the past organizations tried to bury the mistakes of the things that haven't worked. I think it's natural instinct for us to move past our failure, but more and more in a business landscape, it is more acceptable to linger a little bit on those failures, to really dissect what did work and didn't work. In the past you'd just blame it as a bad idea, when sometimes it's an excellent idea that was executed poorly.

Interview with Zach Abraham, Director of Global Campaigns,
WWF International

also be present because finding the cause is only the first part of dealing with failures; the second part is fixing it.

Once the cause has been identified, it needs to be mitigated in a way that's beneficial to the team and its leaders. That's to say, the solution can't be a punitive one because otherwise the team will become afraid of failure, innovation will cease, and history will be doomed to repeat itself because fear of punishment doesn't stop failures from occurring again – it just delays them temporarily.

Proven Methodologies

Methodologies to use for iterative projects

There are many different methodologies you can blend together to successfully run iterative projects. For example, I highly recommend reading *The Lean Startup* by Eric Ries, which details an excellent blended method based on those used by start-ups that companies can use to iteratively innovate. The two methodologies outlined here, Agile and Design Thinking, are among the most commonly used by start-ups, tech companies, and agencies alike – as well as traditional organizations trying to overcome significant culture and digital capability barriers.

That said, the detail required to know and understand these methods fully can (and does) fill multiple books, and many consultants and companies make their entire living from teaching them. As such, the overviews here are more to provide foundational knowledge and incentives for investing in researching and learning them fully – rather trying to act as a guide on how to implement them. For both methodologies described, you can get your teams trained through any number of routes, from taking formal training courses and reading the books and online material available on all three to inviting experts in to coach teams directly.

Whichever methods you choose, be sure to avoid the dangers of jargon discussed in the beginning of this book. Everyone assumes they all share the same definitions for the specialist terminology used in any one of these methods, but that's rarely true. In these cases, the source of the confusion only surfaces after ample lost time, or a few failed rounds of iteration. I regularly come across clients who mistakenly think their organization is running projects using Agile – or worse, that they 'tried Agile' but it didn't work – based on applying new Agile terminology to old ways of working. For example, calling blocks of time in a project plan 'sprints' despite not having any version of a complete and testable product until the very end of the project.

Assumptions like these undermine and sabotage new ways of working without anyone ever knowing the true reason for the failures. Digital transformation for any

> There's always that margin for error when theory hits practice, or rubber hits the road, you've got to ultimately say "how do we make this happen in this organization?" Whatever methodology you use has to work for the team you're working with as well. So if it's a 100 per cent Waterfall organization, as BHF was, introducing Agile could be very difficult and it was very difficult because even if the technical parts were all good, the cultural parts of signing things off, of understanding the process, were missing or difficult for people.
>
> Interview with Dr Charmaine Griffiths, Chief Operating Officer,
> The Institute for Cancer Research
> Former Executive Director of Strategy & Performance,
> British Heart Foundation, 2013–2016

organization requires minds that are open, eager to learn, and ready to experiment, which is exactly how to approach these recommended methodologies.

Agile

Agile is the most commonly used methodology for running iterative projects, but it's rife with specialist terminology and complex processes that are easily misunderstood. For this reason, it's important to know the right way to approach it before even delving into what is it or the benefits it offers. I'll start with the least common approach to adopting Agile, which is to fully adhere to every ceremony, rule, and principle – also known as 'pure' Agile. It's the least common because pure Agile was designed to develop software and, therefore, often doesn't fit the needs of every project, team, or company without some level of customization.

The second approach is the most successful for digital transformation purposes, and it's to learn the pure Agile principles but then experiment with variations until finding an approach that works best for the organization's teams, projects, and culture. This still requires understanding the intentions and core principles behind each Agile method though, because modifying its approach without this foundational knowledge usually results in a major mistakes.

How Agile works

To scratch the surface of the Agile approach and all its specialist terminology, the following is an overview of how it can be used to manage and run an iterative project in a digital transformation programme.

The old way of working would be to use BAs [Business Analysts]. Companies love BAs, because if you or I wanted to do something, we could get someone to sit in front of us and write down everything we want and then we could take it and pass it onto someone who could go and build it, and everyone's really happy. But as we know, despite the comfort it gives at the start, when you actually go to deliver something, the reality is very different – it might cost too much, there may be discrepancies, etc.

We were trying to say let's use Scrum and not use BAs, and the only way we could do it was by going through a process of gathering requirements ourselves, building it, and then saying 'look we didn't have any BAs and we got the product live'.

Interview with Ash Roots, Director of Digital, Direct Line Group

What is Agile?

Agile methodology enables a collaborative and cross-functional team to plan, design, and build complete and testable versions of a product with every project cycle.

Each cycle in an Agile project is called a 'sprint'. Sprints are usually two weeks in duration because this is enough time for the team to plan and build a set of completed features but not so long that it delays producing regular results in case testing reveals problems or needed changes (Scrum Sprint n.d.).

Sprints are managed and planned by getting the team to break down every piece of work into smaller, more self-contained requirements called 'user stories' because they're written from the end user's perspective (Ambler n.d.). For example, 'As website user, I want to access a shopping basket so I can see all the items I've selected for purchasing online'.

Every time a new idea or feature is thought up by the team or uncovered through customer testing, it's captured as a set of user stories that are added to a prioritized list called a 'product backlog'. The user stories in the backlog represent the full scope of the project, describing the desired outputs (Waters 2007). The order that user stories appear in the backlog is determined by the project's sponsor from the senior leadership team, who's given the title 'product owner'. Important and well-defined user stories go to the top of the backlog and less important or incomplete ones sit at the bottom.

What happens to completed user stories?

User stories that have been completed are finished, self-contained pieces of work that can either be tested with customers in isolation as a prototype, or

While I'm a big fan of Agile/Scrum, I don't like to be bound too much by over-engineering methodology. When I first joined American Cancer Society, it was a hodgepodge of a thousand different things. We were a beaten down IT organization and in most cases, we didn't have any proper system process. So, Waterfall was kind of safe way to at least start. You build it, you test it, and you put it in production. Very quickly within the first six months, we started more progressive digital projects, whether it was 'Service Match' or others, and I brought in Scrum Masters and we started doing training. It was really less about checking off little boxes that you're 'Scrum' or 'Agile' or 'DevOps' and more about a mindset change about our business sponsors. They are in the trenches with us. They're at our daily stand-ups. They are at our readouts, and they have skin in the game. This is you're in this with me the whole time and we're going to check on progress along the way.

Interview with Jay Ferro, Executive Vice President, EarthLink
Former Chief Information Officer, American Cancer Society, 2012–2016

added to previously completed work to form an Alpha or Beta release for live testing.

In the example of a website project, the new online order form can now be tested with customers as a prototype to see if it meets the goals set for the project. If it's a later stage of the project, the new form can be deployed to other new parts of the site to test as an Alpha or Beta release, or deployed to the live website to see how it performs against the old ordering form.

Through this repeating process of completing user stories at the top of the backlog, the team can work continuously producing outputs until either the backlog runs out, or the budget or deadline of the project is reached.

Reasons to adopt Agile methods

1. It's the best project management approach for empowering teams and facilitating collaborative working.

Unlike traditional project management where power is held at senior level and work is done in isolated stages, Agile equally empowers every team member and makes them accountable for work done collaboratively in a sprint. It does this through the relationship between the team, project manager, and the owner of the project at senior leadership level.

> If you go very Agile it can go a bit wrong. You need a vision to get to. If you develop everything 'use case' by 'use case', you can end up with a very bitty infrastructure because different use cases can have different solutions. I use a blended methodology of getting the vision established with the board and getting buy-in to that vision, then the next stages are including more people in the planning for how we'll approach this project so we can break it into a few big chunks and a lot of smaller chunks.
>
> Interview with Laura Scarlett, Data & Insight Director,
> Guardian News & Media,
> Former Programme Director, Supporter Loyalty,
> National Trust, 2013–2015

2. Agile projects are easier to govern because of shared responsibility and high transparency.

In addition to sprints giving a regular cadence to projects that helps plan decision-making points and manage stakeholder involvement, Agile is also a very well-governed and transparent project management approach due to its regular project activities (called 'ceremonies'). The simple act of hosting daily stand-ups prevents barriers from adding up until projects are weeks off track and without anyone from senior management even knowing it.

Because these ceremonies take place on the same days and times each sprint, it's easy for stakeholders and senior leaders to know when to drop in for updates and influence progress. Also, because Agile projects use online collaboration software to manage everything, people can even check progress and input remotely without every needing to contact a project manager for an update.

3. Agile easily accommodates change and can be used to maintain the product after the project has finished.

The backlog can be updated or amended at any time and as many times as needed without ever affecting the team's productivity. This is because once a sprint has been planned and started, any items left behind in the backlog have nothing to do with what's being worked on for the two weeks (or however long the sprint is running).

When new ideas or changes are identified through the business or from customer testing, they can be written up as user stories, added to the backlog, and prioritized by the product owner. The same is true for a live solution where the product backlog contains user stories for desired enhancements and needed fixes.

I don't believe in any pure methodologies. I question anyone who shows up at my door as purist. They are generally very smart and can always produce examples of how they've succeeded. But ultimately, they are a form looking for a fit versus taking a look at an organization and saying how do these people work, how are they ready to work, how don't they work, and then adapting based on what the purist sees there. That's because I'm a pragmatist at heart. Ultimately, as much as I want to be someone who as a pure vision for where to go, I've worked too long I think in the reality of organizations to really see anything as the one pure way to work.

I like a lot of things about the Agile approach because it emphasizes results. I like a lot of things about user testing because it gets business people to stop thinking about themselves and think about their customers. I like things about structured traditional development cycles because they seek to predict the future which I don't see as much with the truly 'Lean' methodologies. I think big corporations find it hard to be truly Agile. I've definitively had the most success with blends.

For example, we joke about our development lifecycle for the redesign that won the Webby Award, we called it 'Faux-gile'. When you scratched it a little bit underneath, it was clearly not as free-form as it might have been.

Our approach was definitely more 'Faux-gile' in the testing piece because we have a lot of concerns around methodologies for testing as a bank. We have more concerns about security than any start-up does. In addition, I think there were elements of what it takes to get approval in a large organization where you had to have things go up the line a little more. With the true Agile approach, we would have moved a lot more quickly, but if we'd kept the team working on quick turns of a lot of different items, we would have rapidly moved away from the timelines to reasonably get the buy-in from the different executives who needed to approve it.

Interview with Bryan VanDyke, Managing Director & Head of Digital,
Morgan Stanley

A lot of organizations mistake user stories as final requirements that must be perfected before they can be closed and taken out of the product backlog. Instead, user stories in a backlog represent a current view of what's needed, and as requirements grow or change, new user stories need to be created and added. To hold a user story back or to reopen it after it's been successfully completed in a past sprint is like interfering with evolution and goes against the principles of digital transformation itself.

Think of the project as a prehistoric fish slowly sprouting legs to explore land and eventually leave the ocean for good. The fish you start with isn't the fish that walks out. It takes many generations to evolve an organism, and it takes many user stories to evolve a project to its finished solution. The more user stories the project team completes, the more features get tested with customers and assessed against the project goals. As completed user stories accumulate, this lets you test their performance together in a bigger context. Leaders who hold back user stories until they're 'perfect' prevent their company's digital solutions from growing and improving incrementally, which is the equivalent to expecting a fish to suddenly grow legs and run out of the water.

Design Thinking

Design Thinking is a proven methodology to use throughout a digital transformation project (Christensen 1997) – especially in conjunction with Agile – but it's especially useful at the start when little is known yet about how to achieve the goals set out for the project's route to transformation.

Design Thinking works by making the customer the central figure in all solutioning and decision making, instead of the company's own interests or its existing operations. This results in solutions that are actually based on what the outside world wants, which is usually contrary to what's easy and comfortable for the organization to deliver.

Beyond helping teams, Design Thinking also helps leaders break away from only choosing ideas with instant mass market appeal. Many million-dollar ideas are left undeveloped in big organizations because a methodology like Design Thinking wasn't in place to spot its potential and scale it through an iterative process. Solutions with the power to transform your business are never born fully formed – if they were, they'd already be part of your offering and you wouldn't need digital transformation. Instead, they must be nurtured and developed to understand their full potential and applicability.

Imagine a team in a big retail company working on a new mobile app. In Design Thinking, answers to what the app should do, how it should look, and how it should work would be decided by what works best for the customer, their environment, the competitive landscape, and all the technologies and options available within it.

Compare this to decision making on a traditional project, where the app's features would be decided based on what product categories the company wants to target, designs would be based on what's going to best showcase the company's brand, and its software would be based on what's the easiest to integrate with the existing website and IT platform.

The traditional project will produce an app that's better than what the company had before and it will be easy to build and scale, but it won't do anything to offset the effect of fierce competition, customer disloyalty, or any other growing business threat. The app created through Design Thinking, on the other hand, will be harder to build and slower to scale, but will have an immeasurably bigger impact on sales, brand awareness and other critical business metrics because it's been designed in the interests of the customer and for the realities of the current marketplace, instead of the conditions the company originally designed itself around.

How Design Thinking works

Iterative projects follow a cycle of 'build, test, improve, and repeat' until a solution is ready to scale up to the next stage. Design Thinking is used within each one of those cycles to inform what needs to be built, how it should be tested, and what improvements need to be made.

Design Thinking works in stages to help teams and organizations to:

- Engage better with customers
- Identify the root cause of problems and needs
- Spot innovation opportunities
- Create solutions that aren't bound by what the company already offers
- Test the efficacy of new ideas in real-world settings

Design Thinking starts with methods for engaging with users, observing environments, and asking the right questions also offers techniques and tips for making teams better at collaborating and communicating through the process of creating and refining the solution.

Like Agile, there are many resources and courses available for learning 'Design Thinking', though some are geared towards specific occupations like architects or product designers. For digital transformation purposes, many digital agencies and big consultancies have their own different versions of Design Thinking, but the core principles are usually the same.

Five stages of Design Thinking

For each iteration of a project, the team will complete all five stages of Design Thinking. This might sound like a lot but the methods used in Design Thinking are designed with iterative and Agile projects in mind so have quick set-up and turnaround times, with little need for advanced training to be able to do the basics. Depending on whose version of Design Thinking you're using, there will be different names for each stage.

> Culturally it's been one of the biggest but hardest to measure things. Over the last years we have either comments of people saying everything feels different and asking how we do it. We've been teaching people things like Agile and other specific skills, as well as Design Thinking across the organization.
>
> Interview with Ash Roots, Director of Digital, Direct Line Group

Stage 1: Discover

The purpose of the first stage in Design Thinking is to provide tools and techniques for project teams to engage with customers and develop an unbiased understanding of their needs and wants. It also entails processes for immersing teams in the customer's environment to spot problems and opportunities for brand new innovations.

At the start of an iterative project, Stage 1 is focused on understanding needs and wants to inform ideas for how they can be addressed. Later in the project and after several iterations, Stage 1 becomes more about understanding the customer's behaviour and feedback in relation to what's been developed, whether it's meeting needs and wants, and what other opportunities still exist beyond what's been addressed already.

This is an important distinction and one many organizations get wrong by falsely assuming Design Thinking is a linear process used only at the start of a project and not a repeating cycle to be used throughout. If you stop doing Stage 1 activities after the first iteration of a solution, you'll miss out on enhancements for the solution you're creating, and on ideas for entirely different innovations of equal business and customer value.

Stage 2: Define

The purpose of the Define stage is to determine the needs, wants, pain points, and opportunities identified in Stage 1 in ways that can be understood, prioritized, and actioned by the project team.

This is a critical stage and generally requires experimentation to find the capture method that works best for the team and the organization.

Design Thinking techniques include standard formats for capturing and prioritizing, for example, Customer Journey Maps commonly used. There are also many online collaboration tools of varying complexity and cost to help manage and facilitate these 'Define' processes.

When we went out to go interview doctors in situ as part of an ethnographic approach of gathering qualitative user input and developing personas, we had to be very careful about getting clearance from their line managers because we were doing video interviews and so forth. There's a fair overhead in terms of admin, both to recruit people and get enough numbers to make those methodologies reasonably valid. That takes time and resources, but it's always worth it because if you do have people within the organization who are challenging your approach, there is nothing more powerful than to go back with 'your users tell me this'.

I like interviews conducted with users in pairs because I think it gives you more interesting insights when you have a pair of people talking about something. You videotape them and there's a loose format but you can get a lot of rich insight from that and then play that back internally.

Interview with Stewart Atkins, Digital Transformation Consultant
Former Head of Digital Strategy, British Medical Association, 2011–2015

Stage 3: Ideate

Sometimes also called 'Solution', the purpose of Stage 3 is to come up with creative ways to solve the needs, wants, pain points, and opportunities captured in Stage 2. It includes tools and techniques for helping teams be as creative as possible in finding these solutions, putting a heavy emphasis on collaboration to take advantage of the skill sets of a cross-functional team.

Like Stage 1, companies also often make the mistake in Stage 3 of thinking it's a step that only needs to be done at the beginning of a project. In fact, repeating the 'Ideate' stage in every iteration of a product's development ensures the collective abilities of full team continue to be utilized, especially as customer testing of what's been developed so far reveals problems as well as new insights and behaviours that need to be addressed.

Stage 4: Create

Sometimes also called 'Prototype' or 'Develop', Stage 4 in Design Thinking is the process of creating a version of the solution that is just complex enough to test whether it meets the needs it was designed to fulfil.

The complexity of the build is determined by which stage the project is in (e.g. prototype, Alpha, or Beta) as well as what's being tested. The important part is to determine whether it's achieved its goals and is ready to advance to the next project stage, or if it needs further iterations before it moves on.

The most horrid phrase I can ever hear in my professional life is 'we need to make this go viral'. If any of us knew how to make something go viral, we would be billionaires. You just never know when something fascinating is going to happen or what's going to captivate an audience.

You pilot things, you start small. You show that these approaches can bear fruit. But we can't get cold feet just because we tried something and it doesn't work. The celebration of failure is never more appropriate than in a digital landscape because it's an area where we're all a bit heavy footed from time to time. We are big global brands and the reality is that people want to connect with people.

Interview with Zach Abraham, Director of Global Campaigns,
WWF International

Stage 5: Evaluate

Often called 'Test', Stage 5 provides teams with methods for conducting testing of solutions created in Stage 4 and the means to evaluate the results. The advantage to these techniques is the wide range of options depending on the nature of the solution you're testing, and the environment and customers you're

Digital is all about the customer being in charge, so when I did a special project a few years ago looking at our top-tier customers and what their experience should be, I took a Design Thinking approach. Rather than let everything be decided by the HiPPO [Highest Paid Person's Opinion] in the room, we tested everything with customers to find out their thoughts and expectations. The results were filmed and helped focus the business on what we should be prioritizing. That in turn also helped the culture be a little more customer focused.

In my experience, you need real customer insight rather than just empathy for what you think the customer is feeling, otherwise you're going to go off course pretty quickly. Especially since the customer's expectations are changing so quickly now with all the advances in digital.

Interview with Andy Massey,
Director of Digital Transformation & Innovation, Lane Crawford

testing with. For example, Design Thinking methods for testing include guerrilla testing, whereby teams approach potential target customers in their natural environment for a short, non-recruited test session. This works well when your audience is comprised of members of the public and your solution is something that can be demonstrated on a portable device.

Design Thinking also provides proven methods for evaluating solutions with more niche customer groups and for solutions that require complex set-ups or multiple stages. This is because having a toolkit of different test methods at a team's disposal ensures logistics or access issues don't prevent the customer from staying central to all project decision making and goal evaluation.

Why you should embrace Design Thinking
Here are the top three benefits to Design Thinking and why you should adopt its practices.

1. It's a great way to come up with truly innovative ideas that can transform your business.
Ask an isolated team to brainstorm an offering to transform your company's customer experience and achieve your digital transformation vision, and they will come back with ways to make your current offerings faster, more efficient, and easier to use (Christensen 1997). This is not only non-transformational but it's also a massive red herring. Companies spend fortunes on projects like these and call them digitally transformative because they use new technology – all the while secretly wondering when the 'transformation' is meant to take place.

You're also no better off gathering a team of external experts. Ask a group of digital experts to brainstorm the same transformational offering, and you'll get back a list that corresponds directly to whatever the latest digital trends and product releases have been – possibly also with a quote for how much it will cost for their agency to build you one of your own.

Be prepared to be flexible. Staff need to know they are not going to break it by pressing the wrong button. The people who succeed are the ones who aren't afraid to try, aren't afraid of looking foolish. Consequently, play is very important. Leaders need to be prepared to work around these things, but keep in mind where you want to get to. It's like being a parent. Nobody has all the answers and you learn as you go.

Interview with Stewart Atkins, Digital Transformation Consultant
Former Head of Digital Strategy, British Medical Association, 2011–2015

This is also the reason 'Routes to Transformation' in BUILD Stage 2: Uncover doesn't prescribe the 'how' any of those outcomes should be achieved. The truth is it's impossible for anyone to guess the 'how' – no matter how experienced or how senior they are – without the Design Thinking stages of engaging with customers, defining the areas of opportunities, brainstorming ideas, and testing the efficacy of each to see which is the most likely to achieve your goals.

It's this level of constant interaction and exposure to the people whose needs your organization is meant to serve that real opportunities can be identified. Then, through Design Thinking's techniques for facilitating creative problem solving, people can break out of their usual patterns of thinking and day-to-day routines to come up with truly innovative solutions.

2. It offers an ever-growing plethora of tools, methods, and techniques for creative problem solving.

Rather than think of Design Thinking as a single methodology, it's almost more accurate to view it as a movement. Each year, more companies and organizations adopt its methods and, as a result, there are growing communities online and off for people who practice it to meet, exchange resources, and share new ways of working.

Part of the reason for this popularity isn't just Design Thinking's efficacy at problem solving either. We all work best in environments that are immersive, engaging, and that let us solve problems with all of our senses, and this is exactly what Design Thinking encourages and facilitates.

Compare this to traditional working styles where a lone person fills in lines on a spreadsheet or types bulleted recommendations in a report, and it's no wonder people are flocking to the Design Thinking world of coloured Post-it, customer journey maps, working prototypes, and getting out of the office and into the world where customers live, work, and play.

For this reason, you'll also see reference to Design Thinking in BUILD Stage 5: Disseminate. Because it's not 'owned' by any one company and because as a movement, there is already a wealth of readily available tools and techniques to apply it, Design Thinking is ideal for spreading new ways of working across teams, departments, and entire geographies.

3. It stops teams and leaders from developing tunnel vision without derailing progress.

By repeating the five stages of Design Thinking throughout each stage of an iterative project, teams can refresh their thinking and continuously challenge their assumptions with every iteration they complete. This prevents new and better ideas from going undiscovered because their existence didn't coincide with the project dates. Because of the different methods available in Design Thinking, the team can experiment with those new ideas without losing focus on the solution they're iterating.

My favourite example is when a team from Risk were embedded with us for three months. They wanted to learn about our ways of working, and I said the simple thing to do is just get some of them to come and do their normal jobs, but sit with us, and they can just feedback on what they see.

The main thing they said they would take away was using whiteboards, which was a really amazing bit of insight. They didn't spend any time really thrashing out ideas on whiteboards, which obviously drives collaborative cultures in my view. It was also really good for us because digital teams sometimes get tarnished with the brush of people thinking we want to spend all our time at computers, when that's not true.

Interview with Ash Roots, Director of Digital, Direct Line Group

Imagine a transformation project team at a hospital working on a way to help surgical patients decrease their recovery times. From the first few rounds of the project, the team used Design Thinking to come up with a series of ideas they've now prototyped as a lightweight wearable device that reminds patients when it's time to move around at home, lets them track their post-op routines, and includes an alert button in case they need emergency help.

The device passed testing in the prototype stage and achieved all the goals set out by senior leadership. It's not ready to advance to Alpha stage. Because Design Thinking techniques were used during testing, the team also identified a new opportunity when a patient mentioned the number of follow-up appointments he's needed with his specialist just to get answers to simple questions. The team captures the pain point and comes up with an idea for solving it using a mobile app that connects patients remotely to their specialists via video chat in automatically scheduled five-minute appointments.

The second idea doesn't fit with the first, so while the developers proceed with making the Alpha version of the wearable device, the designer created a simple design of the app to load onto a phone as a simple prototype. The Alpha test proceeds with 100 patients using the new device for a week to see how its platform and network cope with many concurrent users; meanwhile the team also conducts a small test of the mobile designs with just five patients against the goals created for the project. In the next review with senior leadership, the team presents the results of the Alpha testing as well as the smaller test result of the mobile designs, which now has evidence in the form of five patients out of five tested saying they would use the service in ways that could also achieve the goals of the project.

The company's leaders can now make an informed decision using the mobile idea based on the test results. If it passes the evaluate stages, they spin up another team to continue the first team's work, without worrying they'll disrupt the progress on the Alpha version of the wearable device as it scales up to its Beta stage.

What to do with first successes

As soon as your iterative projects start to show any level of successful results, you're ready for BUILD Stage 4: Leverage. Regardless of whether you're running a single iterative project, or many concurrently, the digital transformation leadership group needs to start seizing every opportunity to grow the programme in a way that's going to lead to sustainable transformation.

You'll also want to review and update your vision and your routes to transformation based on the results you're seeing. Innovation teaches us not just about new technology, but about people. As new digital initiatives are tested and launched, you'll need to observe how your customers and staff are interacting with each element, and this is often where the biggest eureka moments occur. Developing the habit of updating your vision as these valuable insights appear also determines your organization's long-term sustainability and adaptability in the years that follow its digital transformation.

The process of transformation itself generally brings enough tools and tricks and inevitably ends up stimulating something in people, which is great. In terms of creating a culture of that, that's the much harder part.

One of the benefits of digital transformation projects like at BHF, is it comes in-built with flexibility and lots more choices. By their nature, digital projects lend themselves more to ongoing innovation because the products themselves are evolving and you usually haven't launched with using all the toys in the toybox to full effect. That combined with the amazing ongoing customer feedback in terms of the user experience and customer journey, means that innovation needs to be part of your ongoing business and your ongoing review process. Several years on, this is exactly how they're working at the BHF.

Interview with Dr Charmaine Griffiths, Chief Operating Officer,
The Institute for Cancer Research
Former Executive Director of Strategy & Performance,
British Heart Foundation, 2013–2016

I start very small, I scale fast and I'm going to kill you with kindness in delivery. You earn credibility through delivery and through understanding how your organization attracts and retains customers. It is not up to them the customer to understand how technology works. It is up to you to understand how business works.

On Day One I would never walk into an organization, whether it's EarthLink, ACS or AIG, and say we're going to start digital transformation because they're all looking around the table going 'you're here because the lights keep flickering and our major applications have been down for two days. Why don't you worry about getting those right first?' You have to stabilize first. Then you begin having a conversation and you weave it into the things that you can and want to do.

We brought the apps and the ideas to the organization because when we had earned enough trust, knew our business processes well enough, and had sunset enough technical debt to earn credibility. No one cares about digital transformation if they can't get their email.

Interview with Jay Ferro, Executive Vice President, EarthLink
Former Chief Information Officer, American Cancer Society, 2012–2016

BUILD Stage 4: Leverage

Leverage successes to remove barriers and access greater resources, influence and space to expand

Why Leverage?

With a big enough lever you can move the earth

Every result achieved through your iterative projects, no matter how small, are points of leverage you can use to get more of what you need to increase the scale of existing projects, expand the digital transformation programme with new projects, and pave the way for permanent changes that will ensure the sustainability of the transformation itself.

A common mistake in digital transformation programmes is thinking that once it's mandated by people at the top, a trickle-down effect will take care of spreading the new ways of working and thinking, or worse, that once digital transformation has taken hold in customer-facing areas of the business, the work is already done. Either misconception leads to the same outcome, which is that the pockets of transformation you've fought so hard to establish start to dissolve the moment senior leadership's focus shifts to a new major initiative.

In fact, the feeling your digital transformation programme is finally gaining momentum is reason to put additional effort into advocating for it now, so it can grow and accelerate more than at any other stage. Not only do you now have the project results to leverage to be able to do it, but you also face new threats to the programme's success that didn't exist when the programme first started.

The first part of this section delves into the types of leverage you should use, reasons why you need to leverage, and the areas where it can be applied. The second part is a deeper dive into how to use leverage internally and externally to sustain the programme and pave the way to bigger, more permanent changes.

It's all about communicating progress and success. Having the forum to do that is really critical in the organization because if you don't have the ability to talk about success and talk about approaches, then it's very hard to maintain the profile that's needed to move onto the next stage. We use anything from presenting to senior management teams through to brown bag lunches, through to email alerts and updates about project progress and success. For example, our Digital Workplace manager has now run a series of brown bag lunches across a number of teams and locations.

Interview with Mike Walton, Chief of Section, Digital Engagement, United Nations High Commission for Refugees (UNHCR)

Types of leverage to further digital transformation

There are two types of leverage: the results of the projects and the teams themselves – namely how new ways of working are leading to increased productivity, creativity, collaboration, and happiness. Both are equally important and need to be applied in different ways in order to achieve programme growth.

Project results as leverage

Project results demonstrate the commercial value and tangible benefits of transformation from a business perspective. They relate to the goals set for teams at the beginning of the project. These are the critical business metrics that relate directly to the drivers of your organization's success. This includes profits made, new customer segments attracted, and new categories entered. The most important aspect of using real project results, however, is in communicating them in ways that can be related to other areas of the business, especially when trying to advocate for increased resources or access to markets or business areas they control.

The key to doing this well is to demonstrate results in ways that build people's pride in the organization. It's not about making the iterative teams look better or the digital transformation programme appear special; it's unifying people from across the entire organization under a banner of joint accomplishment and investment into everyone's future successes. Hearing results from any new projects should make people feel excited about what's possible, rekindle the optimism they felt when they first joined the company, and let them know how they're able to directly take part in this new chapter of the company's growth.

> In terms of speed, we went from quarterly releases to every fortnight. When we introduced the new Home Insurance journeys, after the Motor ones, we did them significantly cheaper. The way we did it was we introduced different ways of working, from Agile to different ways of recruiting different skills.
>
> Interview with Ash Roots, Director of Digital, Direct Line Group

You can also trigger people's interest by presenting project results in the context of how much faster, cheaper, and more collaboratively they were achieved compared to projects in the past. To do this, gather averages from past projects, especially those comparable in subject area or audience focus, and draw comparisons with the new iterative project on metrics like time and money spent, rounds of fixes required, and subsequent performance as a measure of return on investment (ROI).

For example, one company I work with used to take eighteen months just to complete the planning stages for a new project. The first iterative project reached Beta stage in just six months and was already turning a profit from real customers. Leveraging these results wasn't just an impressive story for others to hear; it was an outcome stakeholders from around the company were desperate to replicate in their own areas.

Team achievements as leverage

Because the purpose of digital transformation is to make your company better at dealing with change itself, the achievements of your iterative project teams are just as important as leverage for growing the programme and the effects of transformation as the results they produce.

Team results demonstrate the behind-the-scenes benefits of transformation in the form of greater efficiency and productivity, but with less effort and more job satisfaction. These results are further underlined through testimonials and before-and-after comparisons to past projects. Team achievements are often just as compelling to others as the hard numbers provided by project results. This is especially the case in very tradition-bound organizations where one or two positive team results is like an ignition source for managers and staff alike who have been craving new ways of working but didn't know how to go about making change happen themselves.

One university I worked with started sharing one team's ways of working on just one digitally innovative project for recruiting new undergraduates, and the reaction was so positive the transformation leadership team had to immediately grow in membership to stop from becoming a bottleneck for the sheer number of other faculties wanting to contribute their own personnel and resources to take part and do more.

The most important element to use as leverage within team-related achievements is where you're able to show direct before and after comparisons of new skill sets and capabilities that have been developed as a direct result of working in this style. This helps offset the fear other staff will naturally feel about digital transformation in general. It is very powerful to see examples of others like them who were brought into the process without specialist skills and after only a matter of weeks were able to produce something innovative. It also shows leaders and stakeholders not already involved in the programme how effective it is at imparting new skills in areas they've struggled to recruit or get traction with existing staff in the past.

These stories are best told by the team members themselves but can also be presented as comparisons to project skill sets in the past. For example, by working collaboratively with developers, the designers on an iterative project team will have demonstrably more knowledge about what design features are more feasible from a development perspective than past design teams whose work would have to go through many rounds of changes until developers were able to commit to building them.

The other elements of team achievements that can be used as leverage to further the programme include showcasing examples of creative problem solving and innovative use of technology. Like the purpose of sharing project results, these achievements also should be framed in ways that are aspirational and

It's about exposing and recognizing that expertise that exists in country offices already and making sure they get a chance to share that with the network. We started off with a top down HQ centric approach which did not recognize the talent in national offices. A much more collaborative approach now is recognizing that offices have a great deal of expertise and they are the ones delivering a lot of the work directly.

Enabling that kind of ability to share across offices is important. How well do you recognize and mobilize the excellence that sits in the organization versus putting yourselves up as the big gurus of digital for the whole organization.

Interview with Mike Walton, Chief of Section, Digital Engagement, United Nations High Commission for Refugees (UNHCR)

relatable to the audiences you're sharing them with. People from all levels need to feel like the achievements shared are ones they can replicate for themselves.

Last, the direct impact of collaborative working styles on your team's productivity, efficiency, and general happiness is another big point of leverage for encouraging greater adoption of the digital transformation programme. Are fewer people calling in sick or turning up late? Are fewer complaints and issues being raised in review meetings? Are people generally getting more done, in less time and with less supervision? Are people spending less time in meetings and more time producing useful outputs?

All these points of leverage still apply if you had to use external help, such as digital agencies, to supplement missing skill sets. It's also important to show the benefits of closer working relationships with outside partners, including faster turnaround times, more tailored solutions, and exposing staff to extremely specialist skill sets they otherwise wouldn't have access to.

Other types of leverage

There are also secondary types of leverage which shouldn't be overlooked – especially in organizations that have been traditionally averse to change or innovation. These include successes relating to being the first time the company has used a particular technology or worked in a particular way. When sharing successes in terms of project results and team achievements, it's useful to consider these and other examples as points of leverage:

- Did the iterative project team gather surprising insights on any customer segments?

- Did they dispel any commonly held assumptions about customer behaviour or the marketplace?

- Did the project affect external perceptions of the company by appealing to new customer groups or winning awards?

- Are there any new market insights that other senior leaders or staff outside the transformation programme would benefit from knowing?

These added elements of colour and detail all help to paint a full picture of the benefits digital transformation is already bringing in the organization. With these benefits, incentives can be mapped and presented to key people and groups, both inside and outside the company, for why they should help support, grow, and sustain these changes on a much bigger scale.

Threats to leverage against

Digital transformation programmes generally start with a lot of gusto – the teams are full of energy and senior leadership is willing to invest. This creates a natural

You need to have a really good communications team that can get out in front of you, help provide insight and transparency so the rest of the organization understands why we're doing the things that we're doing.

You also have to figure out how to support the current business, not as a consequence of what you're trying to do. I think too many companies start to starve what ultimately is the current value chain, and then people get super frustrated because they're trying to make their numbers and they're trying to make the business work and there's no one there to help them because everyone's going after the bright new shiny object. That's a really good way to get people disengaged.

Interview with Mike Giresi, Chief Information Officer,
Royal Caribbean Cruises
Former Chief Information Officer, Tory Burch, 2011–2015

swell of activity that gets a number of small projects, or perhaps a single large project, through to a set of first results.

Unfortunately, this is also where many programmes end because they fail to establish the momentum needed to carry activities beyond the exciting first phase – especially into areas of the business that offer up any serious resistance. Your digital transformation programme is still new, and most of the company hasn't had any exposure to it.

If you don't seize the early results to influence what's happening across the company, people will quickly start to view the digital transformation programme as an isolated case that had 'something to do with the website'. Leadership will go back to its usual agenda items, project teams will get sucked back into daily routines, and everyone will be artificially lulled into thinking 'digital' has been ticked off on this year's to-do list.

To avoid this fate, pay attention to the following threats, and be ready to use project and team successes as leverage against to remove blockers and ensure transformation efforts continue.

1. People with vested interests in preserving old ways

There will be people with vested interest in blocking transformation either because their established ways of working won't easily transition into new ways, or because their roles and remit are tied into traditional offerings threatened by new solutions. In most cases, these people actually can benefit from transformation and just need to be shown how. The successes you've achieved so far act as powerful lessons if structured in a helpful and non-threatening way.

For those whose roles genuinely are threatened by transformation efforts, leverage is needed to make the case an evidence-based decision rather than a personal or political one. In these instances, people can choose to retrain, or if it's not likely to be an option, they can use the evidence provided to make a rational decision to prepare an exit plan as opposed to fight the transformation efforts at every step.

It's likely there will also be a small minority who don't accept the evidence for why decisions are moving away from their role type or remit. In these instances, leverage is needed more than ever to prevent sabotage, such as spreading misinformation or passively blocking projects from expanding.

I've worked within government ministries, fast moving consumer goods, luxury and retail, and within the military and national security industries. Over the past three or four years, we've all gone from digital transformation being a customer service facing thing, building a website, having a good mobile app, that sort of stuff, to being a revolution of the back office and the fundamental workings of a business as well.

Financial services and professional services organizations are where digital transformation is currently happening the fastest. Many of my clients today see digital transformation as an existential threat to themselves as individuals within the company, and in some cases, to the sector itself. There are a good deal of companies that really don't need to exist anymore.

Senior management, on the other hand, are actually overjoyed because they're looking at massively increased profitability. The threat is to the middle ranking people. For example, if you work in insurance or fund management and your job is to take data, do something to it and then move it on, you're very vulnerable to machine learning and artificial intelligence.

The idea of 'smashing the looms' and fighting this change doesn't work either because the fundamental nature of the digital world is the work can be done anywhere on the planet. So, you can smash the looms in London all you like, but that just means that those tasks are going to be done by somebody in Paris – or rather, by something in Paris.

Interview with Ben Hammersley, Futurist,
BBC World Presenter 'Cybercrime, with Ben Hammersley' and
WIRED Contributing Editor

I've witnessed many instances of senior leaders who withhold critical information until a team has acted without it to try and make the project look misguided and foolish. I've also seen managers of areas threatened by digital competition create unnecessary 'red tape', block an iterative team's access to customers, and even instruct customer-facing staff to share false information about customer enquiries and requests. In each situation, the best recourse was actively sharing the solid base of evidence that showed the projects and their teams were hitting and exceeding business goals with unprecedented measurability and accountability. This put too much political pressure on individuals to resist at the risk of looking like they're trying to hinder the organization's success and not just that of the transformation programme.

2. Unmitigable barriers

There's a limit to the barriers you can mitigate through the iterative project process. Since the beginning of the programme, the transformation leadership group and the iterative project teams have been chipping away at the major people, process, platform, and partnership barriers identified in BUILD Stage 2: Uncover.

For transformation to take hold across the organization, barriers can't just be mitigated; they have to be removed.

We decided we needed an 'omnichannel' approach to create a seamless experience between our online store and our bricks and mortar experience. The term was a big buzzword about four years ago, and it's easy to say, but actually to deliver it is something completely different.

I did a deck explaining why the technology was a limiting factor. That was quite a defining moment and I think the penny dropped for people that actually we couldn't build on top of what we had and that we had to almost tear up our technical architecture, which had basically grown organically, and then actually plan out the strategy of what we needed to do.

We also realized it's not just about IT – it's about change management and making sure the people are comfortable with the change and why it's happening. To non-digital people, it is not always abundantly clear why you're making that much of an investment when the return maybe isn't as immediate as what their expectations of return would be if you had made that same investment offline.

Interview with Andy Massey,
Director of Digital Transformation & Innovation, Lane Crawford

---

For example, a firm with a digital platform that doesn't support integration with other systems or automation of simple tasks is a major barrier to being able to offer any kind of personalized online services at scale.

At the beginning of its transformation programme, the investment wasn't there to replace the system upfront, so iterative teams worked around it – experimenting and getting excellent results with solutions that avoided the firm's existing platform in favour of mobile and social channels. To fully digitally transform, the platform needs a complete replacement, but there are many other managers outside the programme who rely on it for their own work. Leveraging those early successes is not only needed to help sell the need for the new platform and determine the necessary features; it can also help plant seeds of inspiration to get those other leaders thinking differently about how they can use it to transform their own areas.

3. Risks from major change

Major changes in the form of department restructuring, reducing staff numbers, or altering the core offerings and operations of a company all carry big risks if managed and implemented incorrectly. The nature of digital transformation means you're likely already coming across major changes that need to be made,

For me selling 'Service Match', it was tough at first. It was threatening. I was talking to thirteen different groups in thirteen different geographies and they read the tea leaves and said 'you're talking about centralizing and eliminating a lot of jobs'. I had to stand there and say if that's the case. When you confront people, and say this is not technology or transformation for transformation's sake. This is taking technology in an attempt to save more lives. Now who can argue with that?

You can apply the same thing, although maybe not as dramatic, with a retail experience, an insurance experience, and say 'do you agree we exist to service our customers, to sell more product and to provide an amazing customer service experience?' Sometimes having conversations about facts and not emotions is the best way to start. I learned very quickly you don't die taking certain hills and you go in and you need three things and you can get two and the third one can actually have you killed, then I'll take two and come back and get that third one some other day.

Interview with Jay Ferro, Executive Vice President, EarthLink
Former Chief Information Officer, American Cancer Society, 2012–2016

and to do so without first leveraging current achievements is the equivalent to flying blind into a storm. Testing how people react and seeing what objections and questions are raised is the first part to using the existing results to plan the transition. More so, you're helping people understand the reasons why it makes sense from both a business and staff perspective for these major changes to take place.

Not all major change will have a negative impact on large groups of staff, but anything requiring fundamental changes to people's work environments, team structure, or daily routine is likely to cause temporary upset and stress unless it's been properly bedded in first. You can use positive team achievements to try and build excitement and even demand for some of these big changes well ahead of them being implemented.

Objectives for using leverage

The iterative projects you've currently got running are only pockets of success in an otherwise untransformed landscape. Reviewing your shared transformation vision, there will be areas of the company, whether they're individual business units or entire markets in separate geographies, that still need significant effort to identify and embed the right innovations to achieve success.

Now is the time to accelerate current efforts and it's the transformation leadership team that needs to take ownership, create a plan, and delegate work to getting the following goals added to programme's list of achievements.

1. Start bigger, bolder, more all-encompassing projects

Big and bold ideas that are going to have major impact across the entire organization need leverage to win the assets and buy-in needed to make happen. These ideas generally fall into two categories. The first comprise ideas identified through Design Thinking engagement with customers. These ideas have likely already been prototyped by the iterative project team and tested for their value, but a lack of resources, expertise, or the right external partnerships has prevented further development.

The second category of big, bold projects challenges fundamental parts of the organization, its offerings, or its operational structure. For example, changing the business model for a core product from a normal purchasing model to a subscription-based one. To even start the iteration and experimentation process for a change like this, you need to leverage past successes so people across the organization are sufficiently bought-in to the potential digital transformation can bring. Fail to do so and you risk time delays dealing with challenges, uncooperative staff and management, and even acts of passive sabotage at each project stage.

Over two years ago we delivered IBM's Watson. We were the first university in the world providing Watson services to students, and Watson is now our 'business as usual' responding 24/7 to questions from students.

When we delivered a big platform with Watson for students, we had 100 students working with us in that project. We do not work in isolation, we work with them. When we needed to train Watson we received over 200 applications from students who wanted to work with us, and we had 100 students over the holidays testing Watson. We bought pizza for everyone every day and they happily came to help us test.

Probably the most ambitious thing that we are doing is going to be in production next month is 'Deakin Genie'. It's the next generation of Artificial Intelligence for student assistance. It's a platform that's going to be responding to questions like Watson does, but it's going to be really proactive in helping the student keep on track, study smarter, get more done and stay motivated. It is a really, really a very ambitious programme that is already active working with one faculty, and will be expanded to the whole university in the second part of the year.

Interview with William Confalonieri, Chief Digital Officer, Deakin University

2. Scale to new markets, locations, or business areas

A common question asked at the early stages of digital transformation when an iterative project has proven itself successful is 'how do we scale it?' The wrong approach stems from the old-fashioned company growth model of trying to standardize a new way of working or offering as quickly as possible so it can be applied uniformly across every geography and customer segment. As discussed throughout the book, this approach no longer works now that brands like Amazon and Netflix have taught us to expect at least a minimum level of customization to our products and services. The companies that try to resist leave themselves open to niche competitors swooping in, delivering better to specific needs, and quickly eroding market share.

The new offering you've developed needs to be prototyped in the new location to see what localizations or customizations would be needed to scale it there. This still begs the question about how to scale and, fortunately, the answer resides in where you're able to apply the leverage you've already got.

Use your past successes as leverage with stakeholders, influencers, and leaders in those new areas, and wherever you get the most traction is where the transformation programme should scale to next. As this cycle repeats itself,

> Once you've built up trust that you can deliver things, that's helpful. We'd put in place a new technical and data infrastructure and nothing terrible has happened. The world hasn't changed, things have just got a bit more efficient, so that's built up trust. Then after that you're on better footing because future change can be more incremental. An incremental approach is good.
>
> Interview with Laura Scarlett, Data & Insight Director,
> Guardian News & Media
> Former Programme Director, Supporter Loyalty,
> National Trust, 2013–2015

you'll win the assets and buy-in you need to scale completely, but by doing it incrementally and following a path of least resistance, you'll make the most of every success while saving time and resource.

3. Attract new specialist talent and high-profile partnerships

It's a precarious situation to be in if your organization is having to outsource or rely on partners for work that's essential to delivering your core products or services. In addition to being susceptible to price hikes, if the partner changes ownership or priorities, you're vulnerable to the impact this ultimately will have on your business.

Trying to attract high-quality new talent in-house can be challenging though, especially for businesses in unglamorous locations and sectors, or just with lesser-known brands. It's possible that you're currently finding yourself getting better quality work from outsourced specialists in digital, creative and tech, but this dependency is unhealthy – especially as it means you're not building internal capabilities and knowledge in channels and technologies that may stay relevant to your core business for many years.

Fortunately, these are areas where your team successes in particular can act as leverage in attracting new staff. These successes can help strengthen the business case internally for why it's now essential for the business to build a permanent staff base with these new skill sets. For areas of innovation likely to stay outside your company's core offerings, the same type of leverage can be applied to attract better partnerships – not just brokering better deals but also with organizations on the leading edge of their own areas of expertise.

The methods for how to use leverage for these goals are detailed in the next section, divided by whether the leverage you need is for internal purposes (e.g. scaling a successful iterative project) or external ones (e.g. attracting new developers and designers in-house).

When we deliver these projects, in general around new technologies, new systems, new processes, the most important part is that a change is seen by the organization or by the customer community. You don't need very sophisticated metrics because the feedback, you can feel it.

We have here, over 55,000 students and 6,000 staff. When you deliver something that affects everyone, you have a wave of reactions. Our students are our best ambassadors. Every time we deliver one of these things, the noise that they make is so great, they help us to create recognition in the market and help us to attract more students. It's subjective but it is very visible metric for how things are going.

Interview with William Confalonieri, Chief Digital Officer, Deakin University

How to leverage internally

The biggest challenge your digital transformation programme currently faces is people across the company simply not understanding its full potential. Sharing the successes achieved so far on their own isn't going to resolve this – in fact, it's more likely to open a Pandora's box of internal politics.

Your approach to leveraging successes earned so far needs to follow a similar one to the iterative projects themselves. It starts with choosing audiences

Relay metrics the whole time and have a regular programme of communication of success. Not just during programme delivery, so what you're learning and finding out, but actually in the transition into business as usual and how we do things. Routinely emphasizing the achievement and the benefit in whatever way you can, qualitative, quantitative, however you set it up, the whole time it should be reinforcing how you're making progress towards that goal.

Interview with Dr Charmaine Griffiths, Chief Operating Officer,
The Institute for Cancer Research,
Former Executive Director of Strategy & Performance,
British Heart Foundation, 2013–2016

internally, setting measurable goals, engaging with them to understand their wants and motivations, and then experimenting with communication and engagement styles to see what triggers the behaviours you need to achieve your next goals.

Once you uncover the winning formulas and formats for your organization's staff and leaders, they can be incorporated into the ongoing plan for communicating and leveraging successes in order to grow the programme and ensure that transformation takes hold.

Steps for internal leverage

1. Choose your goals, the audience to target, and a set of responses you can measure

What makes 'Leverage' a stage of digital transformation and not just a standard internal communications exercise is that you're using it for a very strategic and targeted purpose. For example, you may need staff with particular skill sets to volunteer for new project teams, or you might need the managers in a particular business area to volunteer their staff, provide resources, or open up access to their customers.

Choose tangible goals and identify the internal gatekeepers and influencers who can help make them happen. Decide specifically what you want from these individuals and assemble a small iterative team (e.g. a designer and a copywriter) to create materials that help to communicate with and persuade them. Even if you're planning to approach people one-on-one, a video or short slide deck to flip through on a tablet can go a long way to clarifying complex concepts.

Depending on the goal, target requests to specifically what's needed and craft calls to action within your communications to get more of any of the following examples:

One of the key things about making your initial investment apply further is choosing your venue so it's highly visible to a lot people as a place where something new has happened, where there's some buzz about it, and where people quickly say that they want to get on board. It's a bad idea to put a lot of time and effort into something that almost no one will see, and then you have to shop around saying it was a win. But you have to be careful too because you don't want to bring a lot of visibility to a project early on that may not be successful. I think balance between the two is important.

Interview with Bryan VanDyke, Managing Director & Head of Digital,
Morgan Stanley

- People: More staff for iterative teams or additional leaders to join the transformation group
- Resource: More working space, equipment for iterative projects, or bigger budgets
- Access: Permission to target new customers, markets, business areas
- Buy-in: Support for business cases that require large investments

2. Map your goals to how you need people to engage

Your goals need to illustrate how you expect people to engage so you can build in methods that facilitate that engagement. This crucial step is almost always missed, and if you don't make it easy and obvious for how people should respond and react, they'll either not bother or they'll ask the wrong person and end up misinformed and misaligned.

For every method you choose, you need a clear call to action, a mechanism in place for people to engage, and someone on the other end ready to react when they do. It can be as simple as an email address to contact, or the instruction to speak to a certain staff members. The important part is that it's consistent and prominent in all communications to avoid any ambiguity.

3. Assign ownership and resources to make it happen

Leaders from the transformation group should take responsibility for overseeing and leading internal leverage activities. The more senior the target, the more senior the leader responsible. That said, resources in the form of design and development capabilities and budget for producing assets are also a minimum requirement. For major internal engagement pieces, an entire temporary team might even be necessary, depending on the size of the organization and the number of people targeted for engagement.

4. Use an iterative approach to test different methods

Every company is different, both in cultural nuances and logistical make-up. If your organization is very large, you'll probably also have major differences across business units and locations. Use an iterative approach to figure out the best fit for engaging your internal audiences. This guards against launching only one approach that might be ignored or accidentally cause more harm than good.

Following the iterative approach and using the stages of Design Thinking, treat your internal audiences like individual customer segments, engaging with them to see what their thoughts and feelings are now about the transformation efforts, experimenting with different solutions for changing hearts and minds, and winning the buy-in you need.

5. Grow projects that work and learn why others failed

Evaluate the results from first efforts to know which ones to continue and grow, but more important to learn why unsuccessful attempts didn't work. The answer

> You need to tell your story. If you have successes and you have metrics and the impact you have provoked, you need to have all that in your briefcase at the moment that you are going to negotiate the next wave of crazy things. Doing things well means you can propose even crazier things and you will need even less energy to negotiate those. Trust gains momentum and in the end you have the support to try even things that can't be understood for really well by anyone else.
>
> I personally play a big role in storytelling, in marketing and in promoting. I use marketing to create the space to then deliver something properly. I pay a lot of attention to that to have a receptive ground where you put your product.
>
> **Interview with William Confalonieri, Chief Digital Officer, Deakin University**

to why failure occurred is important because it can reveal insights about the company and potential future barriers. For example, did the method fail because the messaging and format were wrong, or was it because it touched a nerve among the recipients? If it's the latter, the team involved should be using Design Thinking techniques to engage with internal audiences to uncover what caused the conflict so it can be mitigated in the next attempt.

Methods for internal leverage

Applying leverage internally depends on the nature of your company, including its size, sector, and culture. Most of all though, the power and influence held by individuals on the digital transformation leadership group has the biggest impact overall. The more senior and the greater the representation across the organization, the more effective any point of leverage will be.

The following methods are used most commonly and achieve the greatest success by organizations and transformation leadership groups of all types. The formats themselves are not new, but the methods for using them include the nuances needed to act as powerful internal persuasion.

Official recognition
Awards, acknowledgement, and stories about team successes – especially when reported by senior leadership – in high-profile places (e.g. all staff email, intranet homepage) can be a great source of aspiration and incentive to join. It also demonstrates to people outside the programme that these projects are valued by senior leadership, as well as being fun and innovative.

> The roadshows are about being transparent about what you're doing, getting buy-in, and enthusing people so they are excited and interested in what you're doing. If you can get people excited about a project, they become the driving force for change.
>
> We also brought people together from across the business, creating panels and working groups so they could contribute beyond their particular areas.
>
> Interview with Stewart Atkins, Digital Transformation Consultant, Former Head of Digital Strategy, British Medical Association, 2011–2015

Presentations

Presentations include everything from roadshows, showcases, demonstrations, and talks of different lengths and focus. Within any kind of talk, be sure to make the purpose covers several different aims. First, it should help people feel pride in their organization and what it's achieved, rather than come across as competitive or threatening. Next, the roles played by the teams and the leaders involved should appear aspirational but relatable, emphasizing that not everybody had advanced skills or training before innovation began. Last, make clear associations and suggestions as to where the project and team's successes could be replicated in other areas of the business. This is perhaps the most important, because if people leave a presentation feeling confused about how it relates to their job or their area, the content has failed.

Shareable assets

Videos are very popular as a shareable asset, but case study write-ups and other more detailed assets can sometimes be needed depending on the sector and audience level. When creating a shareable asset, the content needs to include something entertaining or useful in addition to an abridged version of the same sort of content that would go into a presentation. Be careful not to let it appear like a show-off piece or an anomalous set of activities that don't have relevance outside very specific areas of the business. Also, if you opt for video, reduce the length as much as possible and produce clips covering different topics. This will make them easier to consume but also easier to measure which topics and points of leverage are getting the most traction around the company.

Because shareable assets are likely to be leaked outside an organization, be careful not to include anything you wouldn't want customers or shareholders to see.

Events

Drop-in sessions, workshops, tours of workspaces, and hackathons are common examples of the kind of events you can host for specific internal audiences to display your project and team results. Just be sure to match the event to the audience type and make the call to action very clear at the end. Hackathons, for example, should only be used for gaining buy-in and participation from your company's technical people. Trying to boost attendance by inviting non-technical people is only going to muddle its purpose.

Collaboration spaces

Online collaboration spaces include internal social media channels, forums, and blogs, whereas physical collaboration can take place in a dedicated space in a centralized company location. For either format, the purpose is to share results from the projects and the teams involved and also to invite ideas, suggestions, and feedback from staff. Similar to hosting events, the important part of running collaboration spaces is making the calls to action and purpose very clear. A blog with no comments, a status room with no Post-it added, or a forum with no upvoted suggestions will do more to discredit and dismiss the results you've achieved than act as leverage for getting more.

You want to promote what you've done in the same way that anything important to the business gets promoted, including various internal measures such as an email from a senior executive of the company or an intranet spotlight.

Then you need to have some external validation. We won a 'Webby' for our website redesign, which was a great honour for us, but it served a function also of highlighting the quality of the work. If you're introducing something new to people, they may not know to recognize the hard work that your team did, but external validation is a huge additional bit of support.

The last thing I'll say is if it's good, whatever you're creating, it will likely be something people want to share with others. If you're building a new tool for advisors to model out different products, it should be so good that they tell other advisors about it and you should make it easy for them to do that because that kind of promotion is more valuable literally than anything else.

Interview with Bryan VanDyke, Managing Director & Head of Digital,
Morgan Stanley

How to leverage externally

The steps for applying leverage externally are the same as internal leverage with a few notable exceptions.

1. The goals and their audiences are more straightforward.

Unlike internal goals, which can require decoding a complex political and cultural landscape to determine whom to target and how, the external targets are more obvious and the calls to action can be more direct.

External goals for using leverage externally include examples such as:

- Specialist staff: Attracting new developers, designers, and others of digital ilk.

- High-profile partnerships: Inviting businesses to create joint offerings, or new agencies and tech providers to fulfil specialist needs.

- External perception: Changing the company's image to prospective customers, consumers from new segments, shareholders, and influencers.

2. Be prepared to anticipate and prevent internal backlash.

Because leveraging success externally is often more straightforward, there is a dangerous temptation to only focus efforts outside the company to grow and accelerate digital transformation. This approach attracts litanies of complaints and challenges as staff misinterpret, overreact, and read into information in the public space.

Instead, any external leverage efforts need to be countered with internal ones to anticipate and prevent negative reactions before they can occur. This can include preparing answers to criticism about how much money has been spent so far when management could have invested in existing areas of the business instead – especially if those areas have been put through budget reductions.

3. Be prepared to counteract added competition and customer scrutiny

As soon as you start sharing the good news about your organization's digital transformation successes, expect your competition to listen as keenly (if not more so) than your intended audiences. In the immediate term, you should anticipate direct pushback. This can be an increase in competitor's promotions, marketing, and recruitment activities, or it can take more extreme forms including price cutting, major publicity events, and directly incentivizing customers to switch.

However, it's the longer-term impacts you need to plan against. The moment you begin leveraging successes externally, your closest competitors are going to use your project results to make their own business cases to either start or accelerate their own digital transformation programmes – so there's no time to lose.

We had great success with pilots and proofs of concept. Once we felt we'd struck gold with the technology, we wanted to scale very fast but it wasn't just about ramming technology down people's throats. To me it's always about finding evangelists out in the field in the loosest sense. It could be your 77 million customers, 3 million volunteers, or 10,000 staff.

EarthLink is no different. If a customer has 500 locations using our technology, I'm showing up. If they have quarterly business reviews, I don't just want our salespeople there. I want me there. I want my IT people there too and I want them walking into one of our customer's stores, using the technology that we're providing them.

Interview with Jay Ferro, Executive Vice President, EarthLink
Former Chief Information Officer, American Cancer Society, 2012–2016

This increased pressure won't just come from competitors, though. Leveraging successes to attract attention from customers and shareholders can mean added pressure from increased customer traffic, as well as more external scrutiny than usual. If you're not prepared to handle additional business with impeccable standards of service, external audiences will be quick to judge and unlikely to forgive. This is especially the case when an organization publicizes success in one area of the business and customers assume this means better, more innovative services across the full offering. To them, it's all the same company, so inconsistencies aren't seen as exceptions; they're just considered mistakes.

Methods for external leverage

The methods for externally leveraging successes are similar to methods used internally but with the key exception that self-promotion of the company is generally a faux pas – this is directly opposed to internal leverage where building pride in the company is key. The purpose of any external communications needs to be laser focused on benefiting the audience, whether it's teaching something useful, offering a beneficial service, or presenting a well-matched opportunity.

Events
When it comes to conferences and professional events, it's possible to get very granular with audience targeting. To avoid spending inordinate amounts of time at every major digital conference, consider researching the ones that attract the precise audiences you're trying to target. Developers, for example, have their

I'm CIO of the Year here in Australia, I'm the "Global Winner" of the Computerworld/IDG Premier 100 Technology Leaders Award, "CIO of the Year" at the Australian Executive Awards by CEO Magazine, and I was named and showcased as "Global Digital Leader" by the Gartner Symposium around the world. This gives me a level of reputation that opens doors so I can go anywhere and discuss with anyone, so I am making use of that.

There are many other ways to do it though. There are conferences, you can just cold call and say you want to know what someone's doing, and you can be proactive in developing those connections.

Interview with William Confalonieri, Chief Digital Officer, Deakin University

own popular conferences and generally wouldn't attend a conference for digital marketers (and vice versa).

When preparing the talk, the focus should be on teaching the methods used to achieve the project results, with a showcase of team achievements throughout, but with as much effort put into relating how the methods and results are relevant to the audience in the room. The goal is to strike a balance between showing the points of leverage (e.g. 'see how great it is to work here') and providing useful information about how the project was done. This is a challenging balance to strike, and often best done by matching the presenter with the audience members targeted.

For example, if you need to hire more designers, you should arrange for designers from your iterative teams to attend design-oriented conferences. Senior leaders from the transformation group, on the other hand, are best suited to presenting to potential partners and high-profile candidates at more exclusive events and functions.

If hosting your own event, such as a recruitment open house or a developer's hackathon, consider getting a specialist company to run it unless your company is well versed in event management. The last thing any programme needs is to deal with the internal repercussions of a poorly attended or badly run event intended to highlight its successes.

Articles and interviews

The same principles for choosing events and preparing talks apply for granting interviews and submitting articles for publications. It's better to be as targeted as possible when choosing where you want your successful results to appear. You also need to frame the content in a way that's beneficial to the reader first and the programme second.

I'm really hot on trying to attract the right talent and in Insurance it's tough. I want recruitment teams to think differently when they take our roles. For example, one of things that always frustrates me about doing interviews is can't share the culture really, and you spend the first thirty minutes telling them about what the job is. It's boring. I'd rather be talking about what problems we're trying to solve and whether they fit. So we came up with the idea of doing recruitment videos for individual roles. We did it in the afternoon because I have a video person on my team and put it on LinkedIn for the Head of Performance role.

It did two things. First, it solved a problem and did it quickly. Second, when we showed this video, the Recruitment Department is now starting to come up with a plan of how they're going to get the whole organization to do recruitment videos.

Interview with Ash Roots, Director of Digital, Direct Line Group

The other point to consider is the permanency of print. Sharing a great deal of detail in a written piece in the public domain will attract more competition than sharing the same results at a conference or major event. That said, it will also reach a wider audience and exist for longer – just be sure to prepare your offence in case of increased competitive threat.

Digital assets
Well-designed videos, infographics, and other popular forms of shareable online media can be incredibly powerful tools but there is a huge catch – they have to be really good. There is so much of this kind of content out there that unless you've got particularly outstanding results, or a really engaging way to show them off, shareable assets are often created, posted, and ignored. The exception is for organizations in specialist sectors where peers and competitors rarely share information, in which case you can find greater success in targeting these networks.

HR and company promotional assets
A greatly overlooked area that can generate a lot of external success is working with your company's HR and marketing departments to include recent successes in existing company communications. Being careful not to overplay any areas of success by making the transformation look complete, this includes current job ads, the 'About us' page on the website, and the information used to brief recruitment teams and take to job fairs.

Building these relationships now with HR and marketing also leads into the work you'll do next in BUILD Stage 5: Disseminate. This is how the new ways of working and the solutions found through digital transformation are seeded and formalized across the organization.

If you look at our partnerships, whether it's with IBM, PayPal, Salesforce, any of the companies that we've partnered with in terms of technology, certainly leaning on people who have capacity and who are willing to partner with you is huge.

But even internally, when I first started at ACS, I started by going to HR, corporate communications, and legal, building friendships, building transparency, and building trust. That is absolutely imperative because, when my contract gets to Legal it skates through and not because they're not looking at them but because they know that we deliver for them too, that they're an equal corporate citizen, and that they're getting the attention that they deserve, and that they have a partner in IT. When I needed to make org changes, HR was at the table every time. Why? Because I pay attention to them, because I listen to them, because I addressed their pain points just as much as I addressed Finance and Sales. You've got to forge those partnerships, both internally and externally, and build credibility. With some people, you've just got to win over time and you've got to have a thick skin. I'll get them eventually even if it's a begrudging respect for our delivery.

Interview with Jay Ferro, Executive Vice President, EarthLink
Former Chief Information Officer, American Cancer Society, 2012–2016

BUILD Stage 5: Disseminate

Scale new innovations and ways of working to make adapting to change the new 'business as usual'

Why Disseminate?

Self-sustaining digital transformation

The purpose of the final stage of transformation is to incrementally spread iterative ways of working, data-driven decision making, and processes for ongoing customer and external engagement beyond the confines of the digital transformation programme. This is how you'll scale innovative solutions produced so far, but more important, turn your organization into one that continuously innovates and keeps pace with change going forward.

The end state of transformation for any organization is when people from all roles, levels, and departments can use digital technology and iterative ways of working to:

1. Achieve collective goals that drive meaningful gains externally and internally, and contribute to fulfilling the company's overall mission.
2. Connect to customers and relevant parts of the outside world to spot and react to change, threats, and opportunities.
3. Collaborate efficiently to produce results that are consistent, have high impact, and reflect the company's positioning, brand, and values.

Getting to this end state isn't as simple as sharing the work that's been done so far, or providing training on how to replicate it. Instead, this stage is about shifting the balance of power in your organization from being entirely top-down to one that uses bottom-up control mechanisms to react, adapt, and thrive in changing environments.

Have a group whose job it is to wake up every day and scan the market. If you've got people every day looking at all the clever ideas, sorting them by commercial viability, maybe even making investments and joint ventures with them, so that they're constantly looking at how could this transform our customer experience and our business experience, then I think that's better than people trying to do it off the side of their desks. But if you have that, the people in those groups have to be very commercially based and that have a good understanding of the broader infrastructure and business challenges, and the commercial and competitive structures in which you're working.

Otherwise it's like having someone flying the plane at the same time as they're trying to figure out how to change the engine.

Interview with Jan Babiak
Board of Directors, Walgreens Boots Alliance, and Bank of Montreal

Top-down versus bottom-up control

In digitally transformed companies and those born from digital innovation, bottom-up control (The Economist Intelligence Unit Limited 2015) means that staff are empowered to come together to respond immediately to new threats or opportunities. They have direct access to customer insight and feedback to adjust their actions and achieve business goals.

The role of leadership in a bottom-up model isn't to optimize day-to-day operations, because the staff are empowered to do it themselves. Instead, leadership's job is to look for signs of major change, opportunities or threats and equip the company to deal with them through investments in infrastructure, forming new partnerships and bringing in specialist skills and additional talent. This is what allows these companies to respond to change with speed, coordination, and agility regardless of whether the change is caused by new technology, increased competition, or even variations in weather, the economy, social trends, or the political landscape.

Conversely, top-down management control relies on a company's leaders to spot signs of change and pass down instructions for how staff should react. Leaders then have to wait for instructions to be carried out, wait again for impacts of those actions to be recorded, and again for the results to be reported back. Only after all this waiting can they decide whether the instructions were carried out correctly, or if they were even the right responses for the situation in the first place.

At its most basic core, digital transformation is about enabling innovation from all aspects of the business. It is about the drive to innovate and become more agile.

Companies are being very data centric. That is about becoming much more aware about what you do, why you do it, what works, what doesn't, and what is really being said, felt and emoted about the organization that you are a part of and the product that you're offering.

If you take the most simplistic basis, you flip the organization upside-down so it's all about the external-in versus internal-out, allowing the internal model to be defined and driven by the external requirements of the ecosystem you're trying to thrive in. Then you are disrupting yourself on a consistent, ongoing basis so that you can't be disrupted in ways certain industries have been basically relegated to non-consequence due to their inability to evolve and to perform.

> Interview with Mike Giresi, Chief Information Officer,
> Royal Caribbean Cruises
> Former Chief Information Officer, Tory Burch, 2011–2015

Given the inherently slow reaction speeds and delayed feedback loops of top-down controlled companies, it's easy to see how increasing the prevalence of bottom-up control mechanisms is vital for companies to thrive in rapidly changing environments.

How to disseminate transformation

Transitioning a company's organizational model and power structure can't be done by force, and it can't be done overnight. Companies make huge mistakes trying to embed digital transformation solely via policy changes or department restructuring, which amounts to little actual change in day-to-day practices. Other unsuccessful measures include hiring armies of consultants, or acquiring and absorbing entire digital agencies and start-ups. This most often leads to pockets of transformation at best, and at worst, major overspends and a fragmentation of the company's culture and identity.

Dissemination through iteration

Scaling your solutions and embedding new ways of working need to follow the same iterative approach followed by project teams in BUILD Stage 3: Iterate, and used by leadership in BUILD Stage 4: Leverage, to determine the right ways to

That process of continuous improvement and customer focus, that's what you want to embed at the end of your programme for the people who take it forward.

Each programme has a number of capability releases. So, say what I'm doing at the Guardian is an eighteen-month programme and will probably have five capability releases, almost quarterly. Each of those capability releases will enable certain benefits to be realized. That is something the business couldn't do before and it can now. I'm very careful to make sure the business owns and takes responsibility for the benefits realization. My job is to deliver the capability in August, but my programme team will have lined up the corresponding business user to be able to use that capability and start getting benefits from September. If you position the programme in that way it not only gets buy-in, but you get a shared sense of ownership from the business. Now their head's on the block as well for using that capability.

The worst thing you can do in a transformation programme is produce capabilities and then the business don't use them, or the business isn't prepared or geared up to be able to use them. But if you make them responsible for the benefits that come off that transformation, then they're much more attentive to the programme and much more keen to change their processes and get in shape for using the new capability.

Interview with Laura Scarlett, Data & Insight Director,
Guardian News & Media
Former Programme Director, Supporter Loyalty,
National Trust, 2013–2015

turn individual project successes into access and resources to scale. By scaling incrementally and constantly evaluating successes with new customers and new teams, you'll learn what's working versus what needs adjusting in your innovation mission, systems and roles.

Dissemination can't be done remotely

Establishing systems, training staff, recruiting new people – all of this requires hands-on work from the leadership group and members of the original iterative teams. Sending all-staff emails, posting materials on the intranet, or offering video training are viable options as supplements, but they don't replace face-to-face information and skills exchange.

People from iterative teams should be prepared to work in different locations and units to help other teams achieve results. Members of the transformation leadership group should also spend time in other areas, getting to know managers there, and deciding whether additional support from leadership is needed in the form of adding additional members to the group.

This final stage of BUILD covers how to do this by achieving the following three critical steps:

1. Disseminate the iterative approach
2. Scale the cross-functional team model
3. Invest in platforms, partnerships, people, and processes

Before delving into how to disseminate through these two steps, it's important to understand the fundamental principles of a bottom-up model that allows companies that use them to thrive in changing environments. These traits lay

We had a programme called 'Change Champions' in our organization so when we did roll out new technologies and there was a combination of staff and volunteers, our champions were the first ones. We had different champions based on functions; we're not going to roll out a new fundraising technology to research people. They signed up, we knighted them, we created a mobile message board so they could provide feedback and we could get back to them right away, live chat and all these other things. By going to them right out of the gate and saying you are now a deputy for IT and for a product, and we need your help, 99 times out of 100, people got it and were 'hell yeah! I'm in'. They felt like they had skin in the game.

Believe me it's a whole lot easier to roll out technology when you already have evangelists baked into key roles, in staff and in your customer base.

If you're smart, you're cross-functional enough that you're not leaving anybody out. And the whole time you're communicating what your deployment plan is. Pilot, then champions, then champions squared, everybody good, and after that boom boom boom a million, million people.

One of the ways we did is we said we're creating one digital identity for all ACS resources. Within the first couple of pilots we had maybe 10,000 people using it and seven months ago, we had over 2.5 million people using it. Our customers have one identity, one version of you. It was very very successful.

Interview with Jay Ferro, Executive Vice President, EarthLink
Former Chief Information Officer, American Cancer Society, 2012–2016

the foundation for how to disseminate digital transformation, as well as provide a glimpse into how your organization will operate once this final stage is complete.

Three traits to instil for sustainable transformation

In systems theory, bottom-up control is a defining characteristic of complex adaptive systems (The Health Foundation 2010), which are found everywhere. Weather patterns, the economy, or the human brain are all examples of complex adaptive systems that operate through bottom-up control. What allows these systems to thrive in changing environments – whether it's a company or a flock of birds – are a set of principles followed by every member that allow them to achieve individual goals, as well as produce outputs greater than the sum of their roles.

To understand these, picture a flock of hundreds of sparrows, all flying in fast tightly synchronized displays to evade an encroaching eagle. In the flock, each sparrow knows how to recognize signs of danger, and what the appropriate reaction is when detected. So whether it's the biggest, strongest bird or the youngest and smallest who first spots the eagle, it can react instantly and appropriately, triggering a chain reaction of other instant and appropriate responses from the rest of the flock.

Each bird determines its own behaviour based on environmental feedback, and decides the distance and angles it wants to maintain between its neighbours to avoid collisions. When the flock takes flight, these actions and reactions occur in such rapid succession that within seconds the birds naturally settle into an optimum and equalized distance between one another to suit the current conditions and abilities of each member (Jones 2003).

Interestingly, science only recently discovered the flocking ability of birds is actually the output of a complex adaptive system. Prior to this, it was assumed the ability to fly in fast formations was the result of one lead bird signalling changes to others, or animal instinct dictating predetermined flight patterns in every bird (Rungtusanatham and Choi 2001).

It's not hard to see the analogy when you compare this to companies trying to contend with rising competition, new technology, and shifting consumer behaviour. The commonly held assumption used to be that innovation needed to be driven constantly by leadership, or that it required hiring specialist staff from day one. We now know from countless digitally transformed organizations this isn't the case.

Companies that harness key traits of complex adaptive systems are capable of producing outputs far greater than the sum of their parts. These outputs are also impossible to predict because of the many external and internal variables at play – the same for any organization adapting to the changing world around it.

By gradually establishing these traits in your organization, you can turn any company into one as fast moving and agile as a flock of sparrows, but with the creativity and innovation of any start-up or Silicon Valley firm.

People are naturally tribal, and local allegiances are part of the way that information gets siloed. The democratization of information is going to challenge some of these tribal, hierarchical structures in large organizations.

In an era of digital transformation, the individual contributor has many more leadership opportunities. The access to information has enabled individual contributors to see the bigger picture – of their organization, their market, and the world – and people in roles like software developer, content strategist, and data analyst will be able to provide insights that can help realize an organization's goals. They may not have a traditional advancement pathway to the C-level, but ignore this talent your peril. Smart organizations will be harnessing this talent for both insight and agility.

Interview with Perry Hewitt, Vice-President of Marketing, ITHAKA
Former Chief Digital Officer, Harvard University, 2011–2016

1. Universal goals incentivize cooperation and competition

In a flock, all birds share the same goals of evading predators and avoiding collisions with others. They're motivated individually to fly as fast as possible to avoid capture and secure better positions in the flock, but they are also motivated to work together because flying in the largest numbers possible gives them the best protection.

The same is true for people in your organization. They need to benefit directly from the hard work involved in learning new skills, addressing new opportunities and threats as they arise. Without this motivation, they're more likely to miss signs of change and ignore issues that don't fall directly under their area of responsibility or within their regular routines. In a transformed company, staff and leaders alike work to achieve common goals derived from the company's mission. They cooperate because they'll achieve those goals faster, and they work hard because their individual contributions are trackable and rewarded.

Compare this to a traditional company, where individual contributions are hard to track because of complex hierarchical and department-based structures. Cooperation isn't incentivized – in fact, it's discouraged because departments each have different goals. This makes collaborating outside your role or department a risky venture because you might lose control of the work, or be penalized for not focusing on your own department's objectives.

2. Relevant information and real-time feedback enable agility

Sparrows individually track the location of the eagle, along with current wind speed and direction. This constant monitoring allows each bird to adjust its proximity to neighbours and the predator, simultaneously avoiding capture and collisions.

Feedback loops are used to let individuals know straight away whether they're producing positive outcomes or negative ones, which lets them adjust their behaviours accordingly. Individuals can maximize the effectiveness because they have direct access to relevant real-time information and feedback. If their actions cause a positive effect, they know immediately to keep doing it versus trying a new variation if the feedback is bad.

Staff and leaders in transformed companies all track the behaviours of customers, and watch for changes in the competitive and technology landscape. They then test new ideas and monitor changes to current operations, relying on real-time data and insight to know if decisions and outputs are achieving positive results.

Unlike traditional companies where decisions are made based on protocol, past experience or seniority, IT systems aren't set up to allow real-time data, staff aren't encouraged to test regularly or in real environments, and leaders are expected to rely on experience alone to make most decisions. This means the impact of anyone's actions aren't knowable until long after negative results have manifested.

3. Simple processes and specialist skills enable self-governing behaviour
Every sparrow in the flock follows the same simple processes for how to fly, swoop, bank, and dive to avoid collisions and the predator. This enables them

---

We have to be able to have feedback loops. Someone will say we have to deliver every two weeks. You then have to build in some sort of feedback loop to make sure that what we're going to release is actually going to be a positive thing, depending on the size and scale.

At Tory, we would take about 3 per cent of traffic and see what results we get. The feedback loops get from this process can then feed to product teams, so they can see what's working and what's not.

In this day and age, people are so willing to share. If you give people an opportunity to do so, they will. That can help you curate the functions to a better place so that when it does go into production, it's really meeting someone's expectations and needs.

Interview with Mike Giresi, Chief Information Officer,
Royal Caribbean Cruises
Former Chief Information Officer, Tory Burch, 2011–2015

to act quickly and independently, deciding for themselves what action is needed and when, while contributing to consistent flight patterns across the entire group. The same is true for employees: everyone can make good decisions and act quickly when processes for doing so are collectively known and understood. The more complex the rules, unnecessary hierarchies, restrictions, or instructions people have to follow, the more mechanically they'll behave.

Take the complexity away, and people with specialist skills can use their common sense and experience to follow simple processes to fix problems and address opportunities as they arise. This is why processes in a transformed company are intuitive and flexible, letting staff and leaders take appropriate actions without fear of reprisal. This allows everyone to control their own behaviour, reacting and responding in ways that match whatever conditions or situations arise.

In traditional companies, complex policies, rules, and processes make this kind of quick action too risky or difficult to make. People are unsure how to act, and because the rewards aren't in place for working outside one's role or department, there is no incentive to try and learn beyond the day-to-day (Table 5.1).

The culture you want is one where people utilize data. If people are able to try things they generally end up having power, the power then drives the autonomy and the ability to make decisions.

In the old school world, the only power was wielded by the board because they're got seniority. But in the new world, someone can say 'look I've just run a test because I was experimenting and utilizing data', and they're automatically empowered to make new decisions. It's not that you're asked to make the decision, it's that no one could deny you making that decision because you have the data.

Interview with Ash Roots, Director of Digital, Direct Line Group

Table 5.1 *Transformed versus traditional companies.*

Traits	Transformed company	Traditional company
1. Universal goals incentivize cooperation and competition	Staff: Work hard to achieve company goals because it earns them direct credit and reward. Cooperate with others outside their outside skill sets based on what's required to achieve the company goals faster.	Staff: Only work hard enough to not be criticized, or achieve the goals of their direct managers for praise and promotions. Stay within the confines of the department, hierarchical structure, and their role to avoid losing control, being penalized, or not getting credit.
	Leaders: Establish universal goals across the company to achieve its mission by serving the needs of customers and meeting external conditions. Reward collaboration by making it clear how to work across areas of the business or with external partners. Reward competition by making individuals directly accountable for trackable outputs that contribute to accomplishing company goals.	Leaders: Create different goals for each area of the business, which may put areas in direct competition with each other. Discourage collaboration with complex legal policies for working with external parties, and by creating competition between different departments, roles, and levels of the hierarchy. Discourage competition by pooling similar roles and skill sets together and making it difficult to measure individual contributions.
Simple processes and specialist skills enable self-governing behaviour	Staff: Self-manage by following simple processes that keep actions consistent with the company's brand, mission, and values. Self-organize and collaborate to achieve goals, maintain efficiency, and adapt to changing conditions.	Staff: Are managed by leadership in ways that must adhere to complex processes and policies that may not even relate to the company's mission, brand, and values. Are organized in fixed roles and hierarchies regardless of efficiency or whether goals are being met.

Traits	Transformed company	Traditional company
Real-time information flows and feedback loops enable agility	Leaders: Allow staff to self-manage and self-organize by not introducing complex processes or hierarchies that make decision making less intuitive and more politicized. Staff: Connect directly to relevant information flows (e.g. customer insights) to inform decisions and enable quick reactions. Use feedback loops (e.g. customer feedback and system data) to determine their effectiveness and moderate their actions in real time. Leaders: Connect to an array of changing information flows and feedback loops to anticipate the need for major change as technology and the competitive landscape dictate. Enable the organization to cope with major change by adjusting its people, platforms, partnership, and processes to allow self-governing and self-organizing to continue.	Leaders: Manage and oversee all day-to-day activities, including developing policies and layers of approval that require special training to fully understand and comply with. Staff: Are handed down information by leadership on a need-to-know basis that may or may not be accurate or up-to-date. Are given feedback on their effectiveness by management based on yearly HR cycles, except in circumstances of underperformance. Leaders: Are briefed on internal performance and external conditions from the same sources and at the same intervals as the leaders before them, allowing new threats and opportunities to go unnoticed. React to major threats and opportunities with acquisitions, mergers, redundancies, restructuring, rebranding, and various other extreme measures that are costly, disruptive, and carry high risk.

How to scale innovation

A two-part approach to scaling innovation

Disseminating transformation is about embedding the principles that allowed your programme to achieve success. The challenge is that it's less about imparting training or extending access to new tools. Instead, it requires getting a much larger group of people – some with no experience or exposure to digital or innovation – to not only learn how to work in these new ways and see new technology in a different light but also actually want to do it.

For this reason, disseminating transformation takes a two-pronged approach. The first part, 'Establish goals and rewards for innovation', tackles how to establish universal goals and motivation to achieve them, in order to instil the principles and values of the iterative approach across your organization. Then in the second part, you'll find out how to scale the cross-functional team model across your organization to establish a bottom-up approach to thriving in changing environments.

Establish goals and rewards for innovation

Among your iterative teams and digital transformation leadership group, a change in mindset has already taken place. People in the programme understand the value of working differently and of focusing on the customer to solve problems

We have a Digital Future Lab here at Deakin that I have created. It's a big physical space with all kind of toys and new technology, but it's also used to create a specific mindset. People working in that space, work with a very different approach.

We have three approaches. We have the traditional and slow approach that I call it 'the elephant'. That is safe and slow for when the organization can't go faster than that. When We use Agile teams I call that process 'the horse'. And We have 'the cheetah' and that's what is happening in the lab where we experiment and pour different amounts of money on things that probably will fail but very quickly. This is where the new ideas and the new business value propositions appear for becoming projects later.

Interview with William Confalonieri, Chief Digital Officer, Deakin University

and address opportunities, but knowledge outside the group is limited to those who were exposed to its successes only during BUILD Stage 4: Leverage.

What's needed now is a way to spread those methods and that customer focus beyond the confines of the programme. This requires establishing and – to be sustainable – formalizing three new operating principles across your organization.

First, people from all levels and business functions need to understand the new focus of your organization, which is to deliver your company's founding mission by keeping in line with customer needs and changing external conditions. Next, employees and management need to know the supports in place to enable innovation, so when they spot a problem or an opportunity, there are next steps for them to take and be encouraged to follow through. Finally, individuals across the organization need to know that if they put in the extra effort to self-organize and iteratively innovate a solution, their efforts will be recognized and rewarded.

By the end, you'll have established universal goals for self-directing teams to work towards. You'll also have provided clear rewards to inspire cooperation and competition within your organization – the first trait of any successful complex adaptive system.

Universal goals: Customer experience linked to the mission

The purpose of universal goals in an innovative company is to give clarity to what success looks like and what are the acceptable ways to get there. Google has 'Ten things we know to be true', Netflix has its 'Netflix Focus' (Burke n.d.) – these value and mission statements are different from those of a traditional company

> We are empowering offices with the toolsets to do their job more effectively, and with training and investment strategies. It's key to identify the enablers teams need to do their job properly. Expert digital staff, stronger tools, more consistent training and increased digital efficiency means that we can communicate and engage audiences far more effectively. And there couldn't be a more relevant and motivating agenda to try and engage with than the refugee cause.
>
> Interview with Mike Walton, Chief of Section, Digital Engagement,
> United Nations High Commission for Refugees (UNHCR)

because they are kept relevant and up-to-date based on what's happening in the world and with the company. For example, Google's 'Ten things' (About Us (n.d.) Available at: https://www.google.co.uk/about/company/philosophy/ [Accessed 16 February 2017]) are consistent year on year in terms of the title of each 'thing', but the explanations are updated to clarify their meaning in the current company context. This includes statements about the company's position on expanding into areas beyond web search, and why it will never allow misleading ads to appear anywhere on its platform.

Like the transformation vision, you want your organization's common goals to resonate with people and not just reflect numbers or business metrics. They should be personable and relatable across every business function and job role. Beyond these basic principles, the three most important factors for establishing universal goals are as follows.

1. Mission led

Whether you choose one universal goal or ten, you need to be clear on how achieving these goals will actually lead you towards achieving the mission of company. The universal goals are not good enough if, by reading them, a person can't immediately tell what your company does, what it values, and what makes it different from a company with the same offerings.

You can have all the best plans and methodology in the world but if people don't believe genuinely in why you're trying to do something and what you're trying to achieve, it can all unravel pretty quickly.

It's hard to challenge the mission statement, you either get with that or you leave pretty quickly. At BHF we were fighting heart disease, at ICR we're making discoveries to defeat cancer. That should be at the heart of everything we do. It's about holding on to that and linking everything you find or discover to that and asking does it help or hinder? What barriers are between us and making that change in that context is critical, in our case that's better research to defeat cancer.

Interview with Dr Charmaine Griffiths, Chief Operating Officer,
The Institute for Cancer Research,
Former Executive Director of Strategy & Performance,
British Heart Foundation, 2013–2016

2. Customer focused

The means for succeeding in the universal goals must include a focus on customers, including their changing behaviours and needs, as well as other external factors that will affect your company's ability to achieve its mission. It should also be incredibly clear in the goals that doing right by the customer first is the only route to sustainable success.

3. Contextually appropriate

For an employee to see any value in the common goals, there must be context. Seeing a poster with the universal goals in a part of the business very far removed from the transformation programme is going to look more like corporate marketing and a waste of paper versus a bold new step for the business. Instead, share the goals with areas of the business or markets you're starting to scale transformation into. You can also include them in your communication activities for BUILD Stage 4: Leverage for the next areas you'd like to target for transformation.

Prove your support for innovation

In a traditional company, working outside your normal role or with someone from a different department can feel like breaking the rules. In order to adopt iterative working styles, experiment with new technology, and feel comfortable collaborating with people from different skills sets, levels of seniority, or partner organizations, you need to make it very clear how the employees will be supported and encouraged along the way. The supports you provide and how you communicate them need to answer the basic questions any employee or manager would ask if told they're going to work in this new way, for example:

- How do I access equipment?
- How do I find developers or designers?
- How do I get training on Agile and Design Thinking?
- How do we get customers for customer testing?
- How do I engage with external specialists and companies?

To answer these questions, there are two categories of support to consider: authorization and access. Authorization is about permission to work with others and the recognition people will get if collaboration efforts are successful. Access is about the tools, assets, and resources that are available to them, should they be required.

Once both parts are complete, you'll have provided incentive for people to come together and work collaboratively, vastly increasing the number of external changes and variables they'll be able to handle.

1. Authorization: Permission and recognition for collaboration

To establish authorization for innovative working, you need to formalize approval of cross-departmental work, simplify processes for working with external parties, and, when successes are achieved, ensure there are mechanisms in place to track and reward contributions from everyone involved.

Determine with managers which standard practices should be followed when people work outside their normal roles and structures on 'special projects' so they aren't penalized for putting part of their normal work on hold, and so they get recognition once it's done. It also requires working with your company's own legal team to agree things like a standard non-disclosure agreement (NDA) for working with external companies, and agreeing on ways to streamline contracting and bidding processes for digital work.

2. Access: Tools, assets, and resources for innovation

Establishing access to enablers of innovative working is the practical side of encouraging collaboration in your organization. These are the tools, resources, and assets that people will be able to access when coming together to iteratively solve a problem or address an opportunity.

Some companies centralize these resources in an 'innovation lab' or central digital hub. These facilities are typically staffed by new employees or contractors with specialist digital skills, and then any new iterative project takes place in the lab, pulling in people from relevant parts of the company as needed. This is a good approach if the culture is particularly conservative and digital skill sets

---

Many find value in a Centre of Excellence model. An effective model builds capability and best practices, and shares information across the enterprise.

We implemented this approach at Harvard through a series of "Digital Connect" conferences. Held in the Innovation Lab, these meetings brought together one hundred people working on digital products in various roles. We selected professionals who might not ordinarily run across one another to maximize cross-pollination of ideas. And we had success in co-creating the curriculum with participants, encouraging these practitioners to bring their best practices – and even some of their failures – to share with the broader group.

Interview with Perry Hewitt, Vice-President of Marketing, ITHAKA
Former Chief Digital Officer, Harvard University, 2011–2016

are few and far between. That said, it needs careful governance and oversight to ensure it grows in pace with the needs of the company, increasing digital capabilities and skill sets across the business units with every engagement.

Individual recognition and accountability

Constantly innovating and improving to stay on top of customer needs and ahead of the competition is extremely hard work – let alone when you must also learn new skills before even starting it. The first step to motivating individuals to work hard is to make sure their contributions are both tracked and rewarded. Only when people realize it's part of their day jobs, and not just a side project, will innovation become a sustainable and self-perpetuating process.

1. Tracking individual contributions

Tracking individual contributions means adhering to the iterative approach in Stage 3: Iterate. Each team member is responsible for specific tasks that are necessary to the success of the project or outcome.

The results of each person's work should then be translated into metrics and included in formal job evaluation procedures conducted with staff and leadership. This is where HR and management need to brought in early on, made aware of the benefits of transformation through BUILD Stage 4: Leverage, and given the responsibility of embedding measurements and performance indicators into people's regular performance reviews.

Be careful not to do this before tracking and evaluation on a project level is in place, though, because bringing in formal measurements and assessments too early can cause panic and chaos as people feel they are going to be measured against something they don't understand or haven't had the opportunity or resources to get involved in yet.

2. Rewarding hard work

Rewarding individual contributions can be done through publicized awards and recognition by senior leadership for individuals who have done innovative work. It can also take the form of competitions, such as people submitting business cases to request funding or resources for special projects or tasks related to their work, but in ways that incorporate innovation practices.

Regardless of the early rewards used, the end goal must be an inclusion of innovation metrics in every person's formal appraisals and reviews in order to facilitate their personal career development. This should also extend to updating job roles and descriptions to make sure when someone leaves, the role is taken on by an employee with full understanding of the priority innovation needs to take in day-to-day work.

I think HR has to be the enabler of helping you get the right structure and the right people. They might not necessarily be able to find those people per se, but they can help you sell it into the organization and lay it out in a way that's sustainable.

In IT organizations there are a whole bunch of paths people can go. You can be a product leader, an IT analyst, a business liaison, or you can be what I call a contributing person who doesn't know how to lead people, but can lead technology. All those positions need to have career paths leading to them. When I joined Royal, the only way you could get promoted was if you became a manager of people. So even if you were an incredibly capable tech leader or amazing engineer, but with horrible personality skills, the only way for you to get promoted was to take on the responsibility of people. That led to some people being put in the wrong jobs because what they were actually very good at was developing and creating technology and innovation. They were not so good at actually creating teams.

I asked HR to go into some sort of process where we started to carve out different career paths for these different individuals. Someone who can lead an Agile cross-functional team delivering something every two weeks, is a different kind of leader than someone working on a monolithic reservation system, but understands the implications of that system going wrong.

By creating these cross-functional product teams, we now have people overseeing outcomes and capabilities and results, versus technology platforms. That's driving a different behaviour into the organization. HR had to support that and if they didn't then I wouldn't have been able to sell it into the broader business.

HR can't fill the roles per se, they can't really understand the roles, but they have to be able to understand the technology and the disciple and the desire for why it needs to happen. If we can agree upon that, having them sell it in is much easier than trying to sell it yourself.

Interview with Mike Giresi, Chief Information Officer,
Royal Caribbean Cruises
Former Chief Information Officer, Tory Burch, 2011–2015

Do you have things like innovation awards or 'risk taking' awards? Do you have ways to reward and remunerate people, whether that's actual dollars or cultural capital, for trying and doing new things? It goes back to following the money. Find ways to look fundamentally at the ways you're advancing and promoting people across the organization. Build digital behaviours into that.

One of the hardest areas for digital transformation is HR. For example, the famous job description of 'get me an iOS developer with 25 years' experience'. Everything in HR is about longevity, tenure and years served. We don't necessarily want to promote or advance people the same way we have before. In some large and traditional cultural institutions, the most important thing was to retain someone for seven to twenty-five years. If someone left after five years, they were considered a failed hire. We need to think very differently about what a successful hire looks like.

Interview with Perry Hewitt, Vice-President of Marketing, ITHAKA
Former Chief Digital Officer, Harvard University, 2011–2016

Scale the Iterative Team Model

The ultimate goal: No more silos

Iterative teams aren't just for new projects. Companies known for innovation, including Amazon, Apple, and Google, all favour cross-functional teams for running day-to-day activities as well as new initiatives versus operating in traditional department-driven and hierarchical structures (About Us n.d.). At its most basic level, this is because no one works their best when people of the same skill sets are grouped in large numbers, governed closely by managers, and only get to collaborate with other parts of the business during handovers or review meetings.

People on smaller teams benefit from the natural social circle effect of getting to know, trust, and rely on the outputs of the people in their group. Most important though, when teams have just the right blend of capabilities needed to shape, deliver, and maintain a specific product, service, or function within a company, they're directly equipped to act in ways that achieve goals and solve problems.

This is why the second part of disseminating transformation is about systematically and incrementally scaling the cross-functional team model and expanding the effects of the digital transformation programme. This will enable you to start to permeate your organization's departmental silos, reducing its reliance on the top-down control processes to react to change and meet company goals.

The model is still something I feel is very successful. We've done a number of engagements with outside firms to continue to make sure that this makes sense. We engaged with Forrester Research a year or so ago and one of their lead analysts on digital transformation endorsed this model.

It's a Centre of Excellence model, which allows business units to have local execution. For example, our wealth management business has its own chief digital officer and she is in charge of a tremendous number of actions and activities. Our value add-on the centre of excellence side of things is connecting the various teams with the digital agency. For example, her team leverages platforms that we've put into place, and they take advantage of some of the strategic assets that we maintain like MorganStanley.com that has about 7.5 million users per year. We provide additional capability, ready to go services, and at times data and information so that they can achieve their objectives at a local level.

Morgan Stanley has around 55,000 employees, so it makes sense to have a leading Centre of Excellence that provides the core capabilities and services and maintains the strategic assets, leads the way with some innovation, provides services to business units, and allows the businesses to follow the objectives that help them overall.

We give them a framework to work within which should not be too restricting but it also shows that we're a consistent brand and that we're collecting information on campaigns across business units so that we can have global insights. The Centre succeeds because of the ongoing value that it gives back to the business units. I have to be leading a team that adds value to other groups and when that stops happening, it will stop being a structure that makes sense.

I was just looking through our list of initiatives of things we've kicked off since the beginning of the year. There are quite a few. The diversity of initiatives is one of the things that keeps it interesting and engaging.

Interview with Bryan VanDyke, Managing Director and Head of Digital,
Morgan Stanley

Steps to scaling the team model

Scaling the iterative team model takes an incremental approach and should start in the areas where successes achieved so far have gained access to new areas of the business, customer groups, and resources described in BUILD Stage 4: Leverage.

You can either assemble new cross-functional teams to scale a particular innovation, such as customizing a solution from one market to another, or teams can be tasked with using digital and the iterative approach to improving existing offerings or business functions – just be sure to follow the same processes of evaluating success as BUILD Stage 3: Iterate, including assigning tangible metrics as goals for the teams to be measured against in each iterative cycle.

Once you know where to scale, the first step to achieving it starts with the iterative teams that have already been working on transformation projects, as well as the transformation leadership group. Together, they need to establish flexible systems for guiding work on future iterative teams, with a special focus on the four digital disciplines: Customer Experience, Design, DevOps, and Insight.

The next section shows what parts make up these flexible systems to equip teams with the right tools, frameworks, and support to ensure consistency and rapid growth across any number of new iterative teams, while still allowing room for customizations, growth, and adaptations where needed. If done well, flexible systems help disseminate digital skills across your organization, strengthening your ability to anticipate change and innovate to react, without requiring additional levels of management or oversight.

The second part of scaling the cross-functional team model is knowing how to customize it for the needs and nuances of your organization, and where to invest in order to sustain growth. This applies whether you're scaling an innovation to a new area of the business or consumer market, or whether you're starting a new iterative team around an existing product, service, or function in your company. Knowing how to customize the self-directing team model comes from understanding the approaches used by other successfully transformed organizations, including scaling interim models like accelerators, innovation labs, hubs, and internal start-ups.

Establish flexible systems for scale

One of the biggest mistakes leaders make in scaling innovations or ways of working is they fail to accommodate unique needs between consumer groups and across parts of the company itself.

When scaling a solution to a new market, the iterative project process needs to be adapted to look for the customizations required to meet local needs.

> One thing we've done that's been really successful is to have digital outreach officers in New York and in Bangkok to work with offices there that are sometimes harder for us to have regular contact with. They run integrated planning with each of those offices on how they can improve their digital engagement. Those supported offices have increased public engagement and some have won digital awards. They all started at a very low level of digital capacity. You can see from the offices that they find this support incredibly valuable.
>
> Interview with Mike Walton, Chief of Section, Digital Engagement,
> United Nations High Commission for Refugees (UNHCR)

Failing to allow for these nuances results in solutions which are abandoned by parts of the business as negative perceptions of digital innovation start to undo all the good work accomplished in BUILD Stage 4: Leverage. Like any major change, there is no 'one size fits all' approach. But making too many unnecessary customizations, or even starting from scratch with every new area or market, wastes time and resource, and creates duplications across internal processes.

Flexible systems are needed for disseminating both the solutions themselves and the ways of working that produced them. At minimum, you'll need flexible systems for each of your digital disciplines to enable consistency of output across your company's iterative teams. Parts that make up these flexible systems include the examples listed in Table 5.2, but these aren't prescriptive or exhaustive. In fact, there are enough examples in each category to fill entire books (some of which are recommended in the Conclusion).

As such, the intention of this section isn't to list every possible system you can use to scale, but instead to show you how to identify the systems you need, what work you need to do upfront to set them on the right tracks, and then how to create and evolve them over time.

What are flexible systems for scale?

There are four common parts to any flexible system used for scaling innovation, with each part made up of many different elements depending on the digital discipline and ways of working it's meant to support. This list isn't exhaustive or prescriptive, but highlights the areas any new iterative team will need guidance in when it's time to start innovating.

Table 5.2 *Example systems for each digital discipline*

Digital discipline	Areas of work	Examples of flexible systems to support new teams
Customer experience	1. Engage with customers and the marketplace to identify needs, pain points, and opportunities. 2. Test solutions with customers throughout each iterative cycle. 3. Create user flow diagrams to help guide developers.	1. Tips and processes for recruiting and incentivizing users, customisable templates, and guides for running Design Thinking sessions. 2. Subscriptions to software for testing simple interactive prototypes, training for conducting user testing, and interpreting results. 3. Access to an online platform for creating, updating and sharing user flows across the company.
Design	1. Translate ideas into visuals that can be tested with customers. 2. Interpret the brand into elements like interaction behaviours, and layouts for user interfaces. 3. Ensure finished solutions meet design standards and are updated with new design iterations.	1. Templates and guides for creating mood boards and story boards, and licences to design software. 2. Shared asset libraries and guiding principles for brand elements, grid systems by device type, and guidelines for designing modules within each. 3. Software for creating user interfaces and animations, platforms to host master work, and processes for quality checks and updates.
DevOps (Development and Operations)	1. Identify the right technologies to enable the solution. 2. Write code and configure systems to enable features and functions. 3. Work with existing IT platforms to deploy new solutions quickly and securely.	1. Libraries for code sharing and communities for accessing advice and support. 2. Platforms and processes for documenting and managing upcoming features and bug fixing. 3. Software, processes, environments, and standards for testing, deploying, and hosting new solutions on existing platforms within the regulations and parameters agreed across the company.
Insights	1. Monitor real-time data and detect changes in the success of existing offerings. 2. Gathering and interpreting results on new solutions. 3. Assessing the wider marketplace to spot signs of change or opportunity.	1. Customisable dashboards and software for monitoring and automating live data capture and evaluation. 2. Software, processes, and guidelines for accessing customer groups for testing, capturing, and evaluating test data. 3. Subscriptions and access to online platforms for finding insights from other markets and customer groups and processes for acting on changes, threats, and opportunities.

There were three things we established when I came in. One was we had to be able to do the things we said we were going to do, and be consistent and provide stable operations on a day-to-day basis. It's unacceptable if we're releasing new technology with new functionality and breaking something else in the process. It's not okay to say we're learning our way through it. No, you do it, you do it well or don't do it at all.

Two was that we had to get much better aligned with our business partners. I felt like the IT team had become its own island off, both geographically and strategically. It was not relevant to our business.

The third thing was this pivot to digital. Everything we were going to do was about becoming a digital business. The DevOps piece was a part of that. I mean how can you be a digital business and not practice DevOps from an everyday functionality and release perspective?

So, product teams looking at different metrics and chunking down projects, not trying to come out with these major, major releases. It's okay to work on a certain function and get that function out, maybe two other things come with it – who cares, it doesn't matter. You're constantly making progress as long as our business partners see that, and by the way, it'll cost a lot less and they'll be very happy.

Interview with Mike Giresi, Chief Information Officer,
Royal Caribbean Cruises
Former Chief Information Officer, Tory Burch, 2011–2015

1. Common technology

For each of your digital disciplines, flexible systems need to include common technology for designers, user experience specialists, and developers to access on different iterative teams across your company. This can include licensed software and platforms, test environments, and devices. Standardizing this has huge benefits, as you'll save by getting enterprise licences instead of many individual licences. It also means people across the company can build up expertise in the technology, share help and tutorials, learn advanced features, and benefit from shared libraries and other pooled resources.

As a word of caution though, make sure the approach to common technology is flexible and updated regularly. Signing a long-term deal for any device type or

You're always finding a balance in digital transformation of what skills you want to bring in and what skills you want to keep out. It's always important for a business to remember what its core purpose is. As long as you're clear about where the delineation lies, it's about providing an internal resource with the maximum level of support. Examples might be sending key people on a training course or job shadowing. At one point in the BMA, I embedded one of our technical people into our digital agency's studio to have regular interaction between the teams and to facilitate skills transfer.

On the technical side, it can be things like code libraries or even testing protocols designed for load balancing or security for penetration testing. It's very crucial that the mindset is never one of 'build and walk away'. Change and transformation now is a continuous process, so it's very important for people to understand there is no point where they say 'we've done that'. It's a continuous process.

Interview with Stewart Atkins, Digital Transformation Consultant
Former Head of Digital Strategy, British Medical Association, 2011–2015

platform is only going to leave your company behind or cost more money in the long run when a new and better technology product comes out and your teams have to miss out or pay from individual budgets to access it.

2. Adaptable processes

Whether it's teams finding a great way to run Design Thinking sessions, or developers agreeing with IT on how to deploy a new feature into a live environment, the elements that made the approach successful should be captured and shared into a process for the next iterative teams to try out and adapt as needed.

Depending on the geographic spread and overall size of your organization, this might require a specialized platform for sharing as well as existing teams visiting new iterative teams to share best practices. What's most important though is not trying to share a new process completely out of context. Training people before they actually get to work in these new ways, or expecting them to learn new processes via training videos or written instructions, is only going to lead to confusion and people reverting to old ways of working once the course is over.

One of the challenges we have on our ships is that no two ships are exactly the same. When we think about scaling technology across our ships, it's a problem because they're big ships.

The only way you can scale is if the services that need to scale are on a scalable infrastructure. That makes them incredibly simple. Deploying technology this way is a very, very different way than how most organizations are used to working.

We're containerizing applications, looking at deploying services, as opposed to very complicated and complex apps. We're just getting to a place where we can drive much faster versus having to re-architect everything every two years.

Think about a headless engine. We have a certain capability that we can provide and it's just the basics. People can now write to that capability at an API layer, and it allows us to go much faster.

> Interview with Mike Giresi, Chief Information Officer,
> Royal Caribbean Cruises
> Former Chief Information Officer, Tory Burch, 2011–2015

3. Reusable assets

Your flexible systems for scaling need to include libraries of reusable assets for all the digital disciplines. These can take many different forms, including document templates, design components, and code libraries, and they should be set up to allow for growth as future iterative teams use, customize, and add to them.

Because these materials are likely to be stored on digital sites, be sure to also put processes in place for governing and maintaining any reusable asset libraries. There should be vetting processes for checking assets meet the core principles for their discipline, while regular auditing will ensure these areas don't become virtual dumping grounds that are impossible to quickly search.

4. Open communities

One of the best ways to foster innovation and grow digital capabilities in any organization is to make sure the people who are interested in building their skills can access peers and experts for support, guidance, and review.

Something that's worked really well for programme's I've been involved in is having formal champions. If it's a big programme, you set-up a structure that has people who represent business unit need in a discussion but also go back and champion the programme of change. That can be really powerful because in my experience, people trust a peer in a way they won't necessarily with a sponsor or an external consultant.

In terms of rolling out new tools or practices, the best way to do that is with live examples. You can have great training and great support before launching something new, however, having peer-to-peer and shared experiences can be hugely important. Having a few of those quickly and some quick wins.

Speaking peer to peer is one of the most powerful change agents there is, so using peer-to-peer communication is fantastic. Either doing it formally as champions of change, and also informally as people who 'get it', who really get the why of your programme, and who ideally have a vested interest and can sell it and advocate it at every turn. I think having a much more informal network of people you can ask, either sense check things with or to ask them to advocate on your behalf in within the organization is really powerful as well. That combo of formal project champions and find your influencers internally, and most people would know who they are in their organization if they give it a little thought I'm sure.

At BHF we had testimonials from people like content reps who used to spend hours updating pages and could now do it in tens of minutes. Those kinds of testimonials from peers saying how the project or the product of a programme has altered how they think or how they do work. There's a difference between being told it and hearing it from a training or engagement programme, and actually seeing it action from a peer.

Interview with Dr Charmaine Griffiths, Chief Operating Officer,
The Institute for Cancer Research,
Former Executive Director of Strategy & Performance,
British Heart Foundation, 2013–2016

These don't have to take place face-to-face, though large organizations often benefit from hosting meet-ups and providing a centralized and dedicated space for digital teams to work in. This is especially beneficial when your company is still early in its digital transformation journey.

Core principles for flexible systems

Core principles are clear, easily communicated, and universally understood statements that any leader or employee can use to standardize approaches, tools, and resources for innovation and iterative working. They are the founding principles behind your flexible systems that enable work to be more consistent, cost effective, faster to produce, and more collaborative in nature. Many of the core principles needed to create flexible systems already exist in some guise across a company – though it's also likely they're hard to find, difficult to interpret, or buried in department-specific documents with other policies and guidelines.

The job of transformation leadership and the first group of iterative teams, therefore, is to isolate the core principles that were integral to the successes and innovations achieved so far and make them known to new teams. This means ensuring the core principles are clearly stated, easy to access by all necessary parties, and that processes are in place to keep them up-to-date and monitor their use and effectiveness.

Generally speaking, core principles to guide your digital disciplines and iterative teams comprise the following three categories. By establishing and communicating core principles for each category, you'll start to provide the guidance iterative teams need for establishing flexible systems to scale innovation and iterative ways of working beyond the confines of the digital transformation programme.

1. Legal and security
What are the specific legal, regulatory, and security-based parameters your organization must adhere to?

Legal principles can include rules specific to your sector (e.g. compliance regulations for finance), certain customer groups (e.g. testing with under eighteens for higher education), and your IT policies (e.g. data protection and encryption for customer and company data). The challenge is in writing and sharing them in ways that are directly applicable to the innovations and iterative approach you're scaling. This often requires translating legal terms and phrasing into a more direct and conversational tone. It will also help to give examples from recent projects, and point people to where they can access support if they have questions.

2. Values and culture
How does your company want to be perceived by customers and society as whole, and what actions or means for achieving financial success would detract from this?

What a company needs is a community of technology, business and risk experts to look at transformation and especially when you consider cyber security. For example, you can figure out how to use fingerprint technology to let a customer access your app on their iPhone, but if your underlying legacy system has a backdoor that lets people exploit some previous version of SAP, the fact that you're using a front-end fingerprint is not going to help you.

Interview with Jan Babiak
Board of Directors, Walgreens Boots Alliance and Bank of Montreal

Unfortunately, many organizations think they already have clearly communicated values to guide people's decisions and behaviours, when what they really have are a set of generic corporate values that are bland and interchangeable with those of every peer and competitor organization.

When drafting core principles around values, think about how they'll be used by each of the digital disciplines to make moral and ethical decisions. For example, teams need to know whether winning customers is valued more than being completely honest and transparent about the company's offering. For a designer, this can mean the difference between choosing to digitally enhance photos of products and services to make them more appealing but less accurate.

This also applies to decisions around ideas for new offerings or finding new potential partnerships. If there are behaviours by customers or companies that your organization would rather turn away business from than condone, iterative teams need to know.

3. Identity and brand
How does your organization want to be perceived and what qualities should people recognize in every interaction and experience?

The term 'brand' has unfortunately become easily misinterpreted jargon – to some organizations it only means visual elements like a colour scheme and logo – is this a dangerous mistake when it comes to deciding core principles around identity.

In reality, 'brand' is supposed to encompass the entire personality and value system of an organization. An iconic brand, like Apple, doesn't even need to show you a logo to know you're in one of its stores, speaking to one of its staff, or using one of its products. That's because iconic brands devise core principles

One of the interesting questions to ask is 'who is your tribe?' Time and again, we've seen the value in forming these early networks, and maintaining engagement throughout one's career.

For digital transformation, whether it's internal for a large organization or external for the world, you need to hire and develop competencies of people who can form tribes and networks. Because when you come into an organization and they don't have that bandwidth, it is difficult. This is critical – living in an information deluge, people with strong networks bring capability and scale. Sometimes these extended networks are confined to a large organization, and sometimes they extend beyond. But without them, we're toast.

Interview with Perry Hewitt, Vice-President of Marketing, ITHAKA
Former Chief Digital Officer, Harvard University, 2011–2016

based on the qualities they want people to feel when interacting with them that go beyond a list of allowed fonts and colours, or rules for how to use images and the logo.

That's why creating core principles for your identity is more abstract than the previous categories. It helps to think about qualities that can be associated with any part of your company and not just the visual elements. For example, developers should know if state-of-the-art is a better perception of your company's digital platforms than familiar, and designers should know if being perceived as stylish is better than practical.

When it comes to identifying core principles for visual elements of the brand, think about which of these abstract qualities the colours, fonts, images, and other 'rules' were originally supposed to convey and challenge teams to try to outperform them. Providing they test in real environments with high-quality customers, you might accidentally discover the steps to a needed brand refresh without the million-dollar price tag that normally comes with an agency redesign.

Defining the right corporate governance was crucial in terms of realizing our goals in the digital space. We wanted to have a unified voice in the digital marketplace, but also wanted to remain loose enough that people in different areas could innovate and experiment. You need a flexible kind of environment where people can work independently, but they also understand they're part of a larger whole.

To manage this, we established a governance function that met on a monthly basis, called our 'digital planning forum'. It is a place where people who work in disparate parts of the company, and who don't have any natural reason to interact, come together to talk about the different digital things they're working on, the different platforms and technologies that are being leveraged. An employee in our asset management group and an employee in our institutional business would find that they're actually doing very similar things. They can share information and learn something new, or leverage an investment that someone else has already made. This kind of connection lowers the cost of some of the activities of the different groups overall as we leverage our time and money further. And we begin to move as a group towards common objectives without resorting to a command and control system. You have this shared sense that we're all invested in a common brand and we're aligned on best practices and technology platforms.

Interview with Bryan VanDyke, Managing Director and Head of Digital,
Morgan Stanley

Rules for creating flexible systems

Adhering to the following rules will help you create flexible systems that enable different teams across your organization to work iteratively, produce new innovations, and utilize digital technology at scale.

1. Flexible systems are more than just technology

Flexible systems include technology like the software, platforms, and IT environments your iterative teams are going to use in customer experience, design and dev-ops, and insight areas of work. But this is just one category of the many parts that make up flexible systems. Really, the parts you or your teams define for a flexible system come down to the needs of a particular market or solution, as well as your company itself and what's going to enable it to anticipate and react to change faster and better.

2. Specialists and team members must play a big role in establishing systems

The core principles that underpin flexible systems need leadership guidance and approval (e.g. core principles around security, brand, and values). However, most of the parts that make up your flexible systems for scale will actually be decided by the first iterative teams that achieve success with a new innovation or way of working, under the guidance of subject matter specialists. Those parts will then evolve and grow as future teams start using them and adapting them to their needs and according to the changing digital and competitive landscape.

The purpose of leadership, therefore, isn't to impose systems or police their use. Instead, these systems should be viewed as toolkits and resources that need ongoing investment and governance to support your organization's iterative teams and growing communities of specialists.

3. Don't try to plan too far in advance

To start scaling your iterative solutions, you only need to create the systems needed for those particular innovations, rather than try to anticipate every part you're going to need going forward. This is partly because real-world experimentation and testing in the iterative approach is the best way to identify what should become a new standard part of a flexible system going forward. However, it's also because anticipating which parts you'll need in the future can be difficult to predict.

4. Flexibility comes from modular, open frameworks

Systems for scaling are composed of self-contained parts that can be combined and interchanged with others to produce different outputs or meet different needs. Each self-contained part must be standardized and adaptable for ease

> Where culture change happens is a tipping point. You do lots of little
> interventions and they all add up. The ones that work, you push harder.
> The ones that don't work, you pivot. This is a standard digital Lean Start-up
> approach. I know we've got to scale this thing, so at every opportunity I'm
> going to prod it and if it works, I do more of it.
>
> Interview with Ash Roots, Director of Digital, Direct Line Group

of use and flexible arrangement. That's to say, each part of the system can be
altered and adapted to their market, customer, or business area's needs without
affecting the system as a whole.

5. Consistency comes from standardization

Standardization within each part of your flexible systems is what will allow your
iterative teams to adapt those parts to provide the customizations needed for
their unique business areas or markets, yet still produce outputs consistent
in quality and aligned to the ethos and identity of your organization. However,
standardizing for the digital age isn't the same as it was in the past. Instead of
trying to prescribe every detail of a self-contained part, standardization for digital
requires identifying the core principles that are going to govern and drive each
part, as well as the system as a whole.

> Show them you have no pride of ownership. This was not about building a
> fiefdom in IT. In fact, we reduced headcount in IT by over 100 in my first few
> years at American Cancer Society. This was about a smarter application of
> technology, both for our current business processes and to enable new lines
> of business. My budget went down every year and because I voluntarily said I
> was going to self-fund digital transformation.
>
> You get smarter about the choices, you get more aggressive about sun-
> setting, and all the buzzwords de jour come into play whether it's migration
> into the Cloud or getting rid of non-core competencies.
>
> Interview with Jay Ferro, Executive Vice President, EarthLink
> Former Chief Information Officer, American Cancer Society, 2012–2016

Investing in growth: Platforms, partnerships, people, and processes

The very beginning of this chapter talked about the different roles of leadership in a transformed company versus a traditional one. One of the key differentiators is the transformed leaders' focus on enabling and empowering teams, instead of micromanaging and restricting them.

As the number of iterative team grows, you'll encounter new barriers to transformation across the categories described in BUILD Stage 2: Uncover: people, platforms, partnerships, and processes. To overcome these obstacles, you'll need to make strategic investments to ensure your teams stay self-directing and accountable to allow your company to thrive in changing environments like a true complex adaptive system.

1. Major platform upgrades

Beyond the obvious needs for platforms that are fast, secure, intuitive, and reliable, your investments into new platforms should enable capabilities such as real-time data gathering and analysis, plus the ability to instantly parse and link mass quantities of data from disparate sources. Even this is just the beginning though. For example, artificial intelligence has quickly turned from the stuff of science fiction into real platforms that today already power faster and more accurate thinking processes – from health diagnoses to tax rebates (Berger 2014) – than their human-powered predecessors.

2. Invest in people and new skills

Disseminating the team model is going to be limited by how many people you can recruit or train into digital and innovation roles. Investing in new people, therefore, means deciding which permanent staff changes are needed in order for the transformation to be sustainable in the future – for example, replacing an agency or outsourced team with permanent employees. This will likely require

---

I have a very good understanding of other industries through a global network. We also have forums here in Australia where all the IT and digital heads in the sector come together twice a year and we share and discuss issues. I'm in a permanent process of engaging with this industry. Everything I'm seeing here isn't specific to Higher Education, it's really applicable to most industries.

Interview with William Confalonieri, Chief Digital Officer, Deakin University

There's no more important word in digital transformation than 'culture'. It's very easy to get down a rabbit hole of technology and there are various vendors and agencies who will convince you that your technology selection is what will make or break your digital transformation. It's not incidental: technology is of course important. However, the way you leverage it internally is by promoting and engaging with people who are the right mindset to implement this transformation.

Forming cross-functional ways to promote learning and engagement is a big piece. Then externally, co-creation and innovating alongside your customers is the best way to advance digital transformation. What Apple did with its App Store as a platform was to build a place for developers to become partners by building the apps that sat on the platform. As companies look to be more digitally capable, they're going to need to find ways for their customers to help form their products, and that's how you're going to leverage your transformation externally.

Interview with Perry Hewitt, Vice-President of Marketing, ITHAKA
Former Chief Digital Officer, Harvard University, 2011–2016

transforming your company's hiring processes and internal training programmes to ensure the right people are being brought in and the best staff are retained.

3. Automate and enhance processes
Unpicking, automating, and enhancing complicated processes that get in the way of common sense are the first investments to make to enable greater scale. Then tackle the hierarchy: every superfluous approver, round of internal consultation,

Whiteboards have actually introduced a new skill because of the importance of collaborative working: how good are you at whiteboarding? You train people in how to use Excel, but you also need to train some people on how to write on a whiteboard because people get really good at it, and when they're really good, you know how bad you are and that can stop you from contributing.

Interview with Ash Roots, Director of Digital, Direct Line Group

and hoop to jump through chips away at peoples' ability and willingness to take the risk of expending time and energy away from their day jobs to experiment and innovate.

4. Forge new partnerships

Partnerships help you fill gaps and build bridges across your entire organization, so if you're cutting loose your digital agency because you've managed to hire enough designers and train enough developers, now is the time to find new tech partners with skills you don't yet need, but you recognize they could help you tackle the next change already peering over the horizon. And of course, it's not just about technology. The partnerships you invest in at this stage can open up access to new markets, new customer groups, and provide your staff with access to skills they've never been exposed to.

In essence, the investments you'll make in this final stage are also the ones that bring you back to start to begin BUILD Stage 1: Bridge with the next round of changes in the outside world to contend with – only this time, you're prepared. Therein lies the beauty of real digital transformation: becoming truly innovative means being self-rejuvenating and self-perpetuating in response to constant change.

I live by many mantras but one of them is R&D or 'Rip-off and Duplicate' Learn from partners and leverage existing technologies. If someone's been there before and has stumbled, I certainly want to learn from it.

The CIO community and the technical community, is an extremely collaborative group. I don't know if it's because misery loves company, but we're always willing to share. If I read something in CIO magazine or IBM's doing something cool, I'll pick up the phone or send an email and say 'hey, do you have 15 minutes to talk about that? I'd love to figure out how you did that'. Don't feel like you're on an island.

We can be terrible about asking for help because we're not used to doing it or it's the corporate culture that we're in. For me, picking up the phone or tweeting someone even if it doesn't turn out to be applicable for me, still means I made a new contact and I learned something new.

The best way to retain authority is to give it away. That works internally and externally. Things change so quickly that at best you have half the cards, so reach out to someone and maybe together you can make a full deck.

Interview with Jay Ferro, Executive Vice President, EarthLink
Former Chief Information Officer, American Cancer Society, 2012–2016

CONCLUSION:
Final Thoughts
for your Journey

The essentials of digital transformation

In the beginning, I said digital transformation is your company's *Rocky* moment. Like a champion boxer, digital transformation isn't about quick-fixes or one-off solutions. It's about finding a new 'Business as Usual' that keeps your organization fight-ready for the next challenger, be it threat or opportunity, that enters the ring.

Throughout the stages of BUILD, you've seen that sustainable digital transformation is achievable, as evidenced by a myriad of successful organizations around the world. That for any business, transformation is really about imparting a mindset that embraces change in all forms, and making sure you have the right people to tackle it – not by role, but by attitude and inclination.

You've also seen that by approaching transformation holistically and adopting a continuous iterative approach, you can equip yourself with the networks, capabilities, and mindsets your company needs to adapt, react, and thrive in the changing world around it. This is also why the BUILD model itself is designed to be reusable, acting as an ongoing resource base to help you as you lead your organization through a continuous process of evolution. This is important because 'change' has never been such a constant as it is today.

Next month marks the three-year anniversary I decided to write this book. While the BUILD model was founded from my own experiences, I started validating it immediately through research and by interviewing others far outside my own network and range of experiences. This is because it was essential to me that BUILD not be developed in isolation. I have immense gratitude to the many wonderful and insightful people around the world, both named and unnamed throughout the book, who generously gave their time and shared their expertise. It's this diversity of experience that gives BUILD its depth and breadth, letting it act as a guide for any organization trying to find its path to transformation. It has been an incredible privilege to learn from, share stories, and compare lessons learned with so many truly gifted agents of change.

In many ways, this three-year journey developing the BUILD model and writing this book has been a transformative one in itself. The world isn't the same place it was when I started, nor do I look at it through the same lens. It's by reflecting on these changes, both personally and on the global stage, that I want to share a few final thoughts on the right way to digitally transform in the hopes it will help you in finding your own path on this challenging and ever-evolving journey.

1. Vision and implementation are inseparable bedfellows

The word 'why' came up in so many of my interviews and for good reason. If you don't know why you're transforming – or for some, why you even exist as a business – how will you be able to recognize success, let alone agree on a path to get there? I was often disappointed though during my research on the number of books and articles about digital transformation that focused solely on strategy or implementation, but never the necessary marriage of the two. This fundamental link is perhaps what I find most exciting about BUILD as a model. By accepting the premise that all organizations exist to serve external needs and must adapt to conditions they can't control, the question 'why do you exist?' becomes the core thread that connects everything you do to transform and ensures your success in doing so. From creating your shared vision and determining your best routes to transformation, to deciding which projects with measurable outputs to implement, this focus on 'why' is what delivers the critical changes needed to keep your business relevant and thriving no matter what the needs it's trying to meet – whether it's improving the customer experience for luxury retail shoppers in China, or improving access to life-saving treatments for cancer patients in America.

2. Small failures are the safest learning tool

Change can be unnerving, even for those of us accustomed to leading others through it. Over the course of researching and writing BUILD, I went from being the Global Head of Digital at a mid-sized international digital agency to a digital transformation lead in one of the world's largest and most influential tech and consulting firms. The culture shock and steep learning curve that came with this transition gave me a deeper understanding and greater empathy for the anxieties felt by employees of companies that are mid-transformation, or who have transformation thrust upon them. It's through my own experiences adapting to my new environment that I understood the profound significance and importance of the third stage of BUILD: Iterate. We're all hard-wired to avoid making mistakes – especially in front of others – so de-risking failure by starting small is the first step to encourage experimentation and innovation. But even more important is creating and supporting a culture where failure is embraced as a learning opportunity – something that requires more internal transformation, executive sponsorship, and senior leadership support than adapting to any new platform, partnership, or process.

3. Transformation often starts in the mundane

In all my research and interviews, I found more examples of major innovation and change stemming from what began as a boring, practical project than successful digital transformation programmes that started out as such. This is because, and has been said throughout the book, it can be very hard to win internal buy-in for 'transformation', but it's very easy to convince people of coming together to achieve practical tasks. The more you achieve and deliver, the more you can leverage those successes into space to truly transform. Or perhaps the mundane start is down to circumstance, and the opportunity lies in how to make the most creative use of it. Here is where the real magic happens: where a major building renovation at a national museum can become an opportunity to digitize the entire collection and launch the world's largest virtual museum. Or where an army of students can be fed pizza over a school holiday period to train the world's first university helpdesk powered by artificial intelligence.

Last words for the road

Following all the great insights from experts and leaders quoted throughout this book, I'd like to close on some wise words from a more personal source. I'm very fortunate to have two smart parents, but it's my mother in particular who's influenced the way I make decisions in my professional life. As a former biology teacher, she's always espousing the importance of continuous learning and adaptability, but it's one piece of her advice I'd like to end with in the hopes it will help inspire you on your journey in the same way it continues to inspire me on mine.

> *Controlling change is an illusion, but holding static really is the worst thing you can do. Instead, revel in the wonder and experience the joy of how much there is to learn and discover in the world, then make it your mission to share it with those around you.*
> Cathy Davis-Herbert, Executive Director, Grant MacEwan University

Recommended further reading

There are so many topics in BUILD that are entire books on their own, but no one has time to read the full plethora of what's out there. These days the workday is too long, the email inbox too unrelenting, and the last thing anyone needs is a long list of books to read. For that reason, I want to share a shortlist of the resources I came across during my research that aren't just incredibly useful in terms of content but are also interesting and well-written enough to make them worthy reading materials in the precious non-business hours.

Innovator's Dilemma

A well-respected and frequently referenced book (Christensen 1997) by professor Clayton Christensen on why large organizations fail at innovation – namely because they focus too much on making existing offerings better, faster, or more efficient instead of facing the facts that entirely new offerings are what's needed. This book was a huge source of inspiration for *The Lean Startup* by Eric Rise, and it's easy to see the linkages.

The Lean Start-up

A widely followed book by entrepreneur Eric Ries, *The Lean Start-up* (Ries 2011) provides a hugely compelling argument and framework for how any company can, and should, innovate like a start-up. It includes a lot of helpful advice for finding the right sustainable business model for your innovations, and calculating return on investment based on elements like how you expect them to proliferate. If you're only going to read one more book before transforming your business, make it this one.

Stanford's d school: http://dschool.stanford.edu/

To determine where you should invest in learning and developing your team's Design Thinking techniques, I definitely recommend first visiting the website for Stanford's d school – specifically its online 'Crash Course in Design Thinking', which includes free tutorials, videos, and reusable templates and assets. Stanford d school's site will give you an excellent idea of where you should invest in areas like Design Thinking training or external consultancy, while providing resources you can use to further any of your existing customer experience and innovation-focused projects.

The Everything Store: Jeff Bezos and the Age of Amazon

A highly entertaining read by Brad Stone about Amazon's rise to world-conquering scale (Stone and Ivonne 2013), and how the entire empire was built from day one entirely (and somewhat ruthlessly) on making customer experience its main priority. It also includes methods used by Amazon to innovate in small teams, continuously test and optimize new and existing offerings, and how measurable and meaningful data matters more than anyone's opinion – even Bezos' himself.

Design to Grow: How Coca-Cola Learned to Combine Scale and Agility (and How You Can Too)

An interesting read by David Butler and Linda Tischler that addresses flexible systems for scale and the relationship between design and innovation. In the book (Butler and Tischler 2015), David Butler personally reflects on his time joining Coca-Cola and his mission to turn an iconic, but very inflexible, brand into a modularized system that enables innovation and scalability across every scenario imaginable – from make-shift shops in remote island huts selling mango juice, to new fountain machines in restaurants that staff can easily restock because the syrup dispensers are designed to feel like familiar printer cartridges.

REFERENCES

How to Digitally Transform

Alfredo (2012). *Chapter 1: History and Mission Statement*. Available at: http://
blockbuster-alfredo.blogspot.co.uk/2012/02/chapter-1-history-and-mission
-statement.html (Accessed 28 February 2017).

Bloch, M., Blumberg, S. and Laartz, J. (2012). *Delivering Large-scale IT Projects on
Time, on Budget, and on Value*. Available at: http://www.mckinsey.com/business
-functions/digital-mckinsey/our-insights/delivering-large-scale-it-projects-on-time-on
-budget-and-on-value (Accessed 28 February 2017).

Leckart, M. (2010). *10 Years After: A Look Back at the Dotcom Boom and Bust*. [online]
WIRED. Available at: https://www.wired.com/2010/02/10yearsafter/ (Accessed 28
February 2017).

McRae, H. (2015). *Facebook, Airbnb, Uber, and the Unstoppable Rise of the Content
Non-generators*. [online] *The Independent*. Available at: http://www.independent
.co.uk/news/business/comment/hamish-mcrae/facebook-airbnb-uber-and-the
-unstoppable-rise-of-the-content-non-generators-10227207.html (Accessed 28
February 2017).

Salem Baskin, J. (2013). *The Internet Didn't Kill Blockbuster, the Company Did It to Itself*.
[online] Forbes.com. Available at: http://www.forbes.com/sites
/jonathansalembaskin/2013/11/08/the-internet-didnt-kill-blockbuster-the-company
-did-it-to-itself/ (Accessed 28 February 2017).

Satell, G. (2014). *A Look Back at Why Blockbuster Really Failed and Why It Didn't Have
to*. [online] Forbes.com. Available at: http://www.forbes.com/sites
/gregsatell/2014/09/05/a-look-back-at-why-blockbuster-really-failed-and-why-it
-didnt-have-to/ (Accessed 28 February 2017).

Chapter 1

Bolt, N. (2013). *Seven Major Trends Facing Public Libraries*. [online] ilceig.wordpress
.com. Available at: https://ilceig.files.wordpress.com/2013/08/trends-in-public-library
-service.pdf (Accessed 28 February 2017).

Longworth, E. (2015). *Why Net Promoter Score Can Seriously Mislead*. Available at:
https://www.linkedin.com/pulse/why-net-promoter-score-can-seriously-mislead
-eddie-longworth (Accessed 28 February 2017).

McCarthy, N. (2015). *The Great Decline of the Landline*. [online] Forbes.com. Available
at: http://www.forbes.com/sites/niallmccarthy/2015/02/27/the-great-decline-of-the
-landline-infographic/ (Accessed 28 February 2017).

Noam, E. (1998). *The Impact of the Internet on Traditional Telecom Operators*. [online] Citi.columbia.edu. Available at: http://www.citi.columbia.edu/elinoam/articles /impact2.htm (Accessed 28 February 2017).

Peterson, H. (2015). *McDonald's CEO Reveals His Massive Plan to Save the Business*. [online] Business Insider. Available at: http://uk.businessinsider.com/mcdonalds-ceo -reveals-turnaround-plan-2015-5 (Accessed 28 February 2017).

Postandparcel.info. (2007). *Post Office® (UK) Insurance Sales Hit Half a Million « Post & Parcel*. [online] Available at: http://postandparcel.info/17392/news/post -office%c2%ae-uk-insurance-sales-hit-half-a-million/ (Accessed 28 February 2017).

Ries, E. (2010). *The Five Whys for Start-Ups*. [online] Harvard Business Review. Available at: https://hbr.org/2010/04/the-five-whys-for-startups (Accessed 28 February 2017).

Shevlin, R. (2013) *It's Time to Kill the Net Promoter Score*. Available at: https:// thefinancialbrand.com/47237/its-time-to-kill-the-net-promoter-score/ (Accessed 28 February 2017).

Systems, S. (2017) *What Is Net Promoter?* Available at: https://www.netpromoter.com /know/ (Accessed 28 February 2017).

Titcomb, J. (2015). *Post Office Launches Offensive on Banking Industry*. Available at: http://www.telegraph.co.uk/finance/newsbysector/banksandfinance/11369440 /Post-Office-launches-offensive-on-banking-industry.html (Accessed 28 February 2017).

Warpole, K. (2004). *21st Century Libraries Changing Forms*, *Changing Futures*. 1st ed. [ebook] London: Building Futures, pp. 16–21. Available at: http://webarchive. nationalarchives.gov.uk/20110118095356/http:/www.cabe.org.uk/files/21st-century -libraries.pdf (Accessed 28 February 2017).

Chapter 2

Butler, S. (2016). *Sainsbury's One-hour Delivery Service Takes on Amazon*. [online] the Guardian. Available at: http://www.theguardian.com/business/2016/sep/26 /sainsburys-one-hour-delivery-takes-on-amazon-bikes-london (Accessed 28 February 2017).

Conroy, Jade. (2015). *A Suitcase-Free Stay at the W Hotel London*. [online] The Telegraph. Available at: http://www.telegraph.co.uk/travel/destinations/europe /united-kingdom/articles/A-suitcase-free-stay-at-the-W-Hotel-London/ (Accessed 28 February 2017).

Cunningham, W. (2016). *Bentley Strikes Deal with Gas Elves to Get Tanks Filled Wherever Owners Park – Roadshow*. [online] cnet. Available at: https://www.cnet .com/roadshow/news/bentley-strikes-deal-with-filld-gasoline-elves/ (Accessed 28 February 2017).

Hoffelder, N. (2012). *Walgreens Launches 'Print to Walgreens' Service for App Developers*. Available at: http://www.adweek.com/digital/walgreens-launches-print -to-walgreens-service/ (Accessed 28 February 2017).

Photo.walgreens.com. (n.d.). *Order Photo Prints, Pick Up in Store Today | Walgreens Photo*. [online] Available at: http://photo.walgreens.com/walgreens/storepage /storePageId=Mobile (Accessed 18 February 2017).

Stone, B. (2013). *The Everything Store: Jeff Bezos and the Age of Amazon*. 1st ed. London: Transworld Publishers, pp. 107–118.

Chapter 3

Ambler, S. W. (n.d.). *User Stories: An Agile Introduction*. Available at: http://www
.agilemodeling.com/artifacts/userStory.htm (Accessed 28 February 2017).

Christensen, Clayton M. (1997). *The Innovator's Dilemma: When New Technologies
Cause Great Firms to Fail*. Boston, MA: Harvard Business School Press.

Corporation, T. M. (2006). *Toyota Global Site | Ask 'Why' Five Times about Every Matter*.
Available at: http://www.toyota-global.com/company/toyota_traditions/quality/mar
_apr_2006.html (Accessed 28 February 2017).

Dhar, D. (2015). *The Hub and Spoke Model – from Aviation to Pharma*. Available at:
http://stanford.biocareers.com/bio-careers-blog/hub-and-spoke-model-aviation
-pharma (Accessed 28 February 2017).

Murray, J. (2016). *What Is a Joint Venture and How Does It Work?* Available at: https://
www.thebalance.com/what-is-a-joint-venture-and-how-does-it-work-397540
(Accessed 28 February 2017).

Nielsen, J. (2000). *Why You Only Need to Test with 5 Users*. Available at: https://www
.nngroup.com/articles/why-you-only-need-to-test-with-5-users/ (Accessed 28
February 2017).

Ries, E. (2010). *Entrepreneurs: Beware of Vanity Metrics*. Available at: https://hbr
.org/2010/02/entrepreneurs-beware-of-vanity-metrics (Accessed: 28 February 2017).

Scrum Sprint (n.d.) Available at: http://scrummethodology.com (Accessed 28 February
2017).

Thrasyvoulou, X. and PeoplePerH. (2014). *Understanding the Innovator's Dilemma*.
Available at: https://www.wired.com/insights/2014/12/understanding-the-innovators
-dilemma/ (Accessed 28 February 2017).

Toyota Production System; Basic Concept of the Toyota Production System (n.d.).
Available at: http://www.toyota-global.com/company/history_of_toyota/75years/data
/automotive_business/production/system/change.html (Accessed 28 February 2017).

Waters, K. (2007). *Step 3: Sprint Planning (Requirements)*. Available at: http://www
.allaboutagile.com/how-to-implement-scrum-in-10-easy-steps-step-3-sprint
-planning-requirements/ (Accessed 28 February 2017).

Chapter 5

About Us (n.d.). Available at: https://www.google.co.uk/about/company/philosophy
/ (Accessed 16 February 2017).

Berger, A. (2014). *The Power of Cross-Functional Teams*. Available at: https://medium
.com/@allanberger/the-power-of-cross-functional-teams-b4815a04996d (Accessed
28 February 2017).

Burke, M. (n.d.). *The Nine Netflix Company Values*. Available at: https://inside.6q.io/the
-nine-netflix-company-values/ (Accessed: 28 February 2017).

The Economist Intelligence Unit Limited (2015). *A Bottom-up Opportunity*. Available at:
https://www.eiuperspectives.economist.com/sites/default/files/images
/ABottomUpOpportunity.pdf (Accessed 28 February 2017).

The Health Foundation (2010). *Complex Adaptive Systems*. Available at: http://www
.health.org.uk/sites/health/files/ComplexAdaptiveSystems.pdf (Accessed 28 February
2017).

Jones, Wendell (2003). *Complex Adaptive Systems. Beyond Intractability*. Eds. Guy
    Burgess and Heidi Burgess. Conflict Information Consortium, University of Colorado,
    Boulder. http://www.beyondintractability.org/essay/complex-adaptive-systems
    (Accessed 28 February 2017)
Netflix Inc (n.d.). Available at: http://netflixcompanyprofile.weebly.com/ (Accessed 28
    February 2017).
Rungtusanatham, M. and Choi, T. Y. (2001). *Supply Networks and Complex Adaptive
    Systems: Control versus Emergence*. Available at: https://www.researchgate.net
    /profile/Manus_Rungtusanatham/publication/222668766_Supply_Networks_and
    _Complex_Adaptive_Systems_Control_Versus_Emergence
    /links/09e4150bfdb013183d000000.pdf (Accessed 28 February 2017).

Conclusion

Butler, D. and Tischler, L. (2015). *Design to Grow: How Coca-Cola Learned to Combine
    Scale and Agility (and How You Can Too)*. Philadelphia, PA: Simon & Schuster.
Christensen, Clayton M. (1997). *The Innovator's Dilemma: When New Technologies
    Cause Great Firms to Fail*. Boston, MA: Harvard Business School Press.
Ries, E. (2011). *The Lean Startup: How Today's Entrepreneurs Use Continuous
    Innovation to Create Radically Successful Businesses*. New York: Crown Publishing
    Group, Division of Random House.
Stone, B. and Ivonne, P. (2013). *The Everything Store: Jeff Bezos and the Age of
    Amazon*. London: Bantam Press.

INDEX